MONSTER MIRROR

MONSTER MIRROR

100 Hours with David Berkowitz,
Once Known as Son of Sam

By Michael A. Caparrelli, PhD

REVIEWS

"A fascinating, helpful exploration of one of America's
most frightening killers. It's easy to call people bad.
It's not easy to ask, why. I highly
recommend this book."

Dr. Daniel Amen, Founder of Amen Clinics

"Monster Mirror is gritty and glorious."

*Michael Franzese, Former Colombo Family Mobster
and Author*

"As a former NYPD officer working in the Tactical Patrol
Force in 1977 on the Son of Sam case,
I often think of the lives tragically cut short.
This book is a sharp contrast between evil and
God's redemptive power...a masterpiece
that I could not put down."

NYPD Detective Philip G. Fehr, Shield #3642

"Dr. Caparrelli covers David's story with a depth unlike
anything about the infamous Son of Sam.
He sifts through the ashes, uncovering
the beauty too."

Rev. Don Wilkerson, Cofounder of Teen Challenge

"In Monster Mirror, the latest book by Dr. Michael A. Caparrelli, Jr., the author makes skillful use of case study methodologies to gather and analyze data obtained during more than 100-hours of in-person interviews with the book's protagonist David Berkowitz (aka ".44 Caliber Killer"; "Son of Sam").

Throughout the book, the author seamlessly weaves relevant historical details, substantiative segments of interview transcripts, and his own observations, into a cohesive narrative that is both scripture and science informed.

The David Berkowitz that emerges from Dr. Caparrelli's methodical and deliberative approach to the interviews and their translation into this book is an intelligent, self-reflective, and sensitive man who struggles daily with feelings of shame and profound guilt.

What emerges in Caparrelli's portrayal of David Berkowitz is a person who is far more human, and far more complex than any of the one-dimensional caricatures of evil-personified that typified the portrayal of Berkowitz in the numerous television documentaries, articles, books, and podcasts that have been published In the 46-years (1977) since Berkowitz was arrested for the "Son of Sam" murders."

Dr. Lee Dalphonse, Psychoanalyst

ACKNOWLEDGMENTS

Special thanks to my wife, Alicia, for your constant encouragement, love, and trust throughout this long journey. Without your sacrifices, this book would not have been possible.

Special thanks to Pasco Manzo, Mary Ann Manzo, Don Wilkerson, Dr. Daniel Amen, Michael Franzese, John Curtis, Paul Conway, Tony Palow, Ed Freeman, Matthew Olerio, Bishop Jeff Williams, and Dr. Lee Dalphonse for your support and critical feedback during this journey.

Special thanks to Patricia 'Trisha' Giramma, my editor for most of the manuscript, for your invaluable literary feedback and running the extra miles to make this happen.

Special thanks to Sarah Vaas for your dedication to excellence, visionary ability, and artistic touch in designing the cover. Also, special thanks to Rebecca Danielle for the exceptional photography.

Special thanks to David Berkowitz for allowing me access into your soul and permitting the Holy Spirit to take you further than you wanted to go for the sake of others at risk.

Special thanks to my Lord and Savior, Jesus Christ, who kept me from destruction since the day I invited you into my heart nearly twenty-eight years ago.

DISCLAIMERS

Though the author is a PhD in Advanced Studies in Human Behavior, he is not a clinical counselor. Any advice provided within this manuscript relating to mental health or otherwise should be discussed with a medical professional before acted upon.

The names and identifying characteristics of some individuals have been changed.

David Berkowitz receives no monetary or otherwise profits from the sales of this book.

Dedicated to David Berkowitz's sister and two nieces. He mentioned you often during our 34 sessions and wishes the best for your lives. Perhaps this book will shed a new light on the man you once called, brother and uncle.

TABLE OF CONTENTS

FOREWORD

The 1970s in New York City is a decade too eventful to ever slip my mind. On Halloween evening 1975, inside a banquet hall in Bensonhurst, Brooklyn, Colombo family boss Thomas DiBella dropped a flaming piece of paper into my cupped hands while stating, "If you ever violate the oath of *La Cosa Nostra*, may you burn in hell like the fire burning in your hands." That induction ceremony was the moment I got "straightened out" as a made-man of organized crime, where I was told, "Now you are born again. You are *Amico Nostro* (a friend of ours)."

Outside that catering hall, where a flame barely charred my hands, other bigger fires ignited throughout the city. In 1977, an electric blackout struck all five boroughs for twenty-five hours resulting in the looting of over 1,600 stores. That same year, the *New York Times* reported that the city was virtually bankrupt as Mayor Abraham Beame scratched his head for a solution. Most frighteningly, a maniac was at large randomly whacking young pretty ladies with his .44 caliber bulldog. The city I called "home" was at the cusp of collapse just as I made my ascent to the top.

During those days, I had my hold on nightclubs where New Yorkers danced the night away to *The Bee Gees* with Pina Colada breath to escape the problems outside the glittery atmosphere. Many of those nightclubs were closing early so that ladies could return home at a safe hour to their anxious fathers and mothers. Years later, I found out that the .44 caliber maniac contemplated the idea of unleashing his terror in a Hamptons disco; perhaps a club where I made my rounds. That would have been an interesting night as I was always prepared for war.

From what I understand, the NYPD requested the help of my associates in searching for the elusive killer dubbed as the Son of Sam. The cops knew that wise guys played the streets close and could yank information out of anyone with just a few slaps. Initially, NYPD believed that we were responsible for at least one of the SOS shootings in the Bronx because of the close-range gunshot wound. Now, these same police pled for our help in finding this madman. Isn't it funny how the feet you step on today are sometimes connected to the butts you have to kiss tomorrow?

Then, on August 10, 1977, a twenty-four-year-old, baby-faced postal worker named David Berkowitz was arrested outside his home in Yonkers. If I ever saw that face on the streets of New York, I would have never figured him for having that kind of brass. Yet, David Berkowitz had more weapons sprawled out on the backseat of his Ford Galaxie than most wise guys ever owned in their life. I've learned in my years in *La Cosa Nostra* to never underestimate anybody. You never know what madness lurks behind dimples and light blue eyes.

Sipping espresso while reading the *New York Times* headline on August 10, 1977, "Suspect in Son of Sam Murders arrested in Yonkers," my eyes locked upon this nut-job so starkly different from me. David Berkowitz was a curly-haired Jewish-American kid from the South Bronx. I was an Italian American from Greenpoint, Brooklyn, with slicked-back hair.

He killed people with no rhyme or reason, at least that I could detect. I was involved in a systematic criminal enterprise where bloodshed was a means rather than the end. He was ball-and-chained by the state of New York while I traveled wherever I desired. He would wear orange for his remaining days while I dressed in Armani suits.

Yet soon, our paths strangely paralleled in penitentiaries — David being an inmate at Sullivan County while I was later locked up in federal prison. Behind bars in the late 1980s, we both came to the beginning of God after reaching the end of ourselves. Romans 14:11 says it best, "Every (the lowly and the lofty) knee shall bow before me, and every tongue shall acknowledge God."

You know, I always wondered, How did the same guy who struck terror into New Yorkers morph from a man into a monster, then from a monster into a new man? Monster Mirror captures the vivid details of that harrowing journey.

Monster Mirror is a story that is gritty and glorious. I say *gritty* because the book sheds light on the sinister factors behind the SOS serial killings. The book is drenched with scenes from David Berkowitz's disturbing past, along with psychological theories that help us put his dark deeds in perspective. I say *glorious* because the book reveals how the Son of Sam was transfigured into a son of God after a miraculous encounter in his cell many years ago, along with subsequent events that redefined his character.

On a personal note, I have known the author, Dr. Michael A. Caparrelli, Jr., for many years as a friend and a co-laborer in the ministry. Back in 2009, I shared my story at the opening service of a church he planted in Rhode Island known as Sacred Exchange Fellowship. I returned to that same church, year after year, to watch it grow from a tiny handful to a few hundred souls from all different backgrounds — as Mike would say, "We reach people from Yale and from jail."

In addition to being a PhD in Behavioral Science, a man who studied human makeup on a scholarly level, Mike shepherded that congregation for over a decade, where he deeply cared for addicts, felons, and outcasts. As you'll learn, Mike is a man who possesses a sharp intellect and a burning heart.

Monster Mirror is about Mike's fascinating, heartfelt friendship with New York's most infamous criminal. Like any genuine friendship, it consists of peaks and pits, moments of closeness and tension. Yet, Mike stays by David's side even against a backlash of public criticism. After all, Mike and I both follow in the footsteps of the Savior, "a friend of the sinners." Open up your hearts to a story that you just might surprisingly find yourself hidden within its gritty yet glorious pages.

Michael Franzese,
Author of *Quitting The Mob,*
God the Father (Good, Bad, Forgiven),
I'll Make You An Offer You Can't Refuse,
Blood Covenant, This Thing of Ours,
Mafia Democracy

INTRODUCTION

"Nothing is easier than to denounce the evildoer. Nothing
is more difficult than to understand him."
Fyodor Dostoevsky

I took the horns off a convicted killer named David
Berkowitz, once known as the "Son of Sam". David put the
frighteners on New York City from July 29, 1976, to August
10, 1977 through multiple confirmed and alleged crimes.
Six people were gunned down while seven were severely
wounded with a close range shot from a .44 caliber
handgun. A young lady was nearly stabbed to death on her
way home several months before the shootings. Two
Molotov cocktails were flung into neighbors' homes while
several dogs were executed. Police and media were taunted
with *catch me if you can* letters signed by the doodled
monikers, "Wicked King Wicker", "Duke of Death," and
"Son of Sam".[1] The "Son of Sam" was loose and the city
that never sleeps suffered its worst historic insomnia.

The horn effect is a cognitive bias that blinds us from fully
knowing someone because of a hyper-focus on their
character defects and/or dastardly deeds.[2] Surely, it's easy
to come under the horn effect when analyzing a brutal
killer. Once the horn effect comes over you, you no longer
perceive that despised person as a human but a hellish
creature; hence, the reason it's called the horn effect.
Chances are, you've been blinded by the horn effect in a
relationship with an ex-spouse, an employer who

---

[1] Molly Ivins, "Second Letter from .44 Slayer Has Police Chasing 4 Nicknames, New
York Times, June 7, 1977.
[2] Aparna Sundar, Frank Kardes, and Theodore Noseworthy, "Inferences on Negative
Labels and the Horns Effect," in NA - Advances in Consumer Research 42, eds. June
Cotte and Stacy Wood (2014): 377-380.

mistreated you or some political figure you can't stomach (If you don't believe me, just scroll Facebook - everyone's ex is a narcissist).

Why remove the horns from the "Son of Sam"? Over the last several decades, movies, media and medical professionals portrayed mass shooters and serial killers as monsters. Actually, the term used is psychopaths. [3] Psychopaths are a bloodthirsty species unlike the rest of us, so they say. Psychopaths are nearly irredeemable, so they say. These depictions of psychopaths have not helped society in terms of reducing violence. Senseless killings escalate every year as our nation continues demonizing the perpetrators.[4]

So, over the course of 34 face to face sessions with David Berkowitz at Shawangunk Correctional facility in Wallkill, New York, rather than focusing on the monster in the man, I unveiled the man in the monster. Perhaps this humane approach will intercept some mentally troubled reader from succumbing to their destructive impulses. People rarely seek help from professionals capping their heads with horns. So, hopefully this "hornless" manuscript assists the psychologically tormented who can relate to young David Berkowitz's madness but yearn for an escape.

Of course, removing the horns from David Berkowitz enrages folks. Could it be that we secretly love our monsters? Perhaps our beloved psychopaths make us feel at ease about our own iniquities and afford us an elevated platform from which we can boast like the religious

---

[3] *Diagnostic and Statistical Manual of Mental Disorders, American Psychiatric Association*, 5th ed. (2013), "*s.v. Antisocial Personality Disorder.*"
[4] "Mass Shootings," *Gun Violence Archive*, last modified July 20, 2023, *https://www.gunviolencearchive.org/reports/mass-shooting.*

leaders in the gospels, *Thank God, I am not like those monsters*.[5] Tony Montana, the villain from the classic flick, *Scarface*, makes this same point when hollering at the morally fastidious patrons who snub him at a restaurant – *you want me to be a bad guy so you can feel like a good guy.*[6]

No doubt, it's easy for a father to demonize David. My oldest diva, Ashley, flaunts the same golden blonde hair as 20-year-old Stacy Moskowitz, Son of Sam's final victim. I torture myself by imagining Ashley making the same statement that Stacy recited to her mom, Neysa, the night of her death, "Don't worry. I'll be okay. He's not targeting blondes."[7] My middle child, Hannah, exhibits the Mediterranean features of 18-year-old Valentina Suriani, shot twice just a few blocks away from her Bronx home. Oddly enough, Valentina was an aspiring actress with a theatrical flair just like my Hannah.[8] My youngest princess, Livi, possesses the same mystical eyes as Christine Freund, the 26-year-old secretary struck with a bullet after seeing the movie, Rocky. I envision Livi, my tomboyish beauty, seeing Rocky the night of its 1976 premier too.

Despite my qualms, throughout the 100 hours, David was no longer demonized but humanized. 100 hours with David Berkowitz was not like chatting with an extraterrestrial with whom I shared no mutual experiences. Instead, I met a shockingly relatable man.

---

[5] *A reference to Luke 18:11*
[6] *Scarface directed by Brian De Palma, written by Oliver B. Stone (1983),. Universal Pictures.*
[7] *Andrea Peyser, "A Mom Dies – Forgiving the Son of Sam," New York Times, September 28, 2006.*
[8] *Albert Davila, etc. "Son of Sam Shoots and Kills Couple Sitting in Parked Car in Bronx," Daily News, April 18, 1977.*

Contrary to the popular depictions of serial killers, this specimen felt basic emotions throughout his life with certain periods when these feelings seized up. Like you and I, he experienced sorrow at the loss of loved ones, gratitude towards people who did him right, embarrassment over his blunders, and yes, even empathy. Either I'm crazier than I believe, or the line between the populace and psychopaths is thinner than we all suppose.

Throughout most of our journey, I refrain from using terms like psychopath or other clinical labels that conveniently distance us from David Berkowitz. Instead, I focus on universal mental health breakdowns such as isolation, anger, and shame — struggles we all relate to on some level. Sure, psychopathy applies to the "Son of Sam" in a forensic evaluation. But psychopathy is a particular lens, like any other theory, that has its blind spots. Flying in the face of Cancel Culture, I'm offering you a theory that says men are not monsters but mortals susceptible to certain influences that can sweep anyone away.

We presume that "other" people are capable of heinousness. Other kids are potential mass shooters — *not my son or daughter*. Other men are sexual deviants — *not my husband or brother*. Other women are Jezebels — *not my wife or sister*. Other people are pawns of Satan — not *me!* But what if there are no "other" people? When Jesus charges his dearest disciple with being a devil in Matthew 16:23 [9], He insinuates that anyone with certain vulnerabilities is capable of being swept away by evil.

If devout Peter was a tool, then who can escape from Satan's tricks among us? The fact that Jesus' right-hand man acted like a devil tells us that anyone is capable of

---

[9] *The Holy Bible, King James Version.*

anything. Providing the right circumstances, even a sweet, aging Catholic nun could crack your skull with a tire iron.

Criminal profiling began in the late 1800s under the doctrines of Cesare Lombroso, an Italian neuro-psychiatrist and professor who authored, *L'uomo Delinquente* (The Criminal Man). Lombroso believed that criminals were a closer link in the Darwinistic chain to apes, what he considered "evolutionary throwbacks," as evident in their supposed abnormally large craniums and asymmetric facial bones.[10] Lombroso believed that criminality was exclusives to these freaks of nature. David Berkowitz chuckled about this notion during one of our sessions.

Imagine law enforcement zeroing in on a suspect because the dude had a massive skull. *That's gotta be our guy. Did you see the size of his forehead?*

Undoubtedly, criminal profiling proved useful over the last few decades in pinpointing perpetrators amongst a wider population. Pioneers like John Douglas and Robert Ressler (who both interrogated David Berkowitz) helped local agencies solve many cases utilizing psychological tactics. However, the number of profiles keeps expanding. From the socially savvy serial killer Ted Bundy to the relationally awkward Ted Kazinsky, from the methodical Dennis Rader to the maniacal Ed Gein, the range of personality types keeps expanding. Columbine shooters Eric Harris and Dylan Klebold were two starkly dissimilar dispositions behind the same massacre. I predict that law enforcement will return to the ancient, biblical idea that anyone is capable of anything.

---

[10] *Cesare Lombroso, Criminal Man (New York: Putnam Press, 1911).*

David made the following statement in a conversation during one of our sessions,

> Who were these Nazis prior to World War II? Who were these men that cranked up the gas chamber's temperature? That led women and children into the slaughter. Many were loving fathers, devoted husbands, decent human beings. You gotta ask, what happened to them? What got into them?

I entered the scene in December 2021 when I mailed David Berkowitz a copy of my book, *Dr. Jesus*, a faith-based book for people with mental illnesses, along with a Christmas card. To my shock, the infamous convict wrote back in just a few weeks. He expressed his wish for me to visit his humble abode at Shawangunk Correctional Institution in Wallkill, New York, a three-hour commute from my Cape-styled home just outside of Providence, Rhode Island. Our chat during that first visit paved the way for a 100-hour analysis of the factors behind Son of Sam as well as his present-day life in Shawangunk. Yet, more than behavioral analysis, a friendship serendipitously blossomed that challenged me to square off with my own self.

My intrigue in meeting with David partly stems from childhood experiences with the mischaracterizations of a man whom I loved. I grew up in a neighborhood where my father earned a reputation of being "whacko". I watched police raid our apartment multiple times, even drawing their guns on me while I played with my GI-Joes® in a warm tub of water. On a Saturday morning, an older girl named Gina approached me at the swings and said, "I'd be afraid to live with your father." Gina parroted the buzz on the streets about my dad. I so badly wanted to respond, *You don't know my dad. He gives me rides on the back of his pickup truck, buys me cool stuff, watches out for my safety, and tickles me until I cough blood (not really). He might be your monster, but he is my father.* All this to say, I'm interested in meeting David Berkowitz the man, not David Berkowitz the monster.

My first visit with David transpires on Friday, April 1, 2022. "What's the inmate's ID number?" the strapping correctional officer questions me as I present the proper documents.

"78-A-1976," I reply.

"Berkowitz? Does he know you're here?" The uniformed Hercules appears flabbergasted.

"Yes," I reply.

"I'm surprised. He's very selective in whom he sees," he counters.

Facts are, David read my book. He knew that I was a resigned pastor of sixteen years who would take demons seriously. He understood that I was a PhD in Advanced Studies in Human Behavior who grasped the mental health factors behind his maniacal deeds. He believed that I would seek to understand the Son of Sam tragedies on every level — psychological, social, biological and spiritual. David believed that I would adequately articulate *what got into him* back in 1976-1977.

What was it that got into David? The oldest theory of abnormal behavior, the oldest explanation of what unhinges a person, is the supernatural model. Ancients believed that *daimonion* interacted with natural phenomena. These demonic entities are vagabonds loitering in the atmosphere in search of a soul that accommodates their dwelling. [11] The teachings of Jesus identified the father of daimonion as Satan in John 10:10, "the thief who comes only to steal, kill, and destroy."[12]

According to Jesus, these demons can be evicted from the human-abode when the owner (God) moves back into the house. Now, this theory might sound horse-and-buggy in our advanced society, but keep in mind that over two-thirds of the world still believe in daimonion.

Modern behavioral science doesn't pose the question, *what is it that got into him* when profiling culprits of mass shootings and serial killings. Instead, it asks, *what is it that came out of him*. Modern psychologists examine the ABCs of a person's makeup to anatomize senseless violence. ABCs signify the (a) affective, (b) behavioral, and (c) cognitive factors at play within humanity. [13] A series of malfunctions in how people feel, think, and behave explain how a postman becomes a psychopath. Throughout this journey, we shall explore David's ABCs and how they were marred by childhood traumas. Along this voyage, we shall examine how his ABCs were rearranged to spell SOS (Son of Sam).

Let me fling an oxymoron at you. I'm a supernaturalist with a PhD in Human Behavior. Yep, I'm a minister of the scriptures and a scholar of human behavior. Don't tune me out just yet. I believe in the supernatural theory without putting the boot to the ABCs. I see demonic interference and mental health factors working in tandem. I perceive

---

[11] Livia Gershon, "Where Demons Come From," JSTOR Daily, October 25, 2001, https://daily.jstor.org/where-demons-come-from.
[12] The Holy Bible, NIV.
[13] Bad Verplanken and Jie Sui, "Habit and Identity: Behavioral, Cognitive Affective and Motivational Facets of an Integrated Self," Frontiers in Psychology (July 2019).

the influence of demons as amplifying the mechanisms inside of someone. Therefore, I'm interested in *what got into someone* as well as *what came out of someone.*

As a clergyman, I respect the reality of evil forces that prey upon vulnerable humanity known as *daimonion*. *Daimonion* is the Greek term used in the Holy scriptures to reference demons that prey upon vulnerable people. [14] David's statement during the *Son of Sam* spree in a terrorizing letter to *Daily News* columnist Jimmy Breslin reveals how *daimonion* played upon his psyche, "Thirsty, hungry, seldom stopping to rest; I'm anxious to please Sam."[15]

Daimonion set souls on fire, but the flammable ones are at greatest risk. Mental health breakdowns discussed in this book — such as isolation, anger, and shame — are what makes one flammable. A closer look into the lives of Ted Bundy, Adam Lanza, David Berkowitz, and a host of others reveals flammable men. When Satan was caught by God "roaming throughout the earth" in the book of Job 1:7, the arsonist was searching for a combustible soul.[16]

Regarding supernatural beings, we typically envision otherworldly creatures that float above the horizons of human existence. Yet, a biblical depiction of the supernatural is when the "super" interacts with and infuses the "natural." For instance, on the divine side, God anoints Moses' staff to split the Red Sea in Exodus 14:21. [17] The superpower of God infuses the natural element of a staff to produce miraculous results. On the diabolical side,

---

[14] *W. Gunther Plaut, The Torah: A Modern Commentary, Rev. ed. (New York: Union for Reform Judaism, 2005), 1403.*
[15] *Ivins, "Second Letter from .44 Slayer."*
[16] *The Holy Bible, New International Version.*
[17] *The Holy Bible, KJV.*

demons infuse the physical bodies of people to accomplish their results.

So, when I say supernatural, I mean how the super leverages natural phenomena to accomplish divine or diabolical outcomes.

What is it like coming under demonic influence? We grasp what it means to come under the influence of an alcoholic substance. A person will say and do things outside their normal behavior when swayed by heavy vodka. You might even make the statement about that person after they strip naked at a party, "That's the booze." Similarly, falling under the spell of a demonic spirit is like coming under influence of a mind-altering drug.

Does coming under the influence of alcohol dismiss human responsibility? Absolutely not. First, we hold people accountable for the decisions made in a rational mind that led to boozing. Second, alcohol has been dubbed, *truth serum*, because it often amplifies suppressed emotions. [18]I've known many stoics who become saps and pushovers who become tyrants all while inebriated. In these cases, the alcohol doesn't change a person as much as it amplifies what's inside of them. In the same way, demons don't force their will upon someone. Rather, these imps help release that person's subdued wishes.

During my seventh of 34 sessions with David, the now seventy-year-old convict smiles at a nearby inmate coddling an infant in the visiting room.

---

[18] *Alicia Gilbert, "The Psychology Behind Getting Drunk and Saying Hurtful Things," Soberish.com, May. 23, 2023, https://www.soberish.co/getting-drunk-and-saying-hurtful-things.*

Noticing the young inmate's yarmulke, David says to the fellow, "Mazel Tov" (congratulations in Yiddish). David's blue eyes water. He says to me:

> It breaks my heart knowing I never gave my father a grandchild. I didn't come home from the army thinking I'd commit crimes. That's just not how it happened. I planned on getting married, settling down with a family, making my father proud. It's hard for me to fathom how quickly everything spiraled. It's hard for me to articulate what got into me without oversimplifying.

Making sense of evil is a task that most people cannot tackle without oversimplifying. Religious folks often crown Satan as the singlehanded culprit behind all violent news headlines. On the other hand, the scientific community digs into the human psyche for clues into mass shootings and serial killings. Attributing the works of evil to any one theory exclusively is as silly as blaming the last Jenga block for the tower's collapse.

An accurate depiction of evil is not causal reductionism, the assumption of a single cause in a case where there are multiple reasons.[19] To avoid causal reductionism, *Monster Mirror* considers all of the blocks that contributed to the collapse. The goal of this manuscript is to analyze each block, mental, social, emotional, biological and diabolical, that culminated into the Son of Sam.

When I asked Dr. Daniel Amen, renowned psychiatrist, and brain disorder specialist, to describe the building blocks of violence, he replied, "I think of violent behavior

---

[19] *Matteo Grasso, et al., "Causal Reductionism and Causal Structures," Nature Neuroscience 24, no. 10 (October 2021).*

happening in four circles — biological, psychological, social, and spiritual."[20] (Dr. Amen was interviewed for this book and offered invaluable insights about the biological blocks in particular). To Dr. Amen's point, the Jenga tower doesn't crumple because of one block — rather, a buildup of blocks culminates into its collapse.

How does David Berkowitz explain the Son of Sam? Answering this question is a rocky road from Brooklyn Hospital to a Bronx tenement to an occult hangout in Yonkers known as Untermyer Park to the shadowy streets of NYC. Replying to this question involves 100 hours of data collection, data analysis, and the entirety of this manuscript. But for now, let's peek into his most recent parole hearing. Let's step into a scenario in spring 2022 that sheds some light on Berkowitz's own self-assessment.

Inmate #76-A-1976 sits attentively at his tenth parole hearing before a televised board. He prays that the board's members, handpicked by the New York State governor, discern he's a new man. He's more intent on bearing witness to Christ than being released. Since his conversion in 1988, he's practiced a consistent regimen — he reads his Bible at 5am with a cup of coffee, works as a mobility assistant helping wheelchair bound inmates obtain their meds, submits uplifting writings to the liaison of a website,[21] prepares Bible studies for chapel services, and responds to mail worldwide. He hopes the board members examine his "before and after" pictures. But, instead of weighing any evidence of David as a new man, the board probes the old man. The senior commissioner, a no-nonsense African American lady, pokes around his psyche. She poses the question that many New Yorkers from David

---

[20] *Daniel Amen, Email to the author, August 2, 2022.*
[21] *The official website of David Berkowitz. Ariseandshine.org.*

Berkowitz's era want her to ask, "Please tell us, David, why you committed those awful crimes from 1976 to 1977?"

David, the careful conversationalist, isn't sure how to respond. He's concerned that whatever he says will sound like some excuse. He chauffeurs the parole board down Freudian Lane — the scandalous circumstances surrounding his birth, the bond disruption from his birth mother at four-days-old, the dramatic sit-down with adoptive parents Nathan and Pearl Berkowitz at five-years-old, and the deep dive into occultism as a young adult. He details the impact of these events but clearly states what he believes to be the crux of his actions, "I fell under some kind of spell."

Considering David's history with forensic evaluators, *falling under a spell* is a gutsy claim to make before a committee determining your fate as a free bird or caged canary. The first time he offered this explanation was on May 21, 1978, in Attica prison. Patriarchs of FBI profiling, John Douglas and Robert Ressler, clobbered their fists against the table. According to David, they hollered, "Enough with this devil made me do it crap, Berkowitz!" (FYI — these are the guys that the *Netflix* series, *Mindhunters*, is all about. John Douglas created the Criminal Profiling Program in Quantico, Virginia and Robert Ressler coined the term, serial killer[22]). At some point during those early interrogations, David retracts his ghoulish testimony to make the agents happy.

> I was and still really am a people-pleaser. Hard to believe, but it's true. So, I dropped the devil story to make people happy.

---

[22] *Andrew Whalen, "Mindhunter True Story," Newsweek, May 29, 2019.*

A short time later, David returns for a moment in describing this almost out of the body experience in his interviews with forensic psychiatrist Dr. David Abrahamsen. David told Dr. Abrahamsen in a letter on August 1, 1979, about a trance-like state during the crimes,[23]

While shooting these people, I actually became transfixed with the event. The gun, the screams, the shattering of glass and windshields, the blaring horn, it all just possessed my mind so that I'd take no notice of anything else. During the first incident, I had become so transfixed that I could not move until that car horn started blasting in the quiet night. That horn brought me back to reality in a way. I got back my senses, realized what I had done, and just took off running to my car.

Nearly a year later, David remained perplexed about the spell that came over him. In his letter to that same psychiatrist in May 1980, in which he stated:

"Was this me?" I said to myself. Truthfully, looking at the writings with the printed slant and looking at the shooting scenes were nothing more than a distant remembrance. Perhaps you could explain this reaction that I have because, to me, it's like viewing the actions of a stranger. I can, till this day, recall all the fine details, the most trivial of events which occurred around me, etc. But still, I sometimes cannot believe that I could be capable of such destruction.[24]

[23], "Dr. David Abrahamsen-Berkowitz Letters," Psychiatrist Letters, The People vs. David Berkowitz, https://thepeoplevsdavidberkowitz.com/berkowitz-psychiatrist-letters.
[24] The People vs. David Berkowitz, "Dr. David Abrahamsen-Berkowitz Letters."

"He's a pure psychopath with manufactured delusions," Dr. Abrahamsen documents in court records. Naturally, the Freudian shrink dismissed David's goblins as a displacement of the killer's own ravenous appetites. Esteeming the well-known shrink, David went along with Abrahamsen's theory even to the point of assisting Dr. Abrahamsen in a psychoanalytical book entitled, *Confessions of Son of Sam*.[25] Years later, he tells me about Dr. Abrahamsen.

> He worshiped a god who committed suicide – Sigmund Freud. Satan didn't fit into his Freudian framework. So, I gave up the demon references and told him what he wanted to hear. Plus, I wanted payback with my attorney who secretly worked on a book about my demon possession with another author. So, I recanted all demon references in my story.

After four decades, the notorious convict comes back to his initial story during the tenth parole hearing. He's not retracting to appease anyone this time. He's too old for that back-and-forth hogwash. Loosen his shackles or not, David believes that he was carried away by evil. The controversial inmate of Shawangunk Correctional insists upon the reality of demonic possession. "I fell under a spell," he insists to the parole committee.

Did David use the devil? Many say that Satan is a scapegoat that the convict uses to evade feelings of culpability. Psychiatrists believed that the devil is just another one of David's defense mechanisms. David himself even admitted this reasoning within interviews from the early

---

[25] *David Abrahamsen, Confessions of Son of Sam (New York: Columbia University, 1985).*

1980s. Pinning it on the devil is a habit we inherited from our progenitor, Eve, who responded to God's reprimand in Genesis 3:13, "the serpent tricked me!".

Or...Did the devil use David? According to the legendary exorcist Father Malachi Martin, who claims that he visited David in prison, "David is a rare and unique person who is perfectly possessed" whom "an exorcist could not dislodge the demons because they had the full cooperation of the possessed person."[26] The question of who used who will be explored from a multidimensional perspective within this manuscript.

The question, *Did David use the Devil,* or *Did the Devil use David,* rattled the minds of people attending David's court hearings. Before New York State Supreme Court Justice Joseph R. Corso in the summer of '78, the courts witnessed David's deranged outburst when he chanted obscenities about his victims in the midst of a legal proceeding along with hollering, "I'd kill them all again!". Photographs of his chaotic apartment showed a watermelon sized chunk of plaster smashed out of a wall alongside inscriptions that said, "Little baby killers live in this hole."[27]

When I asked David about these behaviors, he stated,

> My head wasn't right back then. Psychotic behaviors, yes. Psychopathic behaviors, yes. But none of that means the absence of demons.

Maybe demonic powers manifest in everyday life more

---

[26] *"Hostage to the Devil," Son of Sam Episode 4, Podcast, Causeway Pictures Limited. Video, https://youtu.be/ep9KcYwMXm8.*
[27] *Lee Lescase, "Yelling 'I'd kill them all again' Berkowitz Derails Sentencing," Washington Post, May 23, 1978.*

than we are aware. Have you ever behaved out of character? Some outburst that contradicts your baseline temperament. Perhaps you pound on some dude's car window in a road rage incident worthy of a *Dateline* episode. At the end of the mayhem, you apologetically mutter, *I'm sorry but I don't know what got into me.* Or, *I'm sorry but I don't know what possessed me.* Or, *I'm sorry but I got carried away.* What got into you? What possessed you? What carried you away? Your lingo insinuates a paranormal energy whipping up your irritation into rage, or your lustful fantasies into costly infidelities.

Sidebar: Constant references to Satan pose the risk of making the imp larger than his actual status. Facts are, Satan is a created being with limitations. So why talk about him as if he's everywhere at once? During World War II, every US soldier believed that they were at war with Hitler. Soldiers understood that a "war against Hitler" did not mean an actual combat with his physical embodiment. Instead, it meant a war with Hitler's minions and/or deceptive ideology. Likewise, a war with Satan means combat with all of his underlings and deceptive teachings.

David isn't the only killer to incriminate or insinuate demons. On a summer afternoon in 1893, an elementary school principal named Frank Sheffield escorted his five-year-old princess, Maggie, to Rocky Point Amusement Park in Warwick, Rhode Island. Against the backdrop of blaring organ music and eruptions of laughter, Sheffield bashed his little girl's head in with a rock he found on their oceanic walk. A few hours later, he came out of a trance, alleging that he had no idea what got into him.[28]

---

[28] *Kelly Sullivan, Murder at Rocky Point Park (West Columbia, SC: Arcadia Publishing, 2014).*

Michaud and Aynesworth's 150 hours of conversations with Ted Bundy reveal that the prolific serial killer continually referred to an *entity* when describing the frenzy behind his crimes. The two investigators even recall Bundy's baby blue eyes mutating into pitch blackness when divulging the gory details.[29]

Dennis Rader didn't know how to articulate the mystery of the force behind his B.T.K. spree, so he coined it the "X-Factor."[30] And, of course, the "Milwaukee Cannibal" Jeffrey Dahmer claimed he was swept away by Pazuzu from *Exorcist III* while seated alongside his drugged victim minutes before the slaughter.[31] Could the Entity, the X-factor, Pazuzu, and Sam all be monikers for the same supernatural impetus that carries people away?

Andrew Delbanco, a Columbia University professor, once confessed in his book, *The Death of Satan,* "A gulf has opened within our culture between the visibility of evil and the intellectual resources for coping with it."[32] The late pastor Timothy Keller comments on DelBanco's book by saying that all of our explanations about the origin of evil failed us.[33] We once blamed a lack of supportive social systems as the basis for evil. Then, Marxism taught us that placing the means of production in the hands of the oppressed turns them, too, into oppressors. Evil was once presumed to be resultant from a lack of education. *Only*

---

[29] *S.Michaud and Hugh Aynesworth, Ted Bundy: Conversations with a Killer (Irving, TX: Authorlink Press, 2000).*
[30] *Edie Magnus, Rader Blames X-factor, Dateline NBC, NBCnews.com, August 12, 2005.*
[31] *Jack Rosewood, Jeffrey Dahmer: A Terrifying True Story of Rape, Murder, & Cannibalism, (Pittsboro, IN: LAK Publishing, 2017).*
[32] *Andrew Delbanco, The Death of Satan (Scotts Valley, CA: Create Space Publishing, 2013).*
[33] *Tim Keller, "Spiritual Warfare," January 29, 2012, https://m.youtube.com/watch?v=JcPlfM7w-ZE&feature=youtu.be.*

uncivilized people commit atrocities is what we supposed until we discovered that the Holocaust was orchestrated by mad geniuses.

Mental illness, nowadays, is perceived to be the primary cause of evil as evident by the culture's emphasis upon psychiatric drugs. Global sales of psychotropics will probably reach more than $40 billion in 2025, a giant leap from $27 billion in 2022.[34] Yet, young men still go *postal*, as evident in the twelve mass shootings per week in the United States during 2022.[35] What explains relentless, incurable evil if it's not rooted in a lack of social support, lack of education or mental illness?

After David's parole hearing, David strolls the main yard set against an alpine backdrop. Shawangunk allows him an afternoon walk from 1:00 to 3:45 p.m. He eyeballs the mini-forest surrounding the barbwire fence, in particular two trees he's christened with names based on the autumn colors they splash — Mr. Orange and Miss Goldie. He halts at a spot in the yard that gives him a nostalgic gaze into the Shawangunk Mountains, a.k.a. "the Gunks." He recognizes the exact point he scaled as a rambunctious teenager in the Appalachian Mountain Club. He wonders what became of that youngling with so many ambitions. None of his child-hood fantasies included a .44 caliber gun or dead bodies. The Son of Sam was never in view. David often wonders, what got into me?

Monster Mirror derives from 100 hours of sessions with David, an analysis of many letters between David and his

---

[34] *"Global sales of psychiatric drugs could reach more than $40bn by 2025 due to coronavirus, says GlobalData," GlobalData, last modified April 6, 2020, https://www.globaldata.com/media/pharma/global-sales-of-psychiatric-drugs-could-reach-more-than-40bn-by-2025-due-to-coronavirus-says-globaldata/.*
[35] *Gun violence archive, "Mass Shootings."*

psychiatrist, and years of behavioral science data. Witness the unveiling of truths that surfaced throughout our chats about the interplay between mental health factors and demonic activity. David shares from his own vivid experiences about an unseen adversary that took advantage of his every disadvantage. Come face to face with a man that will tell you enough of his story to decide whether he's a monster from the abyss or the boy next door.

David captures the heart of this journey during our first session:

> Doc, I'm reluctant to talk about what was behind the SOS tragedy [Son of Sam] because I don't want it to sound like excuses. I've been locked up for forty-five years, and that sentence still doesn't satisfy justice. Truly, I deserve to die. An excuse is some reasoning that pardons me from my consequences. No excuses exist. But I do want to explain as best as I can the psychological and paranormal factors behind this madness, as a cautionary tale for other troubled young people. I offer no excuses, just explanations.

Chances are, you've already met the Son of Sam in movies, documentaries, books, etc. May I introduce you to David, a fellow human being with familiar vulnerabilities? The monster you met in print collides with the man I met in person. Irrefutably, the precious lives he ended scream from the graves about his barbarism. Yet, a few hours with him will open your eyes to a guy who resembles your brother or friend. Here's David, a lifer at Shawangunk Correctional, who still scratches his head about what "possessed" him decades ago in a city that has mythologized his crimes ever since. May I warn you that when you meet David, you will not look into the eyes of a monster, but a mirror. I present to you: *Monster Mirror*.

CHAPTER 1

ISOLATION

The Lord God said, "It is not good
for the man to be alone."
Genesis 2:18[36]

UP, CLOSE AND PERSONAL

On April 1, 2022, I'm up close and personal with David
Berkowitz at Shawangunk Correctional Facility for the
first meeting. No media reporters are between us to
sensationalize his every gesture into a deranged behavior.
No religious leaders are between us to deify him as St.
David because of his decision to follow Christ in 1988. His
warm smile says that he wishes for peace with everyone.
The scar across his neck says that he's built for battle. This
is David Berkowitz –– nothing mythical, fully human,
neither monster nor martyr.

The visiting room is not just occupied by objects but
symbols. The dullish yellow walls signify the humdrum
life of every inmate. The series of metal tables and
cushionless chairs represent the coldness resultant from
years of being institutionalized. The out-of-order vending
machines signify the tease of pleasurable things within
view but unreachable. And the masks enforced by COVID-
19 policy symbolize the coverup of painful emotions,
distorted thoughts, and dark secrets. Inmates and visitors
alike are reminded by these emblems of our existential
distance from one another. We are all fundamentally
alone.

---

[36] *The Holy Bible, NIV.*

Feelings of alienation began for me nearly four decades ago in a visiting room that resembled this dreary environment. At seven years old, I detested visiting my father in school (a euphemism Italian American mothers use to explain why daddy won't be home for a while). My disgust had nothing to do with saying hello to my old man. I often belly-laughed at how he poked fun at my young, naïve mother, and how she swore back at him followed up with a kiss. I dreaded that moment when the turnkey (a correctional officer) signaled for Dad to wrap our conversation up. Saying hello to dad kicked off a fun time together, but saying goodbye felt like desertion in a grim alleyway. For me, the ecstasy of hello wasn't worth the agony of goodbye.

At the twilight of his life, David preserved his boyish attributes — unblemished face, striking dimples, and sapphire eyes that bulge when he's excited. All of these features overshadow the cue-bald head that hints toward his sixty-nine-year-old frame. Even his pace, though slumped when he walks, is spunkier than his millennial comrades. He enters the visiting room like he's ready for business. I show up expecting an encounter with a loafer but instead, meet a buoyant personality. Most lifers I know crave a long nap, but not this guy. I'd invite him to jet-ski at Orchard Beach in his old Bronx stomping ground if I'd met him on the outside and didn't know his background. I wonder how David stays so spry.

Before he settles into a chair, he greets several inmates who fist-bump back, "Uncle Dave." COVID-19's social distancing practices can't restrain him from fellowshipping with his fraternity (though he remains respectful to policy by keeping his face mask on while pulling it down every few minutes for air). "Hey Dave, say hello to my girlfriend," a young convict hollers.

David knows the inmates' names, stories, and struggles. He's gifted a few of them with Gideon Bibles, the translation that yanked him out of the abyss over thirty years ago. Some even salute him as "Pastor," though he blushes at the title. Even the elderly Jewish man visiting his son grins at his fellow Hebrew. David finally found a family amongst the outlaws of Shawangunk.

> The guards of Attica took bets on how long I would last in prison when I first arrived in 1978. Can you believe it? You know you're hated when they wanna kill you, even in prison. That's how much I was despised back in the 70s after my arrest.

He arrived in Attica to the sounds of prisoners howling like dogs. Word spread swiftly that Berkowitz killed at the order of his neighbor, Sam Carr's black Labrador named Harvey. News like that became material for agate-busters with nothing to do. "Awoooo!" David heard the chorus of wannabe comedians from his cell.

David, the beast on the streets, was initially a buffoon in the joint. If he thought he'd find his tribe amongst bank-robber Willie Sutton and the likes, he got it wrong. During those days, he was ganged up on regularly by inmates who found his story laughable.

CLEARING UP MYTHS

Attica's atmosphere was combustible since the 1971 riots when over 1,200 inmates overpowered the guards. Forty-two staff were held hostage by inmates fed up with being treated like dregs, screaming at the staff, "We are men! We are not beasts!". The uprising ended on the fourth day,

September 13, 1971, with thirty-nine casualties and years of tension between guards and inmates. [37] When David arrived in the late 70s, tear gas canisters looming above were ready to detonate over the slightest feud. Attica was not a communal but contentious environment.

I started changing my story about demons really quick. I didn't want any trouble with anyone, so I changed my initial confession, omitting any mention of the devil.

On February 23, 1979, the *New York Times'* headlines stated, "Berkowitz says that he faked tales of demons."[38]

That retraction didn't change anything. It wasn't until after I got stabbed in the neck that I gained some respect.

David, a new jack in prison, was doing a detail when he was assaulted on July 11, 1979. Another inmate slashed his jugular with a sharpened object as he dispensed hot water into a bucket outside the inmate's cell.[28] Though the wound was a split hair from the artery (which would have resulted in death), David zipped his lips about the attacker's identity when pressed by authorities. The only name he called the inmate was "a real pain in the neck." Other than that, he kept his mouth shut about the fella who opened up the entire left side of his jugular, a 6-inch-long wound requiring sixty stitches. Refusing to snitch made him a star overnight in prison, a status every inmate desires. Social

[37] *Marvin Mayfield. "A half century after Attica..." New York Daily News, September 8, 2021.*
[38] *Richard Meslin,"Berkowitz Says That He Faked Tales of Demons," New York Times, February 23, 1979.*

acceptance is a highly desirable carrot, even amongst calloused outlaws.

"Tell me how you became the Son of Sam." After fifteen minutes of establishing common ground experiences such as Adult & Teen Challenge (a faith-based recovery ministry), Times Square Church, and familiar spots in NYC — I probe my new friend. I purchase us White Castle® burgers from the nearby vending machine, hoping that the savor of New York City's beloved patty sparks enough nostalgia to fuel our conversations. David is a well-mannered eater, usually requesting several napkins. He talks in a thick Bronx brogue, but only after he swallows his food, so he's clearly understood. Connection with fellow humans is valuable to him at this stage of life.

> Doc, when you say that name, it's like a sucker-punch to the gut. Could you not say it so flippantly? That's not a title that I'm proud of anymore. The name makes me sick...like... depressed, to even think about it. SOS was a time of deep anguish, inner torment. Every day, I wish it would all just go away.

Son of Sam, which David refers to by its initials in a quiet tone, was more confining to him than the razor-coiled fences of Shawangunk. Most of us have the privilege of putting the misdeeds of youth behind us — the stuff we stole, the lies we told, and the people we injured. David doesn't have the privilege, and rightly so. The heinous crimes he committed in his early twenties could keep him impounded forever, whether paroled or not. David is locked up inside of David — a cell of his own making. SOS is its own penitentiary, and he fights daily for his release.

Right away, I discern that the SOS tragedies are off-limits within future discussions. The murders are injuries that

David committed against his victim's families but also himself. Simply mentioning the subject jabs a finger into those raw places. Nonetheless, I'm committed to somehow exposing David's wounds to the open air. Here's where the pastor inside of me steps into the scenario. A wound is never healed if it stays concealed. For now, I explore the skin around the wounds.

"I'm sure you have a television in your cell. It can't be easy to get away from.....SOS," I catch myself before verbally spilling that moniker, Son of Sam, again. "...when so many networks feature documentaries about that twenty-four-year-old deranged young man in handcuffs."

Stigma itself is a prison felt by many — former addicts trying to redeem their reputations amongst relatives they betrayed, or abusive men trying to recuperate the trust of the people they wounded. Attica and Shawangunk might be less difficult to escape than the labeled boxes people relegate us to.

You know, the media propagated lots of untruths about me. You probably remember my face from that perp walk after I was arrested in 1977? "The Mona Lisa smile" is how they defined my smirk on that perp walk. They thought I was being smug, but they were wrong.

The perp walk is a long-standing practice in American history, dating back to New York police commissioner Teddy Roosevelt in the 1890s.[39] Police officers escort an arrested suspect through a swarm of reporters for photographs. The custom has been the subject of

---

[39] Clyde Haberman, *"For Shame: A Brief History of the Perp Walk," New York Times,* December 2, 2018.

vehement debate amongst legal scholars. Some argue that a society preaching "innocent until proven guilty" is hypocritical by publicizing the suspect in handcuffs besieged by law enforcement.[40] Let's face it – even the virtuous Mother Theresa would look like a arch-criminal if paraded in such a fashion.

David's perp walk occurred outside the 84th Brooklyn precinct on August 10, 1977, where he was escorted by Detective Ed Zigo into central booking, as reporters captured that eerie smirk.[41] If we had anything in common with the killer, if there was anything relatable about him, that perp walk blinded us from noticing. In that snapshot, all we perceive is a lunatic with a leer rather than the boy next door.

We've all had our share of "perp walks." Facebook and Twitter are the perp walk platforms of the 21st century where haters blast our dirty deeds before the world. Have you ever had a shameful act put on blast on social media — a misconduct with the secretary, a volatile outburst, or mischief with money? "Yes" is likely, since Pew Research Center issued a survey that indicated 58% of US adults believe that calling out people's misdeeds on social media is acceptable.[42] On that perp walk, your flawed humanity is depicted as utter depravity. You didn't just have an affair - the Facebook post says you're a womanizer. You didn't

---

[40] E.F. Lidge, III, "Perp Walks and Prosecutorial Ethics," Nevada Law Journal 7 (Fall 2006).

[41] Carey Winfrey, "Son of Sam," New York Times, August 22, 1977.

[42] Emily Vogels, et al., "Americans and 'Cancel Culture': Where Some See Calls for Accountability, Others See Censorship, Punishment" Pew Research Center, last modified, May 19, 2021, https://www.pewresearch.org/internet/2021/05/19/americans-and-cancel-culture-where-some-see-calls-for-accountability-others-see-censorship-punishment.

just lose your temper - people are posting that you're a rageaholic. Perp walks make monsters out of us all.

Have you ever been so ashamed when caught red-handed that you smiled? Pretty common gesture, right? That's what was behind my smile. I wasn't being cocky. Underneath all that smiling, I was deeply embarrassed. And nervous, to say the least. I was told by the police that I could be attacked or killed by angry New Yorkers.

Initially, I squint at David's explanation. I remember that perp walk, or what looked more like a catwalk. A serial killer flaunts the mug behind six murders, ten injuries, and a series of harassing letters like a model flashing her cleavage. *Yep, I'm the guy that had all of New York City soiling their underwear!* is how I interpreted his cocky countenance.

Then, I give his explanation a second thought. Back in the 1950s, social psychologist Stanley Milgram performed a ground-breaking experiment that revealed something peculiar about awkward laughter. A group of subjects administered shocks to another group (actors pretending to be subjects) when they answered questions wrong. Unbeknownst to the subjects, the shocks were fictional. Strangely, the subjects chuckled loudly when they heard the sounds of screams from those that they supposedly shocked. Later on, the subjects confessed that their laughter was not resultant from callousness but distress.[43]

The other myth about me was that I was a recluse, some kind of weird loner. Believe it or not, I had a

---

[43] Stanley Milgram, *"Behavioral Study of obedience," The Journal of Abnormal and Social Psychology, 67 no.4 (1963): 371–378.*

large group of friends all throughout grade school. We played stick ball, rode subway trains, bicycled for miles, hung out at Orchard Beach, ya know, all the stuff New York City kids do.

Huh? His self-portrait contradicts the letters penned by SOS. On April 17, 1977, New York City Police set foot into a bloodbath on a quiet Bronx neighborhood street lined with row-houses off the Hutchinson Parkway. Alexander Esau, twenty, and Valentina Suriani, eighteen, were found slumped over in a Mercury Montego from gunshot wounds fired by a madman through the driver's side window. Somewhere between the bodies, a letter addressed to Captain Joseph Borelli screeched for the cop's attention. The handwritten memo, all capitalized text, gives a glimpse into the psyche behind the psycho:

I LOOK OUT THE ATTIC WINDOW
AND WATCH THE WORLD GO BY.
I FEEL LIKE AN OUTSIDER.
I AM ON A DIFFERENT WAVELENGTH
THAN EVERYBODY ELSE –
PROGRAMMED TO KILL.[44]

The letter is not penned by a well-adjusted neighbor-hood kid but a freak watching the rest of us from behind a nearby bush. I question David's self-image of being a social person. For now, I change the subject because I don't want to get off on the wrong foot, "Tell me about your relationship with your parents."

---

[44] Carey Winfrey, "Son of Sam," New York Times, August 22, 1977.

DAVID'S CHILDHOOD

As a teenager, I was your typical latchkey kid. My dad worked ten to twelve-hour days at his store, Berk's Hardware on Gun Hill Road in the Bronx. My mom died when I was fourteen. I'd come home from school to an empty house where I'd raid the fridge, make seasoned hamburgers, and watch horror movies. Sometimes, I'd have a group of friends over, and we'd mildly experiment with the drugs of that era. We were on our own, ya know. My dad treated me like a man from a young age. Even as a younger kid, I'd bike as far as I wanted without any questions asked. I planned a trip to Montauk with my bicycle. That would have required an overnight stay somewhere. But my dad would have let me.

The term "latchkey" was first broadcasted on a CBS radio program called "How War Affects Canadian Children" in 1942.[45] Keys were left under the mat for kids between the ages of five to seventeen as dad sailed off to war while mom worked like a government mule. By the 1970s, "latchkey kid" was commonplace in the United States to describe a generation of kids raising themselves on Pop-Tarts® and *Scooby Doo®*.[46]

I'm curious about Berkowitz's relations with his parents because attachment styles, or bonding behaviors, begin within the home long before they manifest in the school yard. Men become what their daddies and mommies make of them, at least to some degree.

---

[45] *Ayden Rudd, When Did the Term Latchkey Kid Start? (NBC Comedy Playground, 6/2020).*
[46] *Todd Perry, Millennials and Boomers May Freak Out Over Social Distancing But It's Gen X's Time to Shine. (Pop Culture, 3/20).*

I contrast Nat and Pearl Berkowitz's parenting style with my own fathering of four children, known as "the helicopter kids." Of course, we helicopter parents presume *I keep my kids snug. I don't have to worry about them feeling lonely or, even worse, becoming serial killers and mass shooters.*

Oddly enough, serial killings and mass shootings are far more common amongst this generation of smothered kids than Baby Boomers and Generation X.[47] How can that be? Baby Boomer and Generation X parents at least engaged their kids over chicken cutlets and mashed potatoes when they returned home from work. Family dinners were more regular. We helicopter parents might hover over our kids, but often with faces buried in video games or iPhones. A 2020 survey indicated that the average parent spent only five hours per week in face-to-face conversations with kids. [48] Helicopter kids are even more lonely than the latchkey kids. *Being* with our kids is not the same as *bonding* with our kids.

> Don't get me wrong, my father tried bonding with me, but I always pushed him away. Something blocked me from getting close to him. I remember dad crying, "I want to get close to you, but you won't let me in, David."

I'm eager to explore this mechanism that "blocked" David's bonding with his dad, but I get the sense to leave it alone for now. David chokes up when recalling the agony

---

[47] Chris Weller, "The Texas Church Shooter was 26 – and it shows a disturbing trend about millennial men and mass murder," Insider, last modified Nov 6, 2017, https://www.insider.com/why-most-terrorists-and-mass-shooters-are-millennial-men-2017-11

[48] Jim Leibelt, "Average Parent Spends Just 5 Hours Face-to-Face With Their Kids Per Week," Homeword.com, last modified February 7, 2020.

he inflicted upon his father, to the point of needing a break.

"What were your friendships like?" I ask.

Staying with his social life, I work my way out of Berkowitz's microsystem into his mesosystem. A key to understanding a man's vibe is to analyze his tribe. David Berkowitz, like the rest of us, is a social creature whose identity was partly whittled by his community.

> We formed a firemen club. We met inside this bicycle room downstairs in a tenement. We had fire extinguishers, axes, scanners. We'd listen for reports of local fires. We'd show up at the scene of a burning building to assist the 45th precinct. I even received a certificate of recognition for helping neighbors stay safe on a street where power lines were down from a storm. I stood at the end of the street with a group of friends, all night long, signaling people away. NYPD supposedly destroyed that certificate after my arrest.

Now, that's peculiar. My research told me that David was a pyromaniac, yet he's putting out fires with friends. This paradox begs my attention.

"You admitted to setting at least hundreds of fires in the Bronx, correct?"

He nods affirmatively.

"Did you set these fires with these same friends, or did you set them alone?"

> I set the fires alone.

Consider this duplicity — David put fires out with his crew but started fires throughout the city alone. What does this imply? David had many comrades, first and last names he drops over five decades later. A comrade is someone with whom you share mutual affinities or activities. But David hadn't any confidants. A confidant is someone in whom you confide your deepest secrets. He was a fireman with comrades but a pyromaniac by himself. Many were his comrades, but zilch were his confidants.

"You were a secretive person, I suspect?" I ask.

I harbored a lot of stuff inside me. So, yeah, I had a lot of friends, but not necessarily people I bonded with on a deep level.

David wrote his psychiatrist on May 29, 1980, a similar confession he made to me.

Ever since I was very young, I committed a multitude of anti-social or criminal actions. Some were more serious than others in that they caused a good deal of property damage. But the main and even tragic similarity is that when I did these destructive things, I did them alone. No other youths were with me to start the garbage and abandoned car fires. No other youths were with me when I wrote graffiti and curse words all over the elevator and stairways of my building at 1105 Stratford Avenue, where I lived when I was young. When I broke windows and car antennas, I did it alone.

So, David was a loner. But not in the *Unabomber* sense of the word, solo in a woodsy cabin with a shaggy face. He was a loner in the likes of Judas Iscariot. Remember Judas? He was the fellow who attended every social gathering

MICHAEL A. CAPARRELLI, PhD

facilitated by Jesus — the feeding of the 5,000, the anointing of Jesus' feet, the last supper. Judas was a master at showing up without ever opening up. His tragic ending revealed a socialized man without anyone he trusted enough to turn to. Like Judas, David had many sidekicks. And like Judas, David had more secrets than sidekicks.

"From what I read about you, I heard you joined the army. That's a place of camaraderie for most people. Any friends in the army?" I ask.

> After I joined the army, I was so lonely. A fellow soldier, John Almond, invited me to church. Then, the bus showed up one Sunday and took us to Beth Haven Church under the leadership of Pastor Tom Wallace. I went because I needed friends. Such a good feeling seeing all the people gathered together, singing hymns, hugging, loving each other. I even got baptized in May 1974, all dressed in a white choir robe. I just wanted to be part of a family, ya know. But my relationships were superficial. The evangelist preaching that first Sunday morning scared me to death! "Who wants to get saved?" he asked. I raised my hand. I knew I needed saving. Then, he asked us to come up front. I thought he wanted me to confess my sins before the entire church. That made me nervous. I wasn't ready to go that deep.

At this point, I could take the easy way out by calling David a psychopath. However, if secrecy is a criterion for psychopathy, then we are all potential madmen. A British survey with over 2,000 respondents revealed that one in five people are withholding a major secret from their spouse.[49] A spouse is almost as close to you as your shadow. How many secrets would you suppose these same people are withholding from their children, close friends, and workplace colleagues?

David highlights the climax of his secrecy within a letter from his Attica cell addressed to Dr. Abrahamsen on June 20, 1980. He cracks open his state of mind after committing the SOS tragedy in 1977.

> I lived a most lonely life in the year before my capture. I was lonely, for I had a deep, deep secret that I wanted to share with friends. It was on the tip of my tongue, and I wanted very much to say it: "Hey, I'm Son of Sam." There were so many times that the temptation to share my hidden secret became overpowering. I often stared at my telephone, hands trembling, as I thought of picking the receiver up, dialing, then saying to the party at the other end: "Hello, is this the Son of Sam Task Force? Well, guess who this is?"[50]

In the midst of our visit, a rabbi approaches us to greet David. The rabbi and the soft-spoken Berkowitz engage in small talk for a minute. I eavesdrop like a mole. The omissions of the letter 'r' in the rabbi's dialect suggested he was from Boston rather than New York City.

I asked him, "Where are you from, rabbi?"

He equivocates, "Here, there, and everywhere."

---

[49] Taryn Hill, "Survey says 1 in 5 People Are Keeping a Major Secret from Their Spouse," Huffington Post, last modified August 1, 2014, https://www.huffpost.com/entry/secrets-survey_n_5642818.
[50] People vs. David Berkowitz, "Dr. David Abrahamsen-Berkowitz Letters.", https://thepeoplevsdavidberkowitz.com

Noticing I'm a news bag, the Talmudist slips away from our company to circumvent any further questions. I look at David, puzzled over the Rabbi's evasiveness.

He's trained by the prison to dodge your questions. Reminds me of when I was in Korea, and I was trained to answer the Koreans discreetly if they questioned me. A Korean might approach in a bar and ask, "What's your name? Where you stationed?" You never know why they ask those questions. They might be working for the enemy. I was good at being discreet.

MINGLING WITHOUT MESHING

The picture of David's isolation becomes less fuzzy. David Berkowitz knew the art of mingling without meshing. Mingling is being with people, but meshing is bonding with people. When you mingle, you chitchat about surface subjects. In the case of David Berkowitz, he liked mingling with others about baseball, geography, cars, and other interests. But meshing is when you step out of the shallows, dive into the deeps. Meshing is the sharing and hearing of each other's secrets and struggles. Meshing is true intimacy, also pronounced into-me-see. Intimacy is when you look into me and see, and I look into you and see.

Violent offenders are often good minglers. Ted Bundy was popular amongst his peers at UPS Law School. Dennis Rader, a.k.a. "Bind Torture Kill", was an esteemed deacon in his church. Gary Ridgeway was a likable john amongst Seattle's sex workers. David Cullen, in his well-researched book entitled *Columbine*, states that the shooters were social bees despite how the media depicted them. The shooter's calendars were packed with recreational activities. On

Friday nights, Eric and Dylan reserved four bowling lanes — enough space for sixteen friends![51] Not all outsiders are hiding in the corners; some are lost in the crowds. Like, Bundy, Rader, Ridgeway, and the Columbine shooters, David was hiding in plain sight.

David wrote his shrink, Dr. Abrahamsen, from his Attica cell on June 29, 1979. The statement shows how his secretive demeanor actually turned into his bargaining chip.

> I must admit that I do love my face. I can fool anybody with it. It's above suspicion, so to speak. My face, my lips, my blue eyes are like weapons I use to my advantage. I was very aware of its usefulness during my crime spree.[52]

Mingling without meshing is not just a characteristic amongst infamous criminals but a growing epidemic. Nowadays, we mingle on social media with 5,000 "friends" we hardly know. People spot our selfies without ever seeing our souls. A Cigna study of 2010 showed that 71% of social media users feel incredibly lonely.[53] Minute-by-minute posting and replying to people across the street and across the world leaves us feeling known by no one. Social media is a nice supplement to face-to-face relationships, but it's a horrible substitute. On Facebook, Instagram, and the likes, we mingle, but we hardly mesh.

---

[51] David Cullen, . Columbine (London: Riverrun, 2019).

[52] People vs. David Berkowitz, "Dr. David Abrahamsen-Berkowitz Letters.", https://thepeoplevsdavidberkowitz.com

[53] Anna Gunther, "Younger generations are lonelier and social media doesn't help, survey finds," Cbsnews.com, last modified January 23, 2020, https://www.cbsnews.com/news/younger-generations-are-lonelier-and-social-media-doesnt-help-survey-finds-2020-01-23.

As David continues dispelling myths about his reclusiveness, I yank my mask just beneath my bottom lip so I can breathe but high enough to remain undetected by Shawangunk's agents of wrath. David responds with a glance of disapproval, like I was caught swiping cookies from the forbidden stash. To appease him, I reposition the mask back to its dutiful position. Ain't that a kick in the head – a compliant inmate seated across from a defiant clergyman. The awkward moment reminds me that the lines between good and evil people are not drawn with a black Sharpie but with a whiteboard marker.

A peculiar isolation surfaces throughout David's childhood; a brand of isolation that the most extroverted among us can relate to. David played on softball teams, hung out with fellow pseudo-firemen, and locked arms with comrades in Korea. Yet, he kept large chunks of his inner self hidden under his hat. He was a mingler but not a mesher. He knew how to be with people but not bond with people. Secrecy, not seclusion, was the cause of his isolation.

How does secrecy foster isolation? Slepian, Chun, and Mason (2017) discovered through an online survey of 200 participants with 13,000 skeletons in the closet that secrecy increased mind-wandering in the presence of others.[54] When I have a secret, I'm physically present with others but psychologically absent. Because of this, I feel estranged even when I'm in the company of people. Swiss physician Paul Tournier says, "Nothing makes us so lonely as our secrets."[55]

---

[54] Michael L. Slepian, James N. Kirby, & Elise K. Kalokerinos, "Shame, Guilt, Secrets on the Mind," Emotion 20 (2020).
[55] Paul Tournier, Good Reads, https://www.goodreads.com/quotes/101973-nothing-makes-us-so-lonely-as-our-secrets.

"Did you feel lonely as a child?" I ask.

I remember, five or six years old, wanting a sister. Mostly everybody in my neighborhood played with a sibling when they returned home from school while I sat alone in my room playing with my toys. I was feeling isolated way back then.

Debates about whether the only child is lonely or lucky erupted for decades. Some studies demonstrate that the only child is better off since they develop a stronger sense of independence. Conversely, a neuroscience study indicated that the medial prefrontal cortex – region of the brain associated with social behaviors — possesses less volume amongst only children. Researchers hypothesize that less exposure to external social groups might have shaped the brain in this manner.[56] For this reason, an only child often feels like a lonely child because of a biological handicap shaped by their experiences that hinders connecting with others.

As a kid, I'd stare out my bedroom window for hours. I'd watch the sky lights shining above Shea Stadium all the way in Queens, or I'd watch people crossing the busy streets. New York City is a busy, populated place. Yet, I felt distance between myself and others.

Ya know, so many of these mass shooters feel disconnected from their communities. Even if they have family and friends, they feel estranged from them. I wrote a piece on my website called Lonely

---

[56] *Peter Dockrill, "Being an Only Child Can Actually Change Structure of Brain,"Sciencealert.com, last updated May 17, 2017, https://www.sciencealert.com/scientists-have-discovered-that-being-an-only-child-affects-brain-structure.*

Girl about Sol Pais, who committed suicide on the anniversary of the Columbine shootings after a trip to Colorado. She was liked immensely by others, known by her peers as a "genuine person with a pretty smile" but still hiding deep loneliness.

"You still feel lonely today?" I ask. I'm curious if he's demolished his own walls over the last few decades of incarceration. Just because everyone knows his name in the visiting room doesn't mean everyone knows his soul. Familiarity and intimacy are not the same thing.

> Funny cause I tell people that I have three families. First, the family of God. I feel blessed when I think about all the believers that I'm connected to within the prison and worldwide. They keep me going. Second, my adoptive family. My adoptive mom passed on when I was a teenager and my dad just a few years ago. Lastly, my biological family. I still have a sister and two nieces somewhere. The distance between myself and them is where the loneliness lies.

While moseying Shawangunk's backyard, David envisions what it would have been like to know his nieces if SOS never occurred. He would have purchased the largest bouquet of roses on his way to their high school graduation or the birth of their babies. He would have introduced his fiancé to his half-sister, Roslyn, with the hopes of the two becoming besties. The deepest loneliness, at least for a "lifer" at Shawangunk Correctional, is the span between your actual and hypothetical relationships.

I ask David if he tried contacting his sister and nieces. He just shrugs his shoulders with a head drop. I surmise that the risk of their rejection might be too great for him. What if he mails a letter and they never reciprocate? I'm reminded of Tony Lip's unforgettable line in the movie, *Green Book*, "The world is filled with lonely people afraid to make the first move."[57]

ISOLATION AND DAIMONION

Isolation is the turf where demons tread. Seclusion and secrecy alike leave a window cracked open for evil to creep into our psyches and vandalize our well-being.

Now, if you are a bona fide believer in Christ, you cannot be possessed by evil (II Corinthians 6:14). God's name is listed on the deed of your temple, and He owns you. Demons have no ownership, but tenancy is a possibility. Evil rents space within your head when you cut yourself off from godly community.

An isolated personality develops through a multiplicity of ways. To name a few, offenses prompt us to pull back from people. Someone makes a hurtful remark, violates your trust, or neglects your needs, and you withdraw not just from that person but eventually everyone. Proverbs 18:19 applies the perfect metaphor to depict how offenses lead to isolation when it says, "A brother offended is harder to win back than a strong city."[58] A strong city is a territory surrounded by walls. Unless the offenses are appropriately handled, as prescribed by Jesus in Matthew 18:15-20, we gradually become walled off from others.

Also, social ties are often sundered by our own indulgent

---

[57] *Green Book, directed by Peter Farrelly, written by Peter Farrelly, Nick Vallelonga, and Brian Hayes Currie (2008), Universal Pictures.*
[58] *The Holy Bible, KJV.*

desires. Proverbs 18:1 says, "A man who isolates himself seeks his own desires."[59] Notice that whenever you're up to no good – boozing, drugging, gambling, porn – you pull away from the people that care about you the most. Why? You make yourself unavailable in order to make yourself unaccountable.

Furthermore, the real tragedy of violating the Ten Commandments is ruptures in relationships. Breaking the first four commandments sever our relationship with God (idols, graven images, taking the Lord's name in vain, neglecting the sabbath), whereas the last six fracture our relationship with people (dishonor of parents, murder, adultery, stealing, bearing of false witness, coveting). [60] Transgressions of any of the commandments work to evil's advantage because they drive wedges between us and community.

Like David Berkowitz, we've all withheld segments of our self from others. Recently, I went to an Al-Anon meeting with a heavy heart. That week, I fell into some classic enabling behavior with addicted loved ones. But what did I do at that meeting? I revealed, not myself, but my shell. With the opportunity before me to bare my soul, I just smiled. "Everything is great," I said to group members. I dropped profound insights on the 12-Step literature but offered no access into my heart. Man, did I feel terribly lonely later that night! The Chinese proverb stands true, *He who builds fences will be fenced in.*

---

[59] *The Holy Bible, The New King James Version.*
[60] Mel Lawrenz, "The Ten Commandments and Our Relationships with Others," *The Brook Network, last modified April 23, 2018,*
https://thebrooknetwork.org/2018/04/18/the-ten-commandments-and-our-relationship-with-god/.

ISOLATION AND VIOLENCE

Let's discuss the link between isolation and violence. Experiments conducted by psychoanalyst Gregory Zilboorg dating back to 1938 revealed a link between loneliness and hostility. Ninety-one participants were given an opportunity to administer annoying noises to an unlikable confederate (Remember, confederates in those post-civil war days were a despised demographic). Participants who scored high on a loneliness inventory administered more noises to the confederate than participants who scored low on that same test. The results imply that we are more prone to harm people when we feel lonely.[61] Next time you snap at someone that gets under your skin, take note of how alienated you felt before that outburst.

Decades later, Ouchi and colleagues (2005) performed similar studies with animals. A sample of mice were removed from their communities and held in segregation. After a period of time, the critters were dropped back into their social networks. Moments after they returned home, they attacked their peers! Somehow, isolation wore their civility thin. [62] In my own life, I've noticed my tolerance towards fellow humanity shrivels the longer I stay by myself. My first day back in society, after quarantining from COVID-19, I snapped at an elderly guy in front of me for driving too slowly. That's not my normal character, but I got *carried away.*

I'm not sure how Adam was behaving in the garden prior

---

[61] Gregory Zilboorg, "Loneliness," *The Atlantic (January 1938).*
[62] Hirofumi Ouchi, et al., "Social Isolation Induces Deficit of Latent Learning Performance in Mice: A Putative Animal Model of Attention Deficit/Hyperactivity Disorder," *Behavioral Brain Research 238 (February 2013):146-53.*

to Eve's arrival when God stated in Genesis 2:18, "It is not good for man to be alone."[63]Perhaps Adam was chasing a pigeon with a stick or pounding his head against a tree. Maybe this is why God swiftly responds to Adam's aloneness by fashioning him a friend. *He needs a friend...quick!* Of course, I'm being waggish, but this monumental event establishes the fact that humans possess a desperate need for social connection. COVID-19 brought our attention to this reality as mental illnesses surged throughout the months of quarantining. The more we lose touch, the more we become out of touch.

EMPATHY EROSION

Is there some mediating variable between isolation and aggression? To answer this question, David's further statements shed light on how the isolated become dangerous.

> I became real isolated in the days leading to my arrest. I withdrew from everyone. My mind was so dark back then. I didn't feel much of anything. It was like another person pulling that trigger. Like I was in some detached trance. I lost all feelings for anything or anyone.

David's loss of feelings for people is known as empathy erosion. Empathy is the brakes that keep us from running someone over. Losing empathy is like the brake pads wearing off.

Simon Baron-Cohen, professor of developmental psychopathology at the University of Cambridge, ex-pounds upon why empathy is so important in his book entitled,

---

[63] *The Holy Bible, The New King James Version.*

The Science of Evil. Cohen defines empathy as a "double-minded attentiveness" that considers the feelings, needs, and views of others in addition to your own. [64] That double-minded attentiveness is cultivated when we mesh with people. We practice hearing and being heard, understanding and being understood, serving and being served. By meshing, we develop double-minded attentiveness. But, in isolation, empathy erodes. Without meshing, we're in touch with our whims but out of tune with our neighbor's wishes.

David once made a statement to a psychiatrist at King's County Hospital after his arrest — an utterance that his sister overheard. The admission flew in the face of everything she knew about the brother who showed up continually with groceries, hugs, and kisses. The confession didn't reconcile with the uncle who lavished his nieces with two beautiful necklaces a year before his arrest. He said to the doctor,

> I've been reduced. I lost human qualities. I'm not human anymore. I have no feelings, no compassion for the human race, no real concern.[65]

Baron-Cohen argues that "erosion of empathy" is a catalyst for genocides, sexual crimes, mass shootings, and other violent outbursts.[66] Take for instance, the Nazis. Emotional detachment made it easier for the Nazis to commit atrocities. The Nazis practiced the utmost degree of social distancing from the Semites. In doing so, they lost all empathy. Jesus told us in Matthew 24:12 that there

---

[64] Simon Baron-Cohen, *The Science of Evil: On Empathy and the Origins of Cruelty* (New York: Basic Books, 2011).
[65] Susan Wisengrad, "First Time Ever - The Startling Story of Son of Sam's Real Mother," *Good Housekeeping*, November 1978
[66] Baron-Cohen, *The Science of Evil:*

would be an "increase of wickedness" in the latter days, not when hate grows hot, but when "love of most grows cold."[67] Note that in your own life, it becomes easier to hurt people when you detach from them. When love grows cold, evil becomes possible.

I'm curious if David knew the SOS victims on any level. Did he know that Stacy Moskowitz's mother, Neysa, worried about her going out that night? Stacy told mom before she left, "Don't worry, Mom. He's not targeting blondes." Did he know that Alexander Esau lived with his dad Rudolph in a Hell's Kitchen apartment, helping him make ends meet? Did he know that Virginia Voskerichian moved from Bulgaria with her parents and little brother in 1968 in pursuit of the American dream? I wonder if firsthand knowledge of these facts would have altered outcomes.

A few months prior to his arrest, a telling talk occurred between David and his half-sister, Roslyn, over lunch within her Queens home. He reconciled with Roslyn as an adult, a story discussed later.

"Is there something bothering you? You're so quiet." She prods gently. Sister knows younger brother isn't his typical self. Deviations from baseline behavior are signs that something is wrong such as chatty people become quiet, quiet people become chatty, etc.

"No, no, just my own problems. They'll all work out," David replies, distracted by a bug in his head.

"Is there anything you want to tell me?" she persists.

---

[67] *The Holy Bible, NIV.*

"I want you to know one thing. I would never do anything to hurt you and your little girls," David fixes his gaze for a second, then swiftly returns to that bug in his head.[68]

Roslyn recalled an overnight at the hospital for a minor surgery. A bond of concern grew between David and his half-sister.

"David came to visit me," she told the reporter of *Good Housekeeping* magazine in 1979. "I was sleeping, and I remember I felt somebody kiss me. I opened my eyes, and there he was."[69]

Empathy serves as a protective factor against violent urges. For instance, an evening occurred when David's hunt for blood evolved into a rescue mission. A lady and her friends were trying to pull her car out of a snowbank when the .44 caliber killer drives by. The stranger requests for David's help, and the empathetic vibes interrupt his murderous mission. David exits his car and assists the immobilized stranger in getting her wheels back on the road. When empathy awakens, even if only for a moment, predators morph into princes.

> As soon as she asked me for help, I couldn't hurt her. Hearing her voice snapped me right out of that violent mindset, ya see what I'm saying. I couldn't hurt someone I knew.

Annihilating a faceless person is painless, but the slaughter of a fellow human is impossible. Ask Pharaoh's daughter how simple it was to watch her daddy mandate the death of every Hebrew baby boy. Yet, it was impossible to obey

---

[68] *Wisengrad, "First Time Ever."*
[69] *Wisengrad, "First Time Ever."*

that edict when she held the Hebrew baby named Moses in her hands. She ended up raising that baby rather than killing him. [70] Stanley Milgram's legendary experiment revealed that 65% of participants were willing to fatally shock subjects when instructed to do so by authority figures. However, the results dropped significantly to 20% when the participants held the hands of the subjects they were ordered to shock. [71] Empathy short-circuits our violent impulses.

So, I question David about whether he had any intimate knowledge with his victims, to which he replies:

> I didn't know them, and they didn't know me. They were simply objects of the devil's wrath in my twisted mind.

Many convicted killers possess a highly selective empathy. Such a picky empathy involved an emotional connection with a small handful of people, sometimes only one person, while aloofness towards humanity in general. For example, Richard Kuklinski, infamously known as the Ice Man, was a devout husband and father but also a merciless killer who murdered for pleasure and profit. Kulinski reported that he shot a man twice in the head on Christmas Eve because he owed him $1600, then returned home shortly after to assemble a toy train for his children. [72]

In most cases, these convicted killers who lack generalized empathy are socially maladjusted individuals. These

---

[70] *The Holy Bible, KJV.*
[71] Milgram, *"Behavioral Study of obedience,"* 371–378
[72] Arthur Ginsberg, *"The Iceman and the Psychiatrist,"* Home Box Office (HBO), 2003, *https://www.hbo.com/movies/the-iceman-and-the-psychiatrist.*

convicted killers are textbook hermits. Or, like David Berkowitz, they hide in plain sight. Isolation, in one form or the other, eats away their empathy like Leukemia erodes white blood cells.

Have you noticed that mass shootings and serial killings are more rampant in western society than anywhere else? As of May 1, 2023, the United States has more mass shootings than days; a total of 350.[73] Fewer lunatics roam the streets of China or other far eastern cultures. Why? Maybe because eastern cultures are collectivist. Collectivist cultures are knitted together like an afghan without any loose threads. In these cultures, you're offered a cup of tea or a home-cooked meal with some quality time if you exhibit signs of distress. In America, you're offered a digital heart emoji when you're fired from your job or lose your pet. We are a lonely culture, hiding behind screens from each other. Violence is prevalent wherever social ties are loose.

When I returned home from the army at twenty-one years old, that was the loneliest time. My mother was long gone, my dad was moving to Florida with his new bride, and all my pals from the neighborhood were settling down with families. I bought a shotgun, hoping to organize a hunting trip with my old pals from the neighborhood. My buddy Lennie moved upstate, and I saw a deer head on his father's wall. I figured hunting would bring us all together again, like in the old days. That trip never happened.

That shotgun was amongst the four firearms collected

---

[73] Kiara Alfonseca, "There Have Been More Mass Shootings than Days in 2023," May 8, 2023, Abcnews.go.com, https://abcnews.go.com/US/mass-shootings-days-2023-database-shows/story?id=96609874.

from his apartment during the 1977 arrest, along with a semi-automatic machine gun, a handgun, and the notorious .44 caliber revolver. David purchased the shotgun to gather his buddies for a hunting trip. When the trip never happened, he used a gun to scatter an entire city. Outlaws are often outsiders fed up with feeling forgotten. Many casualties later, nobody would ever forget the SOS.

"Did anyone, amongst your family and friends, notice your descent into darkness?" I ask, curious if someone reached out.

At that point, when SOS occurred, I had cut off mostly everybody. Especially that six months prior to the arrest, I was isolated from all my family and friends.

David speaks of SOS as an event rather than a person. He references SOS as something that happened rather than someone he was. "When SOS occurred..." is like saying when the comet struck earth. His usage of that name as separate from his younger self hints towards his disintegration into a non-entity. "When SOS occurred..." connotes David being absent from the equation. Young David was out of sync with everyone; therefore, out of sorts with himself.

One of the few connections that felt David in the days before SOS was with fictitious characters. Take, for instance, Travis Bickle, in Taxi Driver, a Martin Scorsese film starring Robert DeNiro as its leading anti-hero.[74] David saw glimpses of himself in the rejection-sensitive, low-class chauffeur, the leading character of the flick

---

[74] Taxi Driver directed by Martin Scorsese, written by Paul Schrader (1976), Columbia Pictures.

released on February 8, 1976, just a few months before SOS.

The first time David saw the film was in Houston with an old army friend he visited on a road trip. He saw the movie multiple times when he returned to the Bronx, and even dressed in an army jacket that resembled Bickle's attire and even took a job briefly as a cabbie. Most notably, he purchased a .44 caliber similar to the one mentioned in the film. In a city of millions, David was more influenced by a virtual friendship than an actual one.

I identified with Travis Bickle, this socially clumsy outcast in search of himself. I especially liked the ending where this nobody becomes somebody. Ya' know, he's loved and celebrated after shooting people inside that brothel. Finally, he belongs.

I ask David to shed some light on why "outsiders" are drawn to the devil. What I discover is that outsiders aren't drawn to the devil as much as the devil is drawn to them.

I have forty-six channels on this 16-inch screen television in my cell. Have you ever seen an episode on the animal channel about how lions stalk their prey? I watched this episode of the animal channel where the lion spots a gazelle at a distance from the herd. Who knows what that gazelle was thinking to be away from the herd? Maybe he was driven out, maybe he drifted away. The bottom line, the bond between the gazelle and the herd was broken. The lion spots the isolated gazelle, and well, you know the rest of the story....

David's fill-in-the-blank statement leaves me room to insert images of a lonely twenty-three-year-old man just before his arrest. There he is, staring out the window of his 35 Pine Street, Yonkers apartment overlooking the Hudson River. There he is, completely solo in America's most populated city. There he is, fidgety, whether he paces the messy floor or lays on the mattress. Here comes daimonion, roaming the earth like a lion. Here comes daimonion, hunting for a lone gazelle.

That apartment in Yonkers was like a hotel for demons. I should have never moved to Yonkers. Big mistake. Those demons were destroying my life. But, at least I had company. That's how I felt back then.

Three hours into our session, David asks me about my own life:

So, what made you resign from pastoring after 16 years?

"Health challenges. I suffered a heart attack in 2018, then a second heart attack known as the Widow Maker a few years later.", I reply with carefully selected fragments of a story too painful to discuss in depth. I, too, have a shell.

David gives a yawn that says, *let's wrap things up.* I surmise he's exceeded his daily dose of socializing. I imagine David heads to his cell to spend the day alone before a television set.

"So, what's your plan for today?" I ask with a yawn that says I've had enough too.

David's reply shows the disparity between the man he was forty-five years ago and the man he is now. His reply also answers my question about how he stays so spry even at his ripened age. Folding up the leftover foil from both of our White Castle Burgers, David says with excitement,

I'm prepping for a Bible study. I set up the Bible study different than your typical church service where the pastor preaches from the pulpit, and the people face him. I situate the desks in a circle so we can face each other, discuss our failures or disappointments. We keep it real. A brotherhood is developing at Shawangunk. Man, I love those guys.

David Berkowitz at 6 years old.

CHAPTER 2

ANGER

Let not the sun go down on your wrath,
Neither give place to the devil.
Ephesians 4:26[75]

A LITTLE INCIDENT

David arrives for the session out of sorts. Quick hellos to fellow inmates rather than his usual personal encounters hints at his bad headspace. A courtesy smile instead of his signature sparkle gives the impression he's bothered by something. Typically, he sits like a man at a Thanksgiving dinner table. Today, he sits without really sinking into the chair. His eyes scan surroundings like a hawk in fight or flight. I'm relieved that the mask mandate has been lifted so I can study his face. He's too edgy to lock eyes with me.

"What's bothering you?" I inquire.

> Ah, just a little incident with an inmate, that's all. No big deal.

A "little incident" is a big deal for sensitive souls like David. I surmise that he's making light of a heavy matter. Perhaps he wants to spare me from his troubles. Either way, his jittery face is more truthful than his soft-pedaled words. Facts are, *little incidents* are the provocations behind many bar room brawls, road rage incidents, and messy divorces. Growing up, most of my family blowouts were set-off by a *little incident*. I was raised in an Italian American family that

---

[75] *The Holy Bible, KJV.*

could fly off the handle over rigatoni being served instead of ziti.

David, like *mia famiglia*, is a deep feeler of little things. I surmise that whatever happened with David and the inmate is a big deal.

Sensitivity in itself is not a character defect. Sensors are mechanisms that rely upon the asset of sensitivity to safely navigate a machine. For instance, your vehicle might have a sensor that helps you park without hitting another car. David is a sensor by temperament, ultra-alert of people, places, and things. In recent years, the trait has served him well. He knows the appropriate words to offer a troubled soul writing to him for help. Newspapers never report on the countless young people that David talked off ledges through his "smoking typewriter" (what other inmates dubbed the apparatus that David strikes so passionately). Sensitivity is David's flair, not flaw.

But in earlier times, this same delicate temperament laced with evil forces shipwrecked his life. A statement from his elementary school report card in 1964 underscores David's long history of sensitivity. His teacher stated, "David could do his work if he wants to, but he upsets easily."[76] Those were the days when fifth-grade teacher, Mr. Fleishacker, applied a headlock to bridle him during an outburst in class. His own father, Nathan, struggled to pin seven-year-old David down when he would take random fits. At one time, David's sensitivity under paranormal influences was volcanic.

Unsatisfied with David's euphemism, *a little incident*, I ask

[76] Leann Fowler, "David Berkowitz, Son of Sam," Radford University, http://maamodt.asp.radford.edu/Psyc%20405.

the question about the inmate again with a whisper. I'm concerned about agitating David even more, so I lower my customary, Italian-American volume. I employ what's known as the late-night disc jockey tone. I've learned that a quiet approach disengages a man's defenses in a heated moment. Solomon said it best in Proverbs 15:1, "A gentle answer turns away a man's wrath."[77]

Mirror neurons are your best ally when dealing with someone upset. Mirror neurons are the brain cells that absorb another's emotions, enabling you to laugh when they laugh or cry when they cry. [78] King Solomon unwittingly alludes to these neurons in Proverbs 15:1 when he says that a wrathful person will absorb your gentleness. I'm banking on David's mirror neurons taking cues from my calm disposition. Solomon winks at me from heaven.

> I'm standing outside the infirmary, and this other guy hollers in front of everyone, 'Hey Dave, did you know that you're ranked the Number One Most Dangerous Guy in New York?'

Right away, I ascertain what's behind David's anger. My blood pressure surged on many occasions when my mother disciplined me in front of my peers, or a teacher insulted me before the class. Discerning what's behind David's anger is easy since it takes one to know one. Nonetheless, I withhold my speculations because it's better for David to discover what's behind his anger than for me to declare it.

---

[77] *The Holy Bible, NIV.*
[78] Eric Jaffe, *"Mirror Neurons: How We Reflect on Behavior," Association for Psychological Science, last modified May 1, 2007,* https://www.psychologicalscience.org/observer/mirror-neurons-how-we-reflect-on-behavior.

"Did you say anything back?" I ask.

Not much.

A man turns quiet after being offended for one of two reasons. Either he's collecting himself or plotting his revenge. Silence after a slight is either an opportunity for the offended party to bury the hatchet or grind the axe. Many years ago, before his conversion, David gave an inmate a vicious beating after feeling disrespected by that cat. The planned attack was so vicious that the guards gave David a hurting and threw him in the "box" for ninety days. David knew how to grind axes.

But it's a new day. David's hush in the moment of the offense, along with his deep breathing now, suggest he's collecting himself. Thomas Jefferson said, "When angry, count to ten before speaking. Very angry, count to 100." Jefferson winks at David from heaven.

It doesn't help that there's no air-conditioning in the cell block.

No cooling system in a prison? Ninety degrees was the weather outside. I can't imagine what the thermostat in a stone-insulated castle reads. My heart sputters at the notion of 600 convicts caged together in Beirut conditions. A 2018 study in Poland indicated that stress hormones surge with the rising of the thermometer. [79] Law-abiding citizens are angrier in humidity, never mind tattooed thugs. Mild-mannered folks are likely to lose their cool on a dog day afternoon, never mind convicted killers. Some anger is instigated by environmental conditions

---

[79] Dominika Kanikowska, "Stress Hormones Spike as Temperature Rises. American Psychological Society, April 25, 2018.

such as a hot day, a crammed room, a traffic jam, or a loud party.

"Do you know why that inmate's comment bothered you?" I ask, hoping to prod him into searching his own soul. Exploring anger is a crawl through a long, obscure tunnel of introspection that usually begins with the question, "Why?"

Can you repeat the question?

David appears stuck outside that infirmary still. His fingers are antsy, like they need something to grab.

Being a Christian of thirty-five years doesn't immunize him from anger. Jesus was angry on many occasions. The apostle Paul actually sanctioned the emotion in Ephesians 4:26, "Be ye angry and sin not."[80] Paul gives permission for the emotion but warns us about its subsequent motions. Paul says, *embrace the emotion but put breaks on your motions.*

David toys with an ice-tea bottle cap rather than mangling the inmate's face. Thirty-five years of walking with Jesus, he's learned how to "be angry but sin not."

MRS. SOSNOFF

I play back the question as he collects himself.

Funny cause I remember Mrs. Sosnoff, the child therapist, asking me that same question during our sessions on Saturdays. "David, why are you so angry?" I never knew how to answer that. I'd just sit

---

[80] *The Holy Bible, KJV.*

there bored. I seen that lady for two years, and we made no headway.

Imagine ten-year-old David tilting his chair back on two legs, eyeballing the ceiling of that midtown Manhattan office. Elderly Mrs. Beatrice Sosnoff leans into the rascal with her question but to no avail. He'd rather be pedaling from his Bronx tenement all the way to Cos Cob, or hopping subway trains to Battery Park with pals. Saturdays are supposed to be fun. He wouldn't be here if those dumb school officials didn't insist upon therapy, and mom didn't bribe him with pie from Horn and Hardart (a popular chain restaurant in Manhattan where they would stop on their way to therapy).

An aversion to psychologists marked David throughout his childhood. I perceive even now as a sixty-nine-year-old man, he shows mild annoyance with any questions that poke his subconscious. As a child, much, much worse. He'd rather peer outside his bedroom window at Shea Baseball Stadium than look into his own soul. Over 2,000 years ago, Socrates coined the phrase "know thy self." If Socrates were alive in the 1960s, little David might tell the bearded Greek to go pound sand.

Introspection is not easy for the angry. Such soul-searching means facing what you feel. The angry prefer fuming over the externals than facing the internals. Listen to angry people fume, and you'll hear them pout about people, places, or things. You hear hardly any mention of their raw feelings. Isn't it easier for you too to shout when your angry, *People are so dumb!* than humbly admit, *I feel so dumb*. The angry are introspectively handicapped.

Believe it or not, venting doesn't get it out of you but only suppresses the real emotions behind anger. Nat purchased

David a Popeye Puncho at six years old, a standup inflatable that rises up every time you whack it. Nat hoped that David could unleash all of his pent-up frustrations, but it never did the trick. The real basis for the anger stayed suppressed. Studies show that all forms of venting, verbal or physical, only leave the angry, still angry.[81]

Furthermore. plentiful data shows that suppressed anger results in misfirings at innocent parties and all kinds of relationship problems.[63] Nobody says it more colorfully than mindfulness expert, Juna Mustard, "Anger is like a wild child that you don't want driving the car. But, neither should you stuff that child in the trunk."[64] To overcome anger, the emotion must be explored, not ignored.

I remember a large chest full of toys inside her office. That was sort of a pleasant distraction from all of Mrs. Sosnoff's questions.

Mrs. Sosnoff, a silvery-headed therapist operating out of an Upper East Side apartment she shared with her sickly husband, practiced a method of counseling known as Play Therapy. Play Therapy has roots that stem out of the Enlightenment period. Rousseau (1712-78) planted the first seed for Play Therapy in his book entitled *Emile*, when he wrote about understanding the child by watching them play.[65] Freud advanced this notion by promoting, "The child takes his play very seriously and expends large amounts of emotion on it."[82] Play Therapy rises to popularity in the 20th century as the child's means of expressing emotions and the therapist's opportunity to observe what they feel.

---

[81] Jennifer D. Parlamis, "Venting as Emotion Regulation," *International Journal of Conflict Management*, 23 no. 1: (January 2012): 77–96.

[82] Jean-Jacques Rousseau, Emile (On Education) (New York: Basic books, 1979).

Trinkets galore topple out of a toy chest in the corner of Mrs. Sosnoff's office — balls, figurines, costumes, stuffed animals, soldiers. None of these novelties win the affections of little Davie. Instead, he uncovers a dart gun buried in the treasure chest. All lads like toy guns, but David stares down the barrel like he's been recruited to raise hell. You might think he's on a mission with that dart gun. Hence, Mrs. Sosnoff asks, "David, why are you so angry?"

> I'd line up the figurines and fire the dart gun at every figurine. Can you believe it? I did that almost every session. Shooting the dart gun at the figurines.

Ominous, indeed. A decade after David's sessions with Mrs. Sosnoff, a psychologist from Oregon Research Institute, Charles W. Turner, investigated a potential correlation between playing with toy guns and future anti-social behavior amongst elementary school kids. Turner's research demonstrated that kids who play with toy guns were more likely to develop anti-social behaviors than kids who prefer toy airplanes. His later studies revealed that additional factors, such as weak family relationships, contribute to the making of a defiant personality.[83] David exhibited both factors — an affinity towards toy guns and strained familial relationships. Angry and lonely is a scary combination.

> Why was I angry? I guess, if I answered that question, I would have said, 'I'm angry with my parents. I'm angry with the neighbors who won't lay off. I'm angry with my teachers.'

---

[83] C. W.Turner, and D.Goldsmith,. "Effects of Toy Guns and Airplanes on Children's Antisocial Free Play Behavior," Journal of Experimental Child Psychology, 21 no. 2 (April 1976): 303–315.

Young David barked at everything in view. Parents, teachers, neighbors, blah blah blah. But the real reason for his anger was out of sight. Mark Twain once wrote, "There are two reasons why anybody buys anything. The real reason, and the reason they give you." The same principle applies for anger. There's the reason you say you're angry, and then there's the real reason. The real reasons for little David's anger were far out of his reach.

God quizzes Cain with the same question Mrs. Sosnoff asked David, *Why are you so angry?* in Genesis 4:6. [84] Of course, an omniscient being already knows the answer to his own inquiry. God's purpose in posing the question is not to solicit information, but to elicit introspection. God asks the question, not for His sake, but for Cain's benefit. *Cain, look within. Identify the true object of your anger because it's not your bratty brother.* Once again, the basis of anger must be explored.

Right after this encounter with God, Cain bludgeons Abel in the field. Cain, just like David, does not like to look in. So, instead of looking in, he lashes out.

SPITE WORKER

My father would call me a "spite worker" when he'd get upset with me.

Nat Berkowitz was a long-suffering man. Even up until his 101st birthday, he spoke with his son at least weekly over the phone. He traveled from Miami regularly to visit David until his frailty made the flights unbearable. Despite the media capping his boy with horns, he'd often tell him, "David, I know you have a good heart." If Nat called little

[84] *The Holy Bible, KJV.*

David a "spite worker," you can bet the reasons stacked high. You can measure someone's rowdiness by a patient man's reaction to them.

"What did you do to deserve such a remark?" I ask. At this point, I notice David has left that infirmary in his head. Thankfully, his agitation towards the inmate dissolved. He's come out of his funk. He's full throttle now while sharing his story. A trip down memory lane remedies the woes of the present.

Ay, what didn't I do? I was just a spiteful kid, ya know. I'd break my brand-new toys, and my mother would replace them. I'd take two trains, smash them together into smithereens. Or, when I'd step off the elevator, I'd press all the floor buttons so that neighbors would have to wait forever. One time, I saw a gallon of paint inside the stairway of my building. Somebody was painting inside their apartment, and they left the gallon in the stairway. The open lid was an invitation. I tipped the gallon over until it poured down the stairway, then left.

Children who pull these antics amongst peers are generally fine. Playing rascal with pals is how juveniles gain social acceptance. But when such antics are one's habitual practice alone, the alarm sounds. A desire to vandalize property for the sheer sake of destruction is symptomatic of a conduct disorder. And conduct disorders set off alarms for what's ahead. Only 1% of all children sprout into adult criminals, but the percentage skyrockets amongst children with conduct disorders to 30-40%.[85]

---

[85] H. Russell Searight, Fred Rottnek, and Stacey L. Abby, "Conduct Disorder: Diagnosis and Treatment in Primary Care," American Family Physician 63, no. 8 (April 2001):1579-88.

Mischief, in the case of David Berkowitz, was more than youthful pranks — it was the seedlings of malice which eventually sprouted into murder. Daimonion had its way with David long before SOS. King Solomon warned centuries ago to pay close attention to the child in Proverbs 20:11, "Even a young child is known by his doings – whether his works be pure and right."[86]

> I wouldn't talk to my parents for two or three days. Walk right pass them, and not a word. I'd give them the silent treatment, ya know. I saw how it upset my father, and I just kept at it. I was spiteful, and they didn't deserve it. My father would ask me what was troubling me. I'd grunt, walk in my bedroom, shut the door, and crank up the music.

Quietness towards others is sometimes an act of punishment. "The silent treatment" or "stonewalling" was a common practice in 19th century penitentiaries. Neuroscience reveals that receiving the silent treatment for even brief periods of time activates the anterior cingulate cortex — the region of the brain that detects physical pain. Victims of silent treatments suffer like their flesh is being pricked. [87] As a young boy, David weaponized silence against his parents.

PHANTOM OF THE BRONX

And then, there were the fires. Picture it, 1970s New York City. The South Bronx has an average of forty fires per day. Eighty percent of housing crumbles within a short

---

[86] *The Holy Bible, KJV.*
[87] *Taishi Kawamoto, et al., "Is Dorsal Anterior Cingulate Cortex Activation in Response to Social Exclusion Due to Expectancy Violation?" Frontiers in Evolutionary Neuroscience 4 (July 2012), https://doi.org/10.3389/fnevo.2012.00011.*

time, displacing 250,000 citizens. To top it all off, twelve fire stations closed due to the city's bankruptcy, leaving citizens to rescue themselves. A cruise up East 138th revealed firemen flinging mattresses out of windows, the stench of charred wood and dead rats, and children playing on heaps of bricks. Bronx native David Gonzales reflected upon a 1969 inferno that nearly shattered his family in a *New York Times* article, "the light flickers on the window, the heat from the narrow hallway where the fire burns, me hugging my father's neck."[88] The Bronx was burning down.

NYPD received bizarre phone calls from the arsonist of many fires shortly after kindled. The perpetrator identified himself as "the phantom," later dubbed by the *New York Times* as the "Phantom of the Bronx."[89] The arsonist's modus operandi was similar to another madman snuffing out bystanders known as the ".44 Caliber Killer" — both taunted the police post-mayhem. NYPD wondered if there was any link between the one who sets fires and the one who fires away.

On August 10, 1977, NYPD raid David Berkowitz' apartment after apprehending him outside his building. Bluecoats discovered a handwritten log documenting over 1,411 fires set throughout the city. Dates, locations, and weather conditions were included in the nefarious chronicles. Fires included vacant lots, abandoned cars, empty buildings, and a host of other landmarks. Most notably, many of the catastrophes occur on the same dates

[88] David Gonzales, *"How Fire Defined the Bronx and Us,"* New York Times, January 20, 2022.
[89] Howard Bllim, *"Reexamination of Berkowitz Files Offers New Insights,"* New York Times, May 12, 1978.

and locations as the SOS murders.[90] Berkowitz was a wrecking ball charging towards anything in open view.

I started lighting fires when I was six or seven years old. I'd place my toys on the windowsill and light them on fire. My parents commented a few times about the burnt windowsill, but I pretended I knew nothing about it. I'd just play dumb, ya know.

What makes a pyromaniac tick (or should I say burn) is highly individualistic. Some pyromaniacs, known as pyrophiliacs, experience sexual orgasms from the sight of an object melting into ashes. Other pyromaniacs are harboring deep anger, and they express their rage through infernos.[91] David's reason for fire-starting — whether lustful or livid — becomes abundantly clear to me after he discusses what happened when his adoptive mother died.

After my mom died when I was fourteen years old, I was so angry that I barked at anyone who tried to console me at her funeral. The place was packed with people. She was so loved. I loved her very much. The Rabbi said it was the largest funeral he ever officiated. So many friends and relatives trying to comfort me, but I would yell at them, "Get away from me!" I was so angry, ya know. I started lighting more fires than ever before.

If anger accelerated David's pyromania, then it stands to reason that anger motivated it. He set buildings ablaze because he was livid, not lustful. The adolescent was fuming, and the flames were an outlet for his fumes. He lit

---

[90] Bllim, "Reexamination of Berkowitz Files."

[91] A. O. Rider, "Fire-starter: A Psychological Profile," FBI Law Enforcement Bulletin 49 no. 6 (June 1980): 6-13.

stuff on fire for the same reason he vandalized property —
to unleash pent-up rage. Can't we all relate to this on some
level? Kick the couch, punch a wall, post a snide remark,
slander your boss, dish out a dig at a rival in dialogue, spit
in his sandwich, wash the toilet with that jerk's toothbrush
— many are the valves that blow off steam.

But, where did all this fury come from? We return to Mrs.
Sosnoff's question, "Why are you so angry, David?"

ANGER WITH THE ALMIGHTY

I flay the layers of David's psyche like an onion. I hear the
crackling in his voice as he reflects upon his earlier views
of God. Onion peeling is a tearful experience.

> I was angry with God. I often cursed him for being
> born into this world.

Anger with the Almighty lies underneath much of the SOS
madness. I'm reminded of that scene from Forrest Gump
when crippled Lieutenant Dan props himself up on the
boat's deck, howling at the heavens amidst a violent storm,
"It's time for a showdown! You and me!" [92] Similarly,
beneath the mask of SOS's hatred towards humanity is a
displaced rage intended for God. Like Lieutenant Dan,
David was in a face-off with his eternal Father.

Even David's early attraction towards Satanism stems from
his detestation of the Divine. When we dislike a person, we
befriend someone with a mutual gripe towards that
despised person. Fraternizing with your enemy's enemy is
what we do when we are mad at someone. David felt drawn

---

[92] *Forest Gump directed by Robert Zemeckis, written by Eric Roth (1994), Paramount Pictures.*

to Satanism probably because of Satan's mutual hatred towards God. I ask David if the slayings and disfigurements were payback towards God. Hurting what our enemy loves — in this case, David shooting God's precious children — is classic warfare behavior.

Well, I mean, all sin is hostility towards God, right?

David turns painfully quiet. Anytime I mention the killings, David forcefully shuts his eyes for a couple of seconds like a man who just stared into high beams. I close my lids the same way when I see surgical procedures performed on television. I wonder if he's having flashbacks of that dark era known as SOS. David never verbally answers my question. A lump of tears in his throat makes it difficult to speak, like swallowing a golf ball. Instead, he offers a shoulder shrug with a muted, affirmative nod. This onion is too tear-jerking for David to peel.

Later on, I dug up David's letter to Dr. Abrahamsen in 1979. David's rants in the letter confirm that SOS was at war with God. Consider the utterances of a madman in Attica just a couple of years after his capture. He wrote Dr. Abrahamsen the following rant towards the almighty:

> I got you back, God! I got my revenge! You took my mother from me, King of Kings! You Indian giver! Payback, payback, payback. I waited so long for the payback. You're cruel. You hurt me. You took from me the only ones I've ever loved.

After a layer is flayed, another layer of the onion remained. Anger by itself is hardly ever the issue. Anger is just a pointer to something else hidden within the soul. Anger is like a flashing light on the dashboard that notifies the driver about something wrong under the hood.

"Can you tell me when the anger began, David?" With this question, I'm snooping under the hood.

About five or six years old, I was dressed in my dungarees, probably playing outside with my friends. Can't remember the exact circumstances. Mom and Dad call me into the living room. They're seated on the couch with serious looks. "David, we want you to know that you were adopted?" Adopted? I had no idea what that word meant. They explained it in simple terms.

"The doctor made a decision between saving your life or your mother at the moment of your birth. Your real mom died, David." I don't know what made me ask this question, but I remember saying, "Did I kick her too hard when she gave birth to me? Did I break something inside of her?" For some reason, I felt responsible for my mother's death.

SURVIVOR'S GUILT

True to Dr. Jean Piaget's theory, an expert on childhood development, a six-year-old squints at the world differently than a grown adult. The pre-operational stage, two to seven years old, is egocentric whereby the child perceives themselves as the center of all existence. *All good and bad happenings are caused by me*, is not a farfetched thought for a runt between the ages of two and seven. Believing he was the cause of mom's death falls in line with Piaget's theory of human development. Lucid causal thinking does not bloom until years later.[93]

---

[93] *Mary Pulaski, Understanding Piaget: An Introduction to Children's Cognitive Development (New York: Harper and Row, 1971).*

Seems like from that point forward, I smashed toys, lit fires, broke the rules, gave my parents the cold shoulder, acted out in class. From there on-in, I was hard to handle.

Ah, survivor's guilt is the problem under the hood! Survivor's guilt is the haunting distress people suffer after an event that struck a deathblow to others but spared them. Auto accidents, combat, and house fires are just a few scenarios that leave its survivors with the conscience-stricken question, *Why am I still here?* Studies show that 90% of catastrophe overcomers experienced survivor's guilt.[94] If you've never experienced such torment, do you recall how bad you felt about being healthy while watching a close friend disintegrate from cancer?

How do we leap from guilt to anger? Defense mechanisms theory argues that anger is the psyche's way of diverting its focus from unpleasant feelings.[95] In the case of David Berkowitz, anger is a diversion from guilt. Guilt feels painful, like a polyester shirt on a rash. Anger feels powerful, like a cape that turns Clark Kent into Superman. David gets angry to deflect feelings of guilt, so he can feel powerful rather than painful. He'd prefer to wear the cape instead of the polyester shirt.

Let me put it this way. Have you ever lashed out on someone right after you cheated on a test, broke a vow, blew it as a parent, or lied to someone you care about?

---

[94] Daniel Amen, "Understanding Survivors Guilt and PTSD," *Amen Clinics*, last modified March 1, 2021, https://www.amenclinics.com/blog/understanding-the-relationship-between-survivors-guilt-and-ptsd.
[95] Leon Seltzer, "What Your Anger May Be Hiding," Psychologytoday.com, last modified July 11, 2008, https://www.psychologytoday.com/us/blog/evolution-of-the-self/200807/what-your-anger-may-be-hiding.

Anger, in those moments, is your subconscious attempt to dodge guilt.

History is filled with examples of the guilt-ridden getting angry to avoid feeling guilty. Why did the Caucasians loathe the Africans so much in the early days of America? Hmm, maybe to placate their guilt-ridden consciences from the act of kidnapping the Africans and enslaving them. The Caucasians perceived the Africans as terrible to justify their crimes against them. The psyche is too fragile to bear the agony of guilt. Therefore, the psyche turns to anger to protect itself from feeling anything unpleasant. Anger is the psyche's bodyguard from all unbearable emotions.

In the 1980s, a televangelist lambasted Catholics over "false doctrines" during his program. A wise mentor of mine told his wife while watching the fiery-faced preacher, "This evangelist is dealing with heavy guilt about something." A few weeks later, the televangelist was caught red handed with prostitutes. When I asked the mentor how he discerned that hidden reality, he said, "A finger pointed at others reveals three fingers pointing back at you. Anger is often a self- incriminating statement."

> I didn't know it as a child, but I can see it clearly now. So much of my anger came out of guilt. I had so much guilt for believing that I killed my own mother.

To review, anger is a flashing light on the dashboard that indicates something is wrong under the hood. Anger points to fear, shame, powerlessness, disappointment, or any vulnerable emotion. Anger also conveniently diverts our attention away from these painful realities by giving us a boost of adrenaline. Adrenaline works just like a painkiller. This sensation anesthetizes the agony of what we're really feeling. For young David, anger was a diversion from survivor's guilt.

Debates ensue amongst criminologist over whether David's anger was misogynistic since he targeted women. Most criminologists theorize that he displaced the anger he felt with his birth mother towards the ladies parked in cars. I believe that the true object of his anger was with himself. All other focuses, which there were many, are diversions from the hatred he harbored towards his own soul over supposedly killing his mother.

ANGER AND DAIMONION

How does daimonion coerce the angry into accomplishing its mission? Ephesians 4:27 clearly states that unresolved anger gives Satan a "place" or some translations say a "foothold." The Greek term for "foot-hold," *topon*, connotes an advantageous position during war.[96] A foothold is like a beachhead during a battle, a position whereby the enemy lands its forces behind its adversary's borders. Simply stated, unresolved anger grants Satan access behind the borders of our shell into our souls.

Another scripture that illustrates this same fatal outcome is Proverbs 25:28, "A man without self-control is like a city broken into and left without walls."[97] Walls were ancient security systems that kept enemies from breaking into a territory. Losing self-control is compared to the disengagement of that security system. Think of your head as the security system that keeps you safe from predators. When you use your head, you make strategic decisions that protect you from any threats. When you lose your

---

[96] "τόπος," *Bible lexicon, https://www.studylight.org/lexicons/eng/greek/5117.html.*
[97] *The Holy Bible, NIV.*

head (a.k.a, getting angry), you disengage your security system. Now, you are wide open for rivals to ravage your land like a city without walls.

Now, let's specifically discuss how anger escalates from the psychological into the diabolical. Let's reference Ephesians 4:26-27, along with scenes from David's story, to witness how an enraged person gets *carried away* by evil. Ephesians 4:26-27 states, "Do not let the sun go down while you are still angry, and do not give the devil a foothold."[98]

First, it begins with *erosion*. Ephesians 4:26 cautions us about not letting the sun go down on our wrath. This phrase, "let the sun go down..." was a popular axiom amongst the Greek philosophers when referring to the act of deferring something or putting it off. For instance, if you realize the sun went down in the middle of a work project, you tuck that undertaking away for the next day. Letting the sun go down on your anger signifies the act of tucking away your hurt feelings for another day. *I don't want to discuss it now – maybe tomorrow.* In most cases, you never get to it. You just keep putting it off.

David had a habit of letting the sun go down on his anger. Every time Mrs. Sosnoff probes David, "Why are you angry," David sucks it up. Every time his father Nat questions him, "What's wrong, son? It hurts me that you won't talk to me," David sucks it up. Over time, the feelings he sucks up eat him up. Hence why I say *erosion*. Mark Twain captures this phenomenon poetically, "Anger is an acid that does more harm to the vessel in which it's stored than any object on which its poured."[99]

[98] *The Holy Bible, NIV.*
[99] *Mark Twain, quoted by https://www.brainy quote.com/quotes/mark_twain.*

I, too, harbored erosive emotions as a child. My mother stood in the kitchen while I sprawled out on the couch when she asked me, "Mikie, did Ben touch you inappropriately?" The simple mention of that pedophile's name, Ben, was a kick to the groin. I cupped my hands against my ears while yelling, "I don't want to talk about it!" From then on, I had problems sleeping at night. My stomach was forever in a state of turbulence. What I sucked up was eating me up. David continues:

> I was in a constant state of agitation. Teachers couldn't get me to sit still. My father struggled to stop me from punching myself in the head. My emotions were inwardly devouring me.

When you suppress uncomfortable emotions, they don't just disappear. Candace Pert, neuroscientist and author of *The Molecules of Emotions*, says that emotions remain shut up inside of you in the form of neuropeptides. Neuropeptides are the biological capsules of emotions, and they modulate nearly all your bodily functions.[100] Suppressing emotions involves amassing these neuropeptides like slowly filling a balloon up. At some point, if you keep going, the balloon pops. When you overreact to someone, let's say you scream at the waitress for screwing up your order, your exaggerated reaction is comprised of all those old neuropeptides surging to the surface. Suppressed shame, guilt, fear, and other unpleasant emotions rush to the top like lava in a volcano. Simply stated, emotions avoided are emotions empowered.

Now, *erosion* results in an *explosion*.

---

[100] *Candace B Pert, Molecules of Emotion: Why You Feel the Way You Feel (New York: Touchstone, 1999).*

Ephesians 4:26 ends with the term, *wrath*. The Greek term for "wrath," *paragismo*, refers to an act of rage or an explosion.[101] Explosions don't just destroy a single object but annihilate everything in its vicinity. The data shows that anger impairs our judgment towards others, essentially turning everyone into an enemy. Anger makes us more prejudice towards outsiders and form hostile opinions about others.[102] For these reasons, Aristotle stated about anger, "To be angry with the right person, to the right degree, and at the right time, and for the right purpose, and in the right way — that is not within everybody's power and that it's not easy." For many of us, anger detonates like an indiscriminate grenade.

When I ask David a question about who he was mad at as a kid, he replies,

I hated my neighbors. I bullied kids in school. I screamed horrible statements at my parents. I'd rip holes in my mother's blouses. I couldn't stand my teachers. I was mad at everyone. The public assumed I was some kind of woman hater, but I hated everyone. During SOS, I threw a cocktail bomb at my neighbor's home because of the family's barking dog. Back then, you didn't want to get me started because I had no breaks.

Here lies the point where we get *carried away*. Here lies the point where anger escalates from psychological to diabolical. Here lies the point where anger becomes more than a mortal emotion but a foothold for Satan.

---

[101] *"parorgismós," Bible lexicon.*
https://www.studylight.org/lexicons/eng/greek/3950.html0.
[102] *Nancy Wartick, "Hardwired for Prejudice," New York Times, April 20, 2004..*

If your anger were purely psychological, you would only target the object of offense. You would storm into the donut shop, holler at the girl for messing up your iced coffee and leave your wrath behind you. But that's not what happens. You holler at the girl, then howl at the kids, the spouse, or your colleagues. If you get *carried away* too far, you pout, *I hate everyone*. You're angry, not just with a single nuisance, but all humanity. In these moments, you've become a conduit for an enemy who wages war against all humanity. At this point, your frenzy is a vessel for satan's fury.

Have you noticed that mass killers do not merely target the object of their hatred, hence the term "mass"? David Cullen establishes within his scholarly depiction of Columbine that school shooters Eric Harris and Dylan Klebold were not raging against bullies on April 20, 1999. Rather, the boys endeavored to massacre the entire school with propane-tank bombs planted in the cafeteria that thankfully never detonated.[103]

Eric Harris ranted in his online diary, "Kill mankind. No one should survive."[104] Even Heath High School killer Michael Carneal stated, "I am seriously mad at the world." Andrew Wurst, the Parker Middle School shooter, told a close friend that he hated the world.[105] Mass killers don't just target someone but rage against everyone. Behind the scenes of these massacres, an unseen nemesis whips up personal offenses into massive onslaughts.

---

[103] *Cullen, Columbine.*

[104] *Cullen, Columbine.*

[105] *Nils Böckler, Thorsten Seeger, Peter Sitzer, and Wilhelm Heitmeyer, "School Shootings: Conceptual Framework and International Empirical Trends" in School Shootings: International Research, Case Studies, and Concepts for Prevention, ed. Nils Böckler, Thorsten Seeger, Peter Sitzer, and Wilhelm Heitmeyer (New York: Springer, 2012).*

On August 10, 1977, David Berkowitz sat dazed behind the wheel of his car outside his apartment building on Pine Street in Yonkers. A paper bag concealing the .44 caliber was just several inches away. A rifle, ammunition, and maps of crime scenes were scattered in the backseat. An unsent letter, addressed to the leading detective of the Omega Task Force, Sergeant Timothy Joseph Dowd, was buried underneath the weapons. Police drew their Glocks swiftly, provoking David's admission, "You got me." Detective John Falotico, standing at the driver's window, asked, "Who do I have?" David replied, almost under a trance, "the Son of Sam."

The New York Times reported that David was headed to a disco club in the Hamptons for a mass shooting just before being besieged by cops with drawn pistols. Berkowitz told a police officer after his arrest that he was fit to die in a blaze of glory while exterminating as many as possible.[106]

A mass killer of mankind is what he would become. When I query David if the claims were legitimate, he gazes down at his now calm hands without saying anything. After a moment of withdrawn silence, he says while choking up,

I was a soldier of Satan.

Before our session closes, I revisit the earlier incident. "Why were you so upset with that inmate outside the infirmary?" To my question, David pops open the hood for us to see what's happening underneath. He's learned over thirty-five years of walking with Christ to answer God's question, *David, why are you so angry?* David knows that's it's better to LOOK IN than to LASH OUT.

---

[106] Maury Terry, *The Ultimate Evil* (New York: Bantam Publishing, 1989).

Anyone insisting that positive trajectories aren't possible for criminals never spent 100 hours with this free bird. Sure, David still gets angry. He even stews in it for a bit. I stewed that same day in a traffic jam on Rt. 84. I've never met a person who doesn't agitate over an impeded goal or a deliberate slight. Don't you? Getting angry is human. But managing that anger is divine.

After a long, heart to heart session, David tears up rather than tearing something up. He's willing to be vulnerable instead of needing to feel powerful. He's okay wearing the itchy polyester rather than the cape. So far away from that little boy in Mrs. Sosnoff's office, David faces what he feels. David reveals the source of his anger. By uncovering the source, he lessens its force. With a deep sob, David replies:

He embarrassed me. I have so much shame over the man I was, and he touched that shame.

David Berkowitz with his adoptive mother,
Pearl, at his Bar Mitzvah.

CHAPTER 3
SHAME

For the accuser of the brethren is cast down, who accused
them before our God, day and night.
Revelation 12:10

TOXIC SHAME VS. TONIC SHAME

In mid-summer 2022, I pay Shawangunk four George
Washingtons for two Polaroids® of David and myself with
a cheesy New York City mural behind us. After the photo
shoot, I hand David a Polaroid® to memorialize our
friendship in his cell. He peeks for a millisecond at the
photo and slides it across the table back to me. I take slight
umbrage over the return, questioning if maybe I've made
more of a fuss over our friendship than what's actual. I'm
embarrassed by my gesture, like a schoolboy feeling stupid
over an unreciprocated invite to his birthday party.
David's sharp intuition picks up on my uneasiness before
I even vocalize my thoughts.

> Don't take it personal. I don't like looking at myself.
> I don't even read what's written about me. My good
> friend, Roxanne Tauriello, did a tremendous job
> capturing my testimony in book form. I couldn't get
> beyond the first few pages because of this thing I
> have with myself.

I'm convinced that the "thing" David has with himself is
shame. Shame is more venomous than guilt. Guilt is the
foulness you feel over what you did, but shame is the
filthiness you feel about who you are. Guilt says, *I hate what
I did* while shame says *I hate who I am.* Most definitely,

David evolved into a new man through the power of the gospel since his conversion, but he's still being shaped on the potter's wheel like the finest saints among us. Shame is a lump in the clay that has yet to be fully smoothed out.

Let's distinguish between two kinds of shame – tonic shame and toxic shame. *Tonic shame* is that blush after you're caught pilfering an Oreo from the cookie jar. You know, that red face that emerges from being caught red-handed? Or the shame that Adam and Eve felt when they hid from the benevolent God they betrayed. *Tonic shame* is healthy and not to be eliminated. Or else you become shameless. The nation of Israel once became so brazen in their rebellion that God expressed disappointment over the fact that they "do not even know how to blush," an utterance that repudiates their shamelessness in Jeremiah 8:12.[107]

Other shame is *toxic,* like the humiliation from being sexually abused. *Toxic* shame is when you see yourself as culprit for circumstances outside your control. *Toxic shame* is poisonous, making us feel antsy in our skin for no good reason. I've had my fair share of *toxic shame*. I remember being humiliated about my bare torso at six years old when my Papa took me for a walk during a family vacation in Cape Cod. I had no time to throw on a T-shirt and felt humiliated because the world could see the hole above my groin. *Toxic shame* makes you feel like a freak for merely having a belly button.

American author Ann Patchett eloquently expounds upon the difference, "Shame should be reserved for the things we choose to do, not for the circumstances that life puts on

---

[107] *The Holy Bible, NIV.*

us." [108] The first shame that Patchett mentions is *tonic shame,* whereas the second shame is *toxic shame.*

David Berkowitz first suffered from a *toxic shame* over believing that he killed his mother as a young boy. The alleged death of mom was completely outside his control, yet he believed a kick on the way out the birth canal put her six feet under. What began as guilt, *I did something bad,* evolved into a shame that said, *I am bad.*

HIDING IN THE DARK

For a long time, I tortured myself with the assumption that I killed my own mother. I started hiding in dark places. I mean, I'd spend hours in closets, under beds, even on a sunny day. My adoptive mom assumed I was playing stickball. That craving for darkness, I believe, was demonic.

One night, I snuck down the fire escape, meandered the streets, and made my way into the scene of a fire. Firemen everywhere. It was probably about 3 or 4 a.m. when my dad found me. Poor guy probably searched the streets for a while after finding my bed empty. I just loved darkness. I remember roaming the dark alleyways of the Bronx when my parents were sleeping.

Hiding in the dark is a habit that begins shortly after David internalized the falsehood that he killed his own mother. David didn't merely tuck away his feelings about killing mom. Rather, he hid himself entirely. Similarly, Adam and Eve didn't bury the crumbs from the forbidden fruit they

---

[108] *Ann Patchett, State of Wonder (New York: Harper Perennial, 2011).*

devoured. *Quick, hide the apple! God is coming!* Nope. Instead, they hid themselves completely.[109] The tragedy of shame is that when you experience it, you don't just hide your secrets, but you hide yourself. Darkness is a comfort zone for those who feel despicable.

> Remember that kid who killed all those elementary school kids in Sandy Hook? What's his name? Adam Lanza. That's right. I remember seeing photos of his bedroom in a news report. Reminded me so much of my apartment in Yonkers. All of Lanza's windows were covered with black tarp. If you go back and look at the photos NYPD took, I had long curtains that kept the sunlight out.

David's mention of Lanza reminds me of my drive through that murky town, Newtown, Connecticut, on every commute to Shawangunk via Route 84. I get the creeps passing by the sign "Sandy Hook." Adam Lanza's google-eyes were apertures into a soul so bleak that black tarps weren't necessary. The twenty-year-old who killed twenty children and six teachers on December 14, 2012, was a darkness dweller. Peter Lanza, Adam's father, once stated, "He did nothing but sit in his dark room staring at nothing." Speculations arose of whether Adam was ashamed of himself due to his speech delays from Asperger's· Syndrome. [110] Likewise, David found refuge from his shame in murky places.

> During my childhood, I hid in closets, inside crevices, wherever I could find darkness. At the same time, I had these ongoing awful nightmares about my birth father. Sometimes, I had pleasant dreams

---

[109] *The Holy Bible, KJV.*
[110] *Andrew Solomon, "The Reckoning," The New Yorker, March 10, 2014.*

of him rescuing me from my misery. But mostly, I had dreams about him hunting me down for payback. "I'm gonna get you for killing my wife, you rotten little boy."

Sigmund Freud theorized that an individual's dream world is a mental safety valve. Through dreams, a person expresses deep fears and wishes that remain unconscious in wake reality. The dream world allows expression of emotions too difficult or taboo to divulge in a wakened state.[111] For instance, David wouldn't have had the mental capacity to articulate his warped self-image at a young age. So, his nightmares do all the talking about his shame. Our nightmares crack open our craniums better than the most probing therapy sessions.

David's nightmares unveil the two sides of shame – *internal shame* and *external shame. Internal shame* is how we see ourselves, whereas *external shame* is how we perceive others see us.[112] Shame is like a concave mirror in a fun house that distorts your reflection. For David, *internal shame* is blatantly evident within his nightmare by perceiving himself as inherently evil. *External shame i*s represented by the father who sees him as evil.

In Numbers 13:33, the spies express their internal and external shame after being confronted by the giants of the land they survey. The spies bellow to Joshua, "We were

---

[111] *Sigmund Freud, The Interpretation of Dreams, trans. A. A. Brill (Hertfordshire, UK: Wordsworth Editions, 1997).*
[112] *Cláudia Ferreira, Mariana Moura-Ramos, Marcela Matos, and Ana Galhardo, "A New Measure to Assess External and Internal Shame: Development, Factor Structure and Psychometric Properties of the External and Internal Shame Scale," Current Psychology 41 no. 4 (April 2022): 1892–1901.*

grasshoppers in our own sight (internal shame), and so we were grasshoppers in their sight (external shame)."[113]

SELF-HARM

I remember punching myself in the head at a young age. I don't even recall what set off these fits. I guess I believed that I was a bad boy. I'd punch myself so hard that my adoptive father would pin me down to keep me safe. I mean, I gave myself a real vicious beating.

Self-harming might seem nonsensical, but it can be self-soothing to the shameful for at least a moment. Physical and emotional pain are processed in the same brain region — the anterior insular. Moments after a person self-lacerates, relief from physical pain is felt. But also, an easing from emotional pain is felt since they both are intertwined in the same region. Self-harmers injure themselves physically to experience the relief that comes, not just physically but emotionally. This is known as pain-offset relief. [114] Simply stated, self-harm is all about alleviating emotional distress.

Cutting oneself is not the only masochistic behavior. All sinful practices are masochistic, a tarnishing of the temple of God, on some level. Even secular studies show that exposure to pornography distorts your psyche,[115] greed

---

[113] *The Holy Bible, KJV.*
[114] *Joe Franklin, "How Does Self-Injury Change Feelings?," Cornell Research Program on Self-injury and Recovery, https://www.selfinjury.bctr.cornell.edu/perch/resources/how-does-self-injury-change-feelings-5.pdf.*
[115] *Robert Weiss, "The Reasons Someone Looks at Porn Matters," Psychology Today, last modified July 18, 2016, https://www.psychologytoday.com/us/blog/love-and-sex-in-the-digital-age/201607/the-reasons-someone-looks-porn-matters-is-why.*

results in unhappiness,[116] and the list goes on. Daimonion comes at you with destructive intentions; self-harm of all forms beat them to it.

After I became a believer, a story that jumped out at me from the Bible was the demoniac man slashing himself with stones in Mark 5. I thought, "Wow! That's me!"

The Mark 5:1-21 account of a deranged man gashing himself with rock-chips in a graveyard plays out like a horror flick. What's this guy's problem? St. Mark tells us that he's demon possessed with an evil spirit known as Legion. The name of the spirit, professed by the man's own lips, might also insinuate how these demons barged into his soul. New Testament historian William Barclay claims that the man survived a massacre known as decimation within his neighborhood at the hands of Roman *legions* (an army of 10,000 soldiers).[117] Chances are that this man witnessed people he loved die by the sword.

Legion is not merely the name of the demon. Legion is also the description of the Roman culprits that possibly killed his community and/or family. Could this man be suffering with the shame of not protecting the people he loved? Could that shame be driving him to self-mutilation? Could that shame be the cracked-open window through which daimonion crept in?

[116] *Shiyu Wei, et. al, "Greed Personality Trait Links to Negative Psychopathology and Underlying Neural Substrates," Social Cognitive and Affective Neuroscience18 no. 1 (July 2022): 1-15.*
[117] *William Barclay, The Gospel of Mark (Louisville, KY: Westminster Press, 1975).*

SHAME AND THE DEATH INSTINCT

Shortly after David's conversion, he reads this Mark 5 story. More importantly, the story reads him. He finds parallels between himself, and this man plagued by legions.

> I had these intense, ongoing urges to throw myself in front of moving traffic. I remember being inside the Westchester Avenue subway station, holding myself against the wall, as far away from the track as possible, because I was afraid I'd throw myself in front of the train. This happened almost every time we took the subway into Manhattan. Also, I had this nudging to jump from my 6th floor fire escape. I sat at the edge, tempted to jump to my death. My father actually removed my bedroom door, he was so scared that I would end my life. I was only six or seven years old.

How could a child possess such bizarre urges to die? Death wishes derive from the flight instinct. The flight instinct is a visceral reaction to bolt from a stressful situation. In threatening moments, a boost of cortisol tightens your chest and speeds your heartbeat. These biological changes scream to your brain that it's time to flee from an actual or perceived threat.[118] We've all thrown on our running shoes when a circumstance outmatches our coping skills. For instance, the enslaved Africans sang the classic hymn while working the cotton fields under their master's whip, *I'll Fly Away.* Young David's urge to die is a flight instinct that says, *get me the heck out of this stressful situa*tion. *Give me wings to fly away.*

---

[118] *Brianna Chu, Komal Marwaha, Terrence Sanvictores, and Derek Ayers, Physiology, Stress Reaction (Treasure Island, FL: StatPearls Publishing, 2023), https://pubmed.ncbi.nlm.nih.gov/31082164.*

What could six-year-old David be so stressed out about? Shame, all by itself, is a manufacturer of stress. For instance, a study was performed amongst forty-four college students that indicated shame correlated with much higher cortisol levels than a control group without shame.[119] Kids are often stressed, not because of deadlines or demands, but a pimple on the forehead or something else that causes embarrassment. David's stress arose from the shame of being a bad boy who killed his mother.

The third chapter of Genesis shows how stress often originates from shame.[120] From Adam's own account, he's afraid. Fear is synonymous with stress. Why was Adam stressed when God beckoned him? Adam's own words in Genesis 3:10 answer the question, "I was afraid because I was naked." Nakedness implies shame. In other words, Adam is stressed because he's ashamed.

Think about it, stress skyrockets at any affair where you feel like an oddity. For instance, you arrive at a party with jeans and a sweatshirt. Looking around, you think, *Holy God, I didn't read the email that said, Black Tie Event!* Or you bump into your attractive ex-spouse with heavy bags under your eyes from a restless night. Right away, the stress activates your flight instinct. Quickly, you bail from her company before she notices how ugly you got since the divorce. Shame makes sprinters out of you and me.

I felt like the universe was telling me I was bad. First, my elementary school teachers. I wasn't an easy kid to deal with, I know. I got out of my seat frequently,

[119] Sarah B. Lupis, Natalie J. Sabik, and Jutta M. Wolf, "Role of Shame and Body Esteem in Cortisol Stress Responses," Journal of Behavioral Medicine 39 no. 2 (April 2016): 262–275.
[120] The Holy Bible, NIV.

stared out the window while the teacher lectured. Nobody knew then that I had severe ADHD. That just wasn't a thing back then. Teachers treated those behaviors as a moral problem rather than a brain problem. Miss Elizabeth Jillson, this young pretty teacher, she would make myself and two other kids from the projects sit in the middle of the class with all our classmates surrounding us. She would say, "These three are the bad kids. And the rest of you, you are the well-behaved ones." God, I hated being shamed like that. I can't tell you how many times I faked sick, I'd place the thermometer against the radiator before handing it to my mother, to avoid all of that.

David's shenanigans intensified the more he was shamed. Being paraded as a buffoon by Miss Jillson in the 3rd grade, head-locked in front of classmates by Mr. Fleishacker in the 5th grade, ridiculed by administrators, and repulsed by brown-nosing classmates only fueled his antics. Just a decade before David endured this humiliation, Abraham Maslow taught the world about our inherent need to feel esteemed. Without being esteemed, Maslow argued that it's impossible for a person to "self-actualize."[121]

The funny thing is, I actually did well for a little while in school when the assistant principal appointed me to be a hall monitor. As a hall monitor, I'd go on these errands for the principal, and it made me feel important. I had an assignment, and it made me feel good. I guess the job gave me some dignity or something. As long as I had a sense of importance, I did

---

[121] Abraham H. Maslow, "A Theory of Human Motivation," Psychological Review 50 no. 4 (1943): 370-396.

112

well. But that job didn't last forever. Right back to being that rotten kid, David Berkowitz.

David proved Maslow right. Treat a child with respect, and you'll get a respectful child. When David was esteemed by the assistant principal, he felt better. When he felt better, he behaved better. Sadly, one progressive-minded assistant principal was not sufficient to offset a city of mockery.

I was also shamed in the neighborhood for being Jewish. My friend from the 3rd grade, Dominick, invited me back to his home after school one day. Dominick, like many of my friends, was Italian. My father's hardware store was next door to an Italian restaurant on Gun Hill Road. We'd eat dinner there all the time, myself, my dad, and mom, and I loved the lasagna. But the love from the Italians towards the Jewish wasn't mutual. Dominick's mother didn't even bother whispering when we walked through the door. She said to Dominick, right in front of me, "I can't believe you brought that Jew back to my home." I just stood there awkwardly.

"Do you recall how you felt when she said that?" I asked, curious to know the level of shame's intensity at that stage of his life.

Not sure exactly, but I never returned to his home again. Even within my own home, I wasn't up to par. My parents were always comparing me to my cousins who excelled in school. The Berkowitz' were all book worms, and I couldn't sit still to save my life.

And then there was my Uncle Milton. Uncle Milton was my dad's youngest brother, and he'd always comment about me being fat. He was an athletic man who jogged all the time. Whenever he'd come around, he'd talk nice to my dad and treat me like I was this fat loser. Ironically, Uncle Milton died from a heart attack while jogging. Go figure. But anyway, I never felt good enough within the Berkowitz family.

Uncle Milton's body shaming fractured David's psyche for years to come. We now know through research that mockery of one's physical appearance during childhood often leads to years of low self-esteem.[122] Think of early childhood experiences as inscriptions on wet cement. Childhood eventually ends, like wet cement eventually hardens. Yet, the inscriptions remain. During SOS, David identified himself within a letter taunting the public as "the Chubby Behemoth." Clearly, Uncle Milton's insults never faded away from his psyche.

Years later, that raven of infamy even followed him out of New York City into the Bible Belt.

Then, there was that incident at the Kentucky church when I was in the army. For a little while, I felt accepted at the church. Ya know, the church people were kind and all. The soldiers ate at church's peoples' homes for dinner after services. But then, the pastor preached this sermon about trying to get over on God. My heart was crushed when he asked the question repeatedly, "Are you Jewing God?" "Jewing" meaning getting over on someone.

America in the 1960s-70s regarded racist statements as innocuous. Hate speech was the common language of

---

122 *Nur Melizza, et. al., "The Relationship Between Body Shaming and Self-esteem in Students," KnE Medicine 3 no. 2 (March 2023): 488–499.*

many folks in urban and rural communities and thought to be a victimless act. Yet, recent data shows a significant correlation between suffering racism and internalized shame. More specifically, racism induces *toxic shame* of the utmost degree. If you criticize my personality, I can conceal the particular trait you mocked every time we are together. For instance, if you shame me for being a big mouth, I'll just talk less. If you attack my ethnicity or skin color, I am left with no place to take cover.

> The inmates and I had a talk last night at my Bible study. We discussed how much society, from Bible days all the way to the present day, shames people for their mistakes. When the woman was caught in the act of adultery, she was flashed before the Sanhedrin, probably half-naked, by the religious leaders. "This woman was caught in the act of adultery," the Pharisees said smugly. Or how about the tabloids blasting people's misdeeds before the world. Man, oh man, I know what that's like.

David's brief homily reminds me of a speech on TED Talk entitled, *The Price of Shame* by Monica Lewinsky. Lewinsky spoke about her suicide attempts amidst the abundant media coverage of the sexual affair with President Clinton. Lewinsky asserts that death was the only way out since "shame sticks to you like tar."[123] Her description of shame carries the historical precedence of founding father Benjamin Rush's words in 1787, "Shame is worse than death." Rush envisioned a nation better than its motherland, where justice was administered privately rather than through public lashings.

---

[123] *Monica Lewinsky, "The Price of Shame," TED Talk, March 20, 2015, https://youtu.be/H_8yOWLm78U.*

With all that shame, death became a fascination to me. I spent lots of time in cemeteries, reading people's tombstones. My family and I would visit dead relatives all the time as a kid. Then I developed a habit of visiting cemeteries by myself. I would visit relatives, but I would also read the tombstones of strangers. I remember wishing I could trade places with them. A death wish kept me visiting that cemetery.

David's mesmerization with death surfaced frequently in his childhood. Hiking towards the back of PS123 Junior High for some baseball, he spotted a swarm of neighbors outside of 1105 Morrison Avenue in the Bronx. A few pals called him over to see something. At the center of the crowd, an unnamed woman known as Mrs. Bulk's daughter sprawled out in a puddle of her own blood. David glared up at the roof, noting that she jumped from the rear so there'd be no attention to her descent. The poor lady wrote the last chapter of her life with a nosedive into concrete.

Nobody knows why Mrs. Bulk's daughter jumped. Maybe she, too, felt skanky in her skin after enduring a shameful trauma. Perhaps she harbored her family's humiliation since her mother, Mrs. Bulk, was a hunch-backed elderly lady in a neighborhood of mockers. Mrs. Bulk was often seen crouched over with a little dog poking its head out of her purse, a sight that made the family laughable amongst taunting urbanites.

When the police barked at everyone to leave, little David stood frozen while staring at the woman's corpse. He was the last one to skedaddle. *Get the heck out of here!* cops hollered, but David remained fixated. Perhaps it was a trance of envy, wishing he, too, could escape his own body of shame. Mrs. Bulk's daughter finalized what he only flirted with.

> As I got older, the darkness thickened. My father and sister talked on the phone about getting me some help. I was spiraling pretty fast in the year before my arrest.

David's father watched him pound his head with both fists in front of a bathroom mirror while visiting him in Florida. Nat phoned Roslyn, David's half-sister, whom he recently reconciled with after being separated at birth. He begged her to get him some psychiatric help. The next time David visited his half-sister, Roslyn tried to convince him to seek help, but he wasn't having it. She even offered to accompany him to a therapist. "I tried it, and they can't help me. I don't like talking to them," David retorted.

By the time David reached adulthood, the reasons for darkness shifted. Once a haven from shame, now a hideout for iniquity. Once a haven from badness-beliefs, now a hideout for badness-behaviors. David wrote his psychiatrist on August 1, 1979, from his Attica cell,

> It is interesting to note my changes in actions during the daylight hours and at sunset. They were two opposites. At night I hunted. During the day, I helped. I became vicious and lethal at night to people I never even knew before and whom I just met by chance. On the other hand, during the day, I was kind, friendly, and courteous to other motorists and pedestrians, also neighbors and strangers. However, these two extremes I cannot explain.[124]

---

[124] The Holy Bible, NIV.

The apostle, John, deciphered the reasons why men love darkness in John 3:19, "This is the verdict. Light has come into the world, but people loved the darkness instead of the light because their deeds were evil." David's relationship with darkness evolved into something more sinister than feeling embarrassed. Darkness became his friend.

I inquire about David's behaviors during the New York City blackout of July 13-14, 1977. The blackout was a euphoric time for nocturnal creatures (later, we shall delve into that period deeper). I imagine that this twenty-six-hour window intensified David's hunting game, though nobody ended up killed by his .44 caliber bulldog during these hours. David is too ashamed to even discuss his prowling the streets during that window.

For David, discussing the SOS era, in general, is like handling a sack of steaming hot potatoes. David skips right over the shootings to life after his arrest. Like the hot potatoes, the shootings are too hot to handle.

> My greatest pain is the shame I caused my family after my arrest. The Berkowitz family cut me off, with the exception of my dad. I'm sure the media made their lives miserable. I left an indelible mark on my family's name forever.

The surname, Berkowitz, was once an epithet of integrity amongst the residents of the Soundview section of the Bronx. Nat Berkowitz was trusted by neighbors every tax season to help get their ducks in order for the IRS. He was also the gentleman who owned the neighborhood's hardware store, the hub everyone visited to purchase the latest security systems for their homes. Back in the 1960s

Bronx, the name Berkowitz made people feel safe and secure. By 1977, the name Berkowitz sent chills up people's spines.

It was like, my crimes smeared the Berkowitz name forever.

After David was paraded on that perp walk, the name invoked a different set of feelings amongst New Yorkers. For instance, a reporter accidentally called Neysa, the mother of victim Stacy Moskowitz, "Mrs. Berkowitz" on live television. Neysa stared at the reporter with daggers, "Don't ever call me Mrs. Berkowitz....he's a bastard."[125]

Alone in my cell after my arrest, the shame of what I did to myself and the people I loved was the hardest part of being alive.

When his half-sister, Roslyn, visited him at King's County Psychiatric Hospital shortly after his arrest, David was beside himself. He jammed his fists into his cheeks, rubbing them around anxiously. His eyes shifted back and forth as if something might jump out from behind the scenes any second. Roslyn tried talking with him, but he was too out of touch.

Finally, she asked, "Would you like me to go now?" He nodded affirmatively. [126] Her next few visits become increasingly difficult, then he furiously drove her away. The shame, along with other factors, was the impetus behind his aggression.

---

[125] *"Neysa's Reaction in Court,"Youtube,*
https://www.youtube.com/watch?v=gFqL3ZvbUGo.
[126] *Wisengrad. "First Time Ever."*

I miss Roslyn so much. And my nieces, man, do I miss them. I was such an idiot. She visited me after my arrest, but I drove her and my birth mother away. I misunderstood their reasons for doing that interview with *Good Housekeeping*. I went off on them, stupidly believing that they were profiteering off my crimes. I have so much shame in how I treated them.

Amidst our talk, David's blue eyes submerge in tears with his hands jittery. I hold his hands, not to control him, but to console him. He's been set free by Jesus from the impulse to punch himself, but the instinct to punish himself remains. A statement spills out of my mouth that takes my cynical nature by surprise. "David, you're a good man," I tell him. Suddenly, the levees break. He sobs for less than ten seconds, then tucks away his tears after remembering his surroundings.

For the last forty-five years, movies, television shows, and books sketched David Berkowitz as a demented bogeyman. David understands that portrayal given the nature of his awful crimes. He empathizes with the general public's disgust towards him. The only assessments that weigh heavy upon him belong to his older half-sister, Roslyn, and his two precious nieces, Wendy and Lynn. The last time he saw his nieces, they were elementary-aged patooties playfully leaping on Uncle Dave's lap when he visited their home regularly for dinner.

I miss them so much. I wish they knew me. I'm not that guy who did those awful things.

SHAME AND DAIMONION

How does daimonion maneuver shame? Revelation 12:10 exposes Satan as the accuser of the brethren.[127] The Greek term for *"accuse," kategoron,* connotes the imagery of a prosecutor sticking his long, bony finger at you in a court room while railing condemnation.[128] I'll bet that when you self-deprecate, you often make second person statements such as, *you're an idiot* or *you're such a loser.* The second-person language hints towards another entity speaking through you and to you. Consider the possibility that when you berate yourself, after committing a misdeed or making a mistake, you are not just talking to yourself; rather, echoes of this accuser's voice from Revelation 12:10 speak through you.

These accusations work like chisels that whittle your self-image. Accusations do more than describe you but they define you. If you've ever been repeatedly insulted by someone, perhaps a parent who branded you as a dummy, or a spouse who ridiculed you as annoying, you eventually live up to the labels assigned to you (In psychology, this phenomenon is known as the Pygmalion effect[129]).

Here lies the point where beliefs metamorphose into behaviors. As a young boy, David believed he was bad. As a young man, he behaved badly. The accusations were a catchy tune that he couldn't stop singing to himself, nor could he restrain his body from dancing along. The tune was a self-destructive mantra that brainwashed him into believing he was the spawn of Satan. Solomon's words in

---

[127] *The Holy Bible. KJV.*
[128] *"kategór," Revelation 12:10, https://biblehub.com/lexicon/revelation.*
[129] *H. Jenner. "The Pygmalion Effect," Alcoholism Treatment Quarterly, 7(2), (1990).*

Proverbs 23:7 succinctly depict David's spiral into a madness, "For as he thinketh in his heart, so is he."[130] Self-image is a powerful impetus for behavior; how you see it determines how you'll be it.

> Ya' know what's always puzzled me. My fascination with horror movies, in particular, *Rosemary's Baby*. From the time I was young, I was drawn into that film.

David Berkowitz identified deeply with the 1968 Roman Polanski film *Rosemary's Baby,* a film that focuses on a mother's evil offspring. The movie became David's mirror in which he saw reflections of his own malevolence. *I am Rosemary's baby* ricocheted across the subconscious corridors of his mind. David believed himself to be just as vile as the evil baby alluded to in that film. Daimonion whispers into David's young soul, *you are my child.*

SHAME AND VIOLENCE

Let's discuss how shame and violence intersect. For example, Germany was globally humiliated prior to World War II. The Treaty of Versailles in 1919 mandated that Germany pay reparations to their World War I opponents, admit their defeat and even cop to initiating the war. The treaty stripped Germans of all dignity and rendered them into the laughingstock of the European world. This treaty of shame is what fueled their metamorphosis into murderers. In Hitler's rise to power, the dictator frequently mentioned that degrading treaty within his speeches to the German people. Hitler knew that shame was a flammable substance that could be set off with just a few words. Hitler

---

[130] *The Holy Bible, KJV.*

whipped up the German's shame into a vicious savagery that could not be obstructed.

Shame morphs into violence through the following stages. First, shame begins with a perceived violation of a role, a failure to meet an expectation, or a defect that cannot be easily repaired. You might think, my *father is not happy with my performance*. Or, it might actually be stated by a second party, *you idiot, you blew it!* David recalls hearing his parents continually compare him to his more studious cousins. David, an undiagnosed ADHD rascal, felt like he never measured up to teacher's expectations, dad's wishes, neighbor's ideals, and the family's glorious name.

Second, shame induces a sense of inferiority. Shame makes us feel stupider, uglier, fatter, weaker, and morally inferior to everyone else. The shameful cannot enter a room without wondering how they rank in a competition of smarts, sexiness, or strength with others. In that shameful mindset, you play your own judge and last-place contestant.

Lastly, shame activates an aggressive pride. Now, shame and pride are two ends of the same axis. Shame says, *I'm lesser than everyone else*, whereas pride says, *I'm better than everyone else*. Violence is the shamed person's attempt to leap from one end of the axis to the other, to feel superior rather than inferior. Author and psychiatrist James Gilligan (1996) states in his research on mass killers and shame, "The purpose of violence is to diminish the intensity of shame and replace it as far as possible with its opposite, pride, thus preventing the individual from feeling overwhelmed by the feeling of shame."[131]

---

[131] *James Gilligan, "Shame, Guilt, and Violence" Social Research 70, no. 4 (2003): 1149–80.*

An excerpt from David's letter to his psychiatrist on May 20, 1980, alludes to this pendulum swing from shame to a fatal pride. In the letter, you can see how his violent crimes were attempts to find something that endued him with a sense of importance; that same significance he felt as a hall monitor for his elementary school principal. David says to his psychiatrist, in reference to his crimes,

I did my job well (SOS). Perhaps this compensated for my failings at everything else.[132]

The synergy between shame and pride is like submerging a beachball into the pool. Pushing down that beach ball is analogous to being humiliated. A lover's rejection, a parent's insult, or a friend's ridicule, real or imagined, is just like being shoved into the water. But the beach ball doesn't stay down! Instead, it doubles up as it thrusts up with aggression, smacking you in the face. Similarly, the shamed party pounces up from the ashes with malevolent energy.

When I think of the shame-violence connection, I'm reminded of my friend's domesticated possum. An older friend of mine told me about how he once trained this possum to follow him to elementary school, wait for him outside, and journey with him back home. He even took the possum into his bedroom and turned it into a house pet. Every person whose ever been shamed can relate to this domesticated possum. You feel like you've been beaten down into something lesser than what you are. Well, the day came when that animal remembered its true nature. The possum suddenly mauled my friend's face. Tragedies occur when the shameful rise up from their disgrace to prove their significance.

---

[132] *The People vs. David Berkowitz "Dr. David Abrahamsen-Berkowitz Letters."*

Ironically, commotion flares up in the visiting room at Shawangunk between two Hispanic ladies and an inmate. The tension rises as the bolder Latina closes the gap between her face and the inmate's mug. She squares off with the hulkish inmate twice her size. She spits out profanity as the other Latina sits quietly. Unholy fragments flying off her tongue imply that she's upset with the way her sister's been treated by this grotesque man. Hulk pivots his head left and right, wondering whose watching. He talks to her through clenched teeth, probably saying, *You better shut your mouth before I....* If shame was propane, his massive cranium would have detonated. Clearly, he's enraged over being made to look like a fool. He's about to snap back at her but looks over at the security guard, who carefully monitors the situation. David says to me about the situation at hand:

> I'm convinced the only two restrainers that keep people behaving properly are the Holy Spirit and law and order. When those restrainers are removed, bedlam breaks out.

David threw those restraints to the wind many moons ago. Back in 1977, NYPD established a task force known as Omega to hunt for him.

"We had a psycho out there, and he had to get caught," Detective James Justus of the task force stated in a 2017 interview.[133]

In public, a madman roamed the streets with a need to flaunt his power. Yet, in private, a disturbed young man saw reflections within the mirror of "the little brat," "the

---

[133] *Sal Bono, "40 Years After Son of Sam Arrest, Detective Reveals How Cops Finally Ended His Reign of Terror," Inside Edition, last modified August 1, 2017.*

outsider," "the chubby behemoth," and "Beelzebub". Law and order couldn't cap this cocktail of deep shame and brewing violence. Law and order couldn't stop that submerged beachball from thrusting up with doubled-up force. Law and order couldn't subdue the domesticated possum from snapping.

Then, on August 11, 1977, that infamous perp walk occurred right after his arrest. The *New York Times* splashes a photo of him smirking with the headline, "Suspect in Son of Sam Murders Arrested: Police Say .44 Caliber Weapon is Recovered."[134] Was it a cocky leer like so many believe? Or was the smirk a manifestation of deep shame and nervousness, just as he claims?

Remember, shame and pride are two ends of the same axis. Probably the best explanation for the smirk — a smile rooted in shame but overcompensated by pride. On the surface, arrogance. Underneath the surface, a deep inferiority complex.

Throughout my session notes, I referred to David by his last name only until the Holy Spirit prompted me to modify my reference to him as *David* rather than *Berkowitz*. A surname makes him sound criminal. His elementary school teachers probably called him by his surname when he was in trouble. But his first name, David, humanizes him. Shortly after I modified all my references, I read a letter that he wrote his psychiatrist on July 4, 1979, in which he stated,

I noticed that you never refer to me as Mr. Berkowitz but just Berkowitz. This is understandable. Truly, I

134 Robert McFadden, "Suspect in Son of Sam Murders Arrested: Police Say .44 Caliber Weapon is Recovered," New York Times, August 11, 1977.

must be a very evil and unrepentant man. In your opinion, do you think there's any hope for me in becoming a productive citizen?[135]

NEYSA MOSKOWITZ

As our session closes, David's eyes glisten as if he watches a pleasant rerun of his life on the movie screen of his mind. He says:

So much healing happened through my friendship with Neysa Moskowitz (a long, tearful silence) ...She was a beautiful woman. What God accomplished by bringing us together is a story in itself. God used that woman to repair my dignity.

Hold up! A friendship with Neysa Moskowitz, the mother of the SOS's last victim? If anyone asked Ms. Moskowitz to identify her enemy in 1977, she would have stated with no delay, "David Berkowitz." Her daughter Stacy's neck and head were pulverized by two.44 caliber bullets, while seated with her boyfriend in a parked car under a moonlit sky. The last words that Neysa heard just before Stacy left the house, "Don't worry, mom. He's not targeting blondes."

Before David's arrest, Neysa vented to the media in her thick Jewish-American, New York dialect, "An animal like this has to be caught — not to die, but to be tortured for the rest of his life...he's not human. I would die right here and now just to see this man punished."[136]

---

[135] *The People vs. David Berkowitz, "Dr. David Abrahamsen-Berkowitz Letters."*
[136] *Neysa's Reaction in Court. https://www.youtube.com/watch?v=gFqL3ZvbUGo.*

I question David with a dropped jaw, "You and Neysa were friends? How did this happen?"

> Only God. We corresponded for a couple of years and even spoke on the phone regularly. We had plans of meeting in person. My friends on the outside offered to pay her way to New Jersey, then meet me. They were gonna take her to Beth El cemetery in New Jersey to see her daughter. Ironically, the same cemetery where my adoptive mother Pearl lays to rest. But then, Neysa passed away from cancer. But, yea, we wrote all the time. I'll give you copies of our letters.

I'm eager to get a copy of these letters. I'm curious to know how Neysa addressed her long-standing nemesis, the one who pled guilty in killing her daughter. Reflecting on the Neysa I knew through the media, she would have called him an evil dog or a devil. Remember how she scolded that reporter who clumsily addressed her as "Mrs. Berkowitz"?

(I later received copies that confirmed Neysa's love for him. She even requested that David, the guy responsible for the death of Stacy, pray for the healing of her only daughter alive).

I ask David, "How did she address you in her letters?"

David's eyes swell up again with that familiar crack in his voice. This time, his tears reek of dignity rather than infamy. This time, he looks up at me rather than down at his hands. This just might be the part of the story where some of that sticky tar called shame was peeled off his psyche.

> She called me Davie.

David Berkowitz with his adoptive parents
at his Bar Mitzvah.

CHAPTER 4

ABANDONMENT TRAUMA

I will not leave you as orphans.
John 14:8

FEAR OF ABANDONMENT

I ask David Berkowitz about the most grueling part of prison over the last four decades. Is it the puny cell no larger than your standard bathroom? Is it the bland chow that hardly appeases his Bronx-conditioned taste buds? A boiled hot dog is a far cry from a sizzling slice of New York City pizza. Or how about the sciatic nerve pains from sleeping on a mattress too shallow to buffer the springs underneath? These are the sixty-nine-year-old inmate's daily hassles.

David's reply has roots that shoot down deep. I surmise his answer traces back to a cataclysmic moment at Brooklyn Hospital four days after June 1, 1953. His response derives from a trauma that his mind can't recall, but his sympathetic nervous system never forgot; a moment that coarsened his soul. His response makes me curious about how many times my own reaction to what's *before* me stems from what's *behind* me.

> The hardest part of being in prison all these years is the relationships you form that suddenly dissolve. People come and go, and it's painful saying goodbye. For instance, I built so many relationships at Sullivan prison. I was there twenty-seven years, ya know. Then, one day, they tell me, "Berkowitz, pack your bags. You're being transferred to Shawagunk." Just

like that, I lost connection with brothers I counseled, prayed with, and walked alongside for years.

The fear of abandonment is more common than you imagine. Haven't you noticed a subtle awkwardness when saying goodbye to someone over the phone? Or maybe it takes you forever to say "good night" when leaving a friend's home? You stand at the doorway, putting on your coat for twenty minutes, striking up new conversations just as the old talks fade. That awkwardness might derive from the fear of abandonment. A subconscious impetus that says, *what if this is the last time I ever see this person?* This could be the reason you dread saying goodbye.

The Annual Chapman University Survey of American Fears of 2022 revealed two of the top five fears relate to abandonment — a loved one getting sick and losing a loved one. [137] Why else would Jesus Christ's pledge in Matthew 28:20 to His followers be, "Surely I am with you always to the very end of the age."[138] The Savior could have offered many promises before His final departure. He might have said, "I'll be there to protect you," or "I'll be there to provide for you." Instead, He simply says, "I'll be there," as if the assurance of a friend's presence is all we really need.

When my adoptive mother, Pearl, withered away with cancer, I couldn't stay in the hospital too long when my dad took me to visit her. I'd disappear. Take long walks outside while he stayed in the visiting room. I couldn't face the reality of saying

---

[137] *"The Top Ten Fears in America 2022,"* Chapman University, last modified October 14, 2022, https://blogs.chapman.edu/wilkinson/2022/10/14/the-top-10-fears-in-america.
[138] *The Holy Bible, NIV.*

goodbye to her. Then she passed. I was fourteen years old and started spiraling quickly.

Most of us adjust to the fact that relationships are like cogwheels. We make contact with someone for a moment, move onward, and sometimes come full circle to touch again. This circuitous motion is a fact of life most people cope with fairly well. Others soothe their feelings of loss with Tito's® vodka, Ben and Jerry's® ice cream, or sex with strangers. And then, a handful of people like David go berserk when people depart.

> I had a tough time when I came home from the army. I remember attending my buddy Eddie's wedding. It was a good time, ya know, mingling with old friends, but everyone went their own way after the wedding. There I was, alone. And then, my dad moves to Florida with his new wife. Mom already passed away a few years earlier. From that time onward, I started spiraling.

David is not exclusive amongst notorious killers in dreading abandonment. When Jeffrey Dahmer's reasons were probed for butchering, dismembering, and canni-balizing a slew of young men, his explanation flew in the face of the media's speculations. Reporters supposed that his disturbing deeds were hate crimes since the victims were mainly African Americans. They presumed that race-related rage was at the heart of this bedlam. Dahmer's stoic response was unexpected, "I didn't hate them. I just didn't want them to leave me...The eating of the heart and the arm muscle, it was a way of making me feel like they were, uh, a part of me."[139]

---

[139] *"Inside the Mind of Jeffrey Dahmer," interview by Inside Edition, https://www.youtube.com/watch?v=iWjYsxaBjBI.*

Why are some people's reactions to abandonment so hysterical? What makes David or Dahmer any different than you and me? Most folks don't pull a trigger when they feel abandoned. However, some snort a line, inject a needle, or sniff glue after losing someone. Some ladies boil their man's bunny if he leaves her (an allusion to the film *Fatal Attraction*). Some dudes become crazed stalkers after reading a "Dear John" letter by a lover who left. When reactions are hysterical, the pain behind the reaction is historical. Let me say that again — hysterical typically means historical.

DISTANCE FROM ADOPTIVE DAD

"Did you get along with your dad and mom?" I inquire, figuring that his relationship with adoptive parents is the root of his pain. Attachment Theory experts argue that relationships with our caretakers lay a foundation for all other relationships. Bonds with caretakers set the tone for all subsequent relationships.[140] I knew some facts about Nat Berkowitz – a hardworking provider, an affectionate dad who sobbed during a press hearing after his son's arrest, saying, "I will live with this heartache for the rest of my life." More important than the facts, I needed David's own feelings on his dad. The poet Anne Sexton wrote, "It doesn't matter who my father was. It matters who I remember he was."[141]

My adoptive mom and I were somewhat close until she passed when I was fourteen. My dad tried a million ways to get close to me. Ten days a year, he

---

[140] David B. Abrams, et al. "Attachment Theory," in *Encyclopedia of Behavioral Medicine* (New York: Springer, 2013).
[141] Ann Sexton, Journal entry, 1972, https://poietes.wordpress.com/2019/01/22/it-doesnt-matter-who-my-father-was-it-matters-who-i-remember-he-was-anne-sexton-from-a-journal-entry-1972.

shut down his shop to take us on vacation to upstate New York for swimming, mountain climbing, camping. Even after she died, the trips continued. I remember our last trip together to Mount Washington in New Hampshire. He tried hard, but for whatever reason, I just couldn't get close to him.

Being a father much like the Prodigal Son's dad in Luke 15, Nat never pushed away his adopted son. Instead, his adopted son drove him away. Why? In the sport of boxing, an idiom is used to describe a fighter who dodges his opponent's punch by striking him first. The idiom is uttered by sports commentators, "he beat him to the punch." When I asked David if he pushed his dad away to avoid being pushed away himself, he paused for a pensive moment. Did he abandon to avoid being abandoned? Was he beating his father to the punch?

It's very possible. I mean, the more he loved me, the more I hated him.

David's distance from dad stunted his own development. Ancient wisdom emphasized sonship as a pivotal factor in a boy's passage into manhood. Men are often introduced in the Bible as the son of someone — Isaac, the son of Abraham. David, the son of a Jesse. Jesus, the Son of God. Many surnames — even in our modern Western culture — still carry the vestiges of this ancient wisdom. Names such as Johnson mean "the son of John," Ben-Hur means "the son of Hur," and McDonald means "the son of Donald." Men were known in respect to their fathers because sonship is a basis for personal identity. Let us not forget what David would later on nickname himself – the *Son of Sam*.

Who you are is shaped by whose you are. Dean Martin hit

it on the head with the timeless lyrics, "You're nobody until somebody loves you."[142] No surprise that the stats show 71% of high school dropouts, 90% of all runaway kids, and 60% of all youth suicides are fatherless kids.[143]

Some fatherless kids are dad-deficient, meaning that dad is nonexistent. Other kids, like David, are dad-distant, meaning that dad is not available. Nat Berkowitz labored twelve-hour days at his hardware store to keep away the wolf at the door. He wished to be present at David's baseball games and other events, but it was impossible without the debt-collectors devouring him.

My dad worked long hours at the hardware store. Gone from sunrise to sunset, ya know. And when he came home, he tried to get close to me, but I just pushed him away. After my mom died, the distance between us was vast. We were like two ships passing in the night, living in that apartment. A lonely time indeed with just my dad and I in that apartment.

So, why did David resist the love of his adoptive father? Surely, he didn't need to be the SOS. He could have been the "son of Nat" a well-respected elder in the community who operated a hardware store, labored tirelessly to support his family, and was known by neighbors as a respectable man. If David was beating him to the punch, what would make him think he had to? Nat only showed himself to be faithful. Answering these questions was the hallmark of David's own journey in 1974.

---

142 *James Cavanaugh, Larry Stock, and Russ Morgan, "You're Nobody Until Somebody Loves You," Peermusic Publishing," performed by Dean Martin, https://www.lyrics.com/lyric/34356218/Dean+Martin/You%27re+Nobody+%27Till+ Somebody+Loves+You.*
143 *"The Statistics Don't Lie: Father's Matter," https://www.fatherhood.org/father- absence-statistic.*

SEARCH FOR BIOLOGICAL FAMILY

In 1974, I ventured on a mission to find my biological father.

According to experts in adoption studies, the leading reasons why adoptees search for biological parents include: to forge a bond with biological parents because of a breach with adoptive parents, to fill an emotional void, and to deepen their sense of personal identity.[144] Not one, but all of these factors stand true for the emotionally destitute David Berkowitz. For some adoptees, finding answers is like scratching an itch. For David, finding answers was more like mending a hemorrhaging wound.

I found a brochure for ALMA, the Adoptee's Liberty Movement Association, on a seat in a classroom at the Bronx Community College. Like it was left there for me. I was a student at that school, my tuition funded by the GI Bill, when my eyes landed on this flyer. Right away, I knew that I should contact the organization. It tapped into an instinct within me.

What is ALMA? Circa 1950s, Jean Paton crusaded for the rights of adoptees to reconcile with their birth parents. Up until that point, birth records were legally inaccessible. Paton, a twice-adopted woman who only felt complete after reconciling with her birthmother at forty-seven years old, preached her message, "In the soul of every orphan is an eternal flame of hope for reunion and reconciliation

---

[144] Tom Andriola, "Top 5 Reasons Adoptees Search for Birth Family Members," last modified August 15, 2016, https://adoption.com/top-5-reasons-adoptees-search-for-birth-family-members.

with those he/she has lost through private or public disaster."[145]

In 1971, Florence Fisher, another crusader inspired by Paton, influenced legislators to overturn the sealing of adoptee's birth records and founded ALMA. Florence herself was a New York housewife who reconciled with her birth family after decades of estrangement. Fisher's words in a New York Times article encapsulated David's feelings at that time perfectly. "The need is not that of a child for a parent, but rather a need to acquire a history and biological relatedness in a world that has asked us to live a contrived identity in a contrived reality, not just as a child, but for all our lifetime."[146] Without Paton and Fisher blazing the trail, no opportunity would have been afforded to David to uncover its roots.

> I started attending monthly ALMA meetings upstairs in a midtown Manhattan church. I shared my story with other adoptees searching for birth parents and birth parents searching for the babies they gave up. I told about how my birth mother died during my delivery. Everyone chuckled. Why are they laughing at me? Then, someone pipes up. Turns out, this was a common tale that most adopted kids were told at that time.

So-called experts told adoptive parents to lie to their kids about their birth circumstances. I guess the lie was supposed to reduce the rejection or something like that. I left that meeting baffled by what I heard. Did my parents

---

[145] Chapin Wright, "Who Am I?," Washington Post, February 26, 1978.
[146] Enid Nemy, "Adopted Children Who Wonder, 'What Was My Mother Like?'" New York Times, July 25, 1972.

lie to me all these years? Could my real mom still be alive? If so, would she want anything to do with me?

Heeding ALMA's advice, David rummaged for his birth certificate at the Vital Records Department on Worth Street in Manhattan. In a large dusty book with tiny print, he located fifteen births on June 1, 1953, in Brooklyn Hospital. Only one record slightly resembled him — Richard David Falco, the son of Betty Falco.

Richard David? But I'm David Richard. Falco? That's Italian. I thought I was Jewish.

David inched into the light of who he truly is and why he never fit in with the Berkowitz tribe. Many success stories are told by people who were adopted as infants and assimilated nicely into their new families. Studies indicate that adoptees older than one years old are more likely to develop attachment problems. [147]Yet, David was the poster child for Reactive Attachment Disorder, a disorder characterized by a fear of getting close to anyone, aversion to affection, and outbursts of anger. [148]Strangely, this curly-haired, husky boy could never bond with his adoptive family even though he was only four days old when rescued by the Berkowitz family.

I didn't want to call my father because he wasn't too happy about my mission. He took it deeply personal

---

[147] Linda Van den Dries, Femmie Juffer, Marinus H van IJzendoorn, and Marian J. Bakermans-Kranenburg, "Fostering Security? A Meta-analysis of Attachment in Adopted Children," Children and Youth Services Review 31 no. 3(March 2009):410-421.

[148] Maria Del Duca, "Kids Confidential: What Reactive Attachment Disorder Looks like," Leaderpubs,asha.org, last modified July 13, 2013, https://leader.pubs.asha.org/do/10.1044/kid-confidential-what-reactive-attachment-disorder-looks-like/full.

that I insisted on meeting my birth family. But the confusion was too much for me to contain. I needed him to set the record straight. And he did just that. He told me, "David, I'm sorry we lied to you all these years. The doctors told us to tell you your birth mother was dead. She's not dead, David. Your birth mother is alive. I'll mail you your original birth certificate. I've kept it locked away in a security box since you were four days old".

All these years, David felt like a lone cub in the Congo. Now, he had a chance to locate the lioness's whereabouts. Had she ever pondered what became of the little boy she bonded with for nine months? After hours of searching though microfilms of telephone directories at a Manhattan library, he narrows it down to a woman on 42nd Street in Borough Park, Brooklyn.

Imagine that! She lived just one borough away from the Bronx. All these years, he meandered through the Congo while his lioness mother remained alive somewhere in the Sahara.

Yahweh thought it'd be an amusing plot detail that David arrived at his birth mom's suspected home shortly after Mother's Day. A Chinese family chowed on white rice with their front door open as he trudged up the stairway. David asked the family if an older lady, maybe sixty years old, lived in the building. Blank stares followed his inquiry. An outsider himself, David smiled at the foreigners and kept it moving. The youngest daughter in the family trailed behind him. "Sir, there's an older lady on the floor just above us," she said.

"Oh, thank you," David replied.

Approaching the door, David noticed a *Mezuzah* hanging from the upper-right doorframe. A *Mezuzah* is a small, decorative case containing a verse from the Torah that memorializes God's commandment to the Hebrews in Egypt. Yep, a Jew lives here. *Mommy?* David smiled broadly. Quickly, he conjured up a plan to reconcile with his first and only love. David left something behind that would hopefully reconcile the cub with the lioness.

On May 12, 1975, a dainty Jewish lady in her sixties walked down several flights to retrieve her mail. An envelope, folded many times until it was small enough to push through the narrow slit above the mailbox, awaited her. The envelope read, "Private: Mrs. Betty Falco (ONLY)." Whomever left the greeting card is a wary individual, emphasizing the exclusive content by writing in heavy print, (ONLY). The individual did not want the world meddling in this sacred moment between a mother and her son as it did once before. The lady opened the card that read "Happy Mother's Day" with an original poem on the inside jacket. The neat print suggested that its author labored over every jot and tittle. The poem read:

So, as it was once before,
We've been destined to meet once more.
And I guess the time is now.
I should say, hello – but how?

A phone number with the Bronx area code — 917 — not so subtly invited her to make a call. Initials "R.F." caught her attention but rang no familiar bell. *Hmmm*, the lady wondered. She returned to her apartment without any haste. She phoned the number as if she's simply called to straighten out a misunderstanding. A gentle voice, like that of a little boy, echoed through the phone waves, "I'm your son, Richard Falco. You gave birth to me on June 1,

1953." Like sudden hail on a sunny day, Betty Falco sobbed with no tissues at hand.

For the next forty-five minutes, mother and son repaired the breach. They shared a moment you'd only see on the Hallmark Channel. Tears of exhilaration burst across the phone line. Betty informed her beloved boy that he had a half-sister, twelve years older, named Roslyn.

> I have a sister! I was totally overjoyed. I always wanted a sister. I couldn't wait to meet my new family. This reunion would plug the hole in my soul, gnawing at me since I was little. Initially, my mother said, "Let's meet in two weeks." We hung up the phone, and she called me right back within a minute or so. "We can't wait two weeks to meet you. What's the soonest you can get to your sister's home in Queens? We want to see you as soon as possible."

"You want to see me as soon as possible?" David was flabbergasted to feel so wanted. That's not to say that Nat and Pearl Berkowitz didn't toil at welcoming him into the family. Expensive toys, yearly vacations, nightly prayers before bedtime, freshly baked cookies after school. Nat and Pearl took their vows at the adoption ceremony seriously. But, like trying to adhere tape to a wet surface, all that affection never stuck. Love-extended does not guarantee love-received. The next day, David drives to Queens to reconcile with his tribe.

> It infuriates me how the media distorted my reconciliation with my birth mother and sister. All these so-called experts speculating on talk-shows about how the reunion sparked my killing spree. Professors speculating that I targeted women that looked like my mother. A bunch of Freudian

nonsense about me displacing anger with my mother for abandoning me onto the victims. Go back and look at the victimology. That's not even factual about all of the victims having a resemblance to my mother. Some with blonde hair, others with dark hair. Anyway, my reunion with my birth family was glorious, unrelated to the crimes.

I ask a question I'm afraid will infuriate him. "You started the killings right after your reunion with your family?" I ask.

Yes.

"And you were killing during the same season you met with them?" I ask.

Yes.

He knows what I'm implying, but he takes no umbrage. Instead, he says without flinching,

My birth family was not the reason for the killings. On the contrary, my family was my refuge.

At first, I was skeptical. Like the rest of America, I saw David as a lunatic taking out his mommy issues on helpless women. After all, didn't Emerson say, "Men are what their mothers made them." [149] A host of dead poets, philosophers, and shrinks agree that many of a man's defects can be pinned on mom. Then, I dug a little deeper, dropping $50 on eBay with a purchase of a *Good Housekeeping* magazine article from November 1978. David called the

---

[149] *Ralph Waldo Emerson, https://www.goodreads.com/quotes/1212701-men-are-what-their-mothers-made-them.*

article "truthful" and insisted I read it. The title says it all, "The Startling Story of the Son of Sam's Real Mother" (Interestingly enough, the reporter of the story, Susan Wishengrad, was David's cousin)[150]

Betty and Roslyn spare no detail in this nine-page spread about building a relationship with David two years prior to his arrest. One particular detail grabbed me by the shirt-collar.

Roslyn recalled how her half-brother didn't want to leave her home after dinner one evening. He asked if he could sleep over since the traffic was so heavy. She remembered thinking it was an odd request because the traffic was light at that hour. David wrestled that evening with the urge to kill and overcame it. Being with his new family was an impetus to do right, not a provocation to do wrong. Just as David described, his new family was not the reason for the killings but his refuge from killing.

> It was the happiest day of my life, meeting my mother, sister, and two beautiful nieces, Wendi and Lynn. Those two little girls called me Uncle David right away. I fell in love. We shared a dinner together, laughed, wept. My mother held nothing back. Turns out, she carried on a seventeen-year affair with a Jewish guy, a married man, named Joseph Kleinman. They fought hard during the pregnancy. He insisted on adoption, but she wanted to keep me. He demanded she list Falco on the birth certificate, the name she bore from a previous marriage. He threatened to withhold money if she kept me. My mother was barely making ends meet cleaning

---

[150] Wisengrad, "First Time Ever."

houses. She knew she couldn't provide for me. Finally, she gave me up, but with a broken heart.

Today, David consoles himself with the heritage of a mother who loved him enough to give him up. How we explain what happened to us bears more of an influence on our psyches than what actually transpired. Proponents of narrative therapy will tell you that your explanations are more impactful than your experiences. How you see it and say it matters the most. A person is responsible for managing their own biographical narrative and the message it conveys.[151] In David Berkowitz's self-narrative, love has two sides. Love is not just a mother's embrace, but it's also a mother's release.

Back in spring 1975, seated around Kasha and split pea soup, Betty spilled her guts about the most traumatic moment of all. She shed light on an affliction that David's mind forgot, but his soul remembered vividly. She unraveled a trauma that his central nervous system relives day after day.

"Four days after your birth, I dressed you up nicely for your new *Mishpacha* (Yiddish for family). I bathed you in my tears on our way to the front stoop of Brooklyn Hospital. There, I handed you over to a liaison of the Berkowitz couple. I learned what great people they were and knew this was the right thing to do. But that doesn't mean giving you up didn't shatter my soul," Betty stated.

A bond between mother and son was severed on June 4, 1953. Of course, women give up infants for adoption every

[151] Courtney Ackerman, "19 Best Narrative Therapy Techniques," *Positive Psychology.com*, last modified March 9, 2023, https://positivepsychology.com/narrative-therapy.

day without causing irreparable damage. But every child responds distinctively to trauma. David, for whatever reason, was marred at the core by that moment.

Oxytocin flooded the blood streams of mother and child as Richard David (now David Richard) cleaved to his mom's womb for nine months prior to his birth. Oxytocin is dubbed by doctors as "the bonding hormone" or "the cuddling chemical" because it produces a sense of attachment between two people.[152] Think of oxytocin like an adhesive, a strong piece of tape, that fastens two items together. Now, imagine removing the tape from whatever it sticks to. Try placing that tape on a second object. The adhesive won't be as sticky, and in some cases, it won't stick at all. When Betty walked away, little David struggled with sticking to anyone else. The seeds of an attachment disorder were planted within baby David on that Brooklyn Hospital stoop; a kernel that gradually sprouted into a barren shrub known as the SOS.

Baby David's first reaction says it all. On route to his new residence at Stratford Avenue in the Bronx from Brooklyn Hospital, an approximate thirty-five-minute drive via the Triborough Bridge (now Robert F. Kennedy bridge), baby David involuntarily laid in the doddering Jewish arms of Nat Berkowitz's mother, Freida, while weeping uncontrollably. No matter how much Pearl and Freida tried comforting him, baby David just kept crying.

My father drove us home from Brooklyn Hospital while my mother and grandmother sat with me in the backseat. I was screaming, completely

---

[152] Naomi Scatliffe, Sharon Casavant, Dorothy Vittner, and Xiaomei Cong, "Oxytocin and Early Parent-Infant Interactions," International Journal of Nursing Science 6, no. 4 (October 2019): 445-453.

inconsolable, for the entire drive to my childhood home in the Bronx. That's what my grandmother Freida told me years later. They kept trying to comfort me, but I refused to be comforted. I just screamed.

Infants sob all the time because they yearn to be held. Pick the infant up, sing the child a lullaby, caress the head, and he or she quiets down. But David still sobbed profusely even after being held and caressed. Perhaps he cried not from the agony of bond deprivation — *I want to be held!* — but from the trauma of a bond disruption – *What happened to the lady who let me go? Where is my mom?* Researchers Hepper and colleagues (1993) conducted a study that showed newborns prefer a mother's voice over a stranger's, highlighting the tangling between mother and child's souls.[153] At four days old, David voyaged miles away from the voice that soothed him for nine months and four days.

PRIMAL WOUNDS

Therapist and adoption expert, Nancy Newton Verrier, classifies what happened to baby David as a "primal wound." A primal wound is defined as a psychological injury inflicted upon a helpless baby when forfeited for adoption. The baby's brain is too undeveloped to identify the well-meaning intentions behind such an action. In-stead, the baby experiences the separation as utter abandonment. Such an injury often leaves the child with a fragile sense of self and a profound feeling of

---

[153] *Peter G. Hepper, D. Scott & S. Shahidullah, "Newborn and Fetal Response to Maternal Voice," Journal of Reproductive and Infant Psychology, 11 no. 3 (1993): 147.*

disconnection. Verrier compares the wounded baby's new relationship with adoptive parents as gluing a broken plate together. The best glue in the world will not override the fragile seam between the pieces. [154]

Statistics confirm Verrier's portrayal of adoption as a particular trauma. Researchers Slap, Goodman, and Huang (2001) conducted a study amongst 6,577 adolescents that indicated adopted kids were four times more likely to attempt suicide than non-adoptees.[126] More frighteningly, a study by David Kirschner, PhD, author of *Adoption Forensics: The Connection Between Adoption and Murder*, showed that 16% of the 500 known serial killers in the U.S. were adopted as children. That might not sound like a substantial figure until you compare it to the mere 2% of adoptees among the general population. A serial killer is eight-times more likely to have been adopted than non-killers. Furthermore, Kirschner also revealed that adoptees are fifteen-times more likely to kill their parents.[155]

At that Queens dinner table in spring 1975, Betty resumed her story. She shared about the only other occasion she saw her beloved son. Eighteen months after her heart broke, she showed up at a legal proceeding where a Family Court judge signs the Order of Adoption. The Order of Adoption officially ended Betty's parental rights while inaugurating Nate and Pearl as the legal father and mother. Betty claimed that baby David locked his eyes upon her as she stood by herself across from the Berkowitz family. Out of all the people inside that tribunal, he stared at her. If the look wasn't enough to yank her heart, he smiled with

---

[154] *Nancy Newton Verrier, The Primal Wound (Baltimore: Gateway Press, 1993).*
[155] *David Kirschner, "Adoption Forensics: The Connection Between Adoption and Forensics," Crime Magazine, October 13, 2009.*

endearing dimples. Perhaps baby David's smile was one of pleasant nostalgia that said, *Hey, I remember you!*

Betty's assertion, back in 1975, probably sounded like wishful thinking. But, in light of contemporary research, her story sounds more credible. One study showed that infants discern their birth mother's armpit odors.[128] (Though these studies focus on post-birth experiences, future research might show that a mother's voice or smell is still distinguishable at later times.)

Was there something Betty uttered in that courtroom that snatched baby David's attention? Years later, David mentioned to me how he adored the sound of her "nasally Brooklyn dialect with a hint of Yiddish," when they first spoke on the phone. Perhaps the mother is an irreplaceable figure within the heart of a child. In the adoption of baby David, a judge could mandate parental rights, but he could not legislate the rhythms of the heart.

> The reunion was glorious. But, right around the time of SOS, I started drifting from my birth family too. Sadly, the reunion was too late to save me. I was already too messed up in the head to bond even with my birth family. I stopped taking calls, stopped paying them visits.

During a recent interview with Dr. Lee Dalphonse (a psychotherapist who was also adopted after spending several years in foster care), we discussed how infants and young children are psychologically impacted when permanently separated from their biological parents. While some experts have labeled these developmental experiences as "primal wounds," Dr. Dalphonse described the impact of being removed from the family of origin with more nuance understanding, acknowledging that ".... permanently removing an infant or young child from their family of origin undoubtedly has a profound impact that lasts into adulthood, thereby shaping adult attachment style and adult parenting style." But, Dalphonse continues with what he believes to be equally or even more so impactful than the disruption at birth. "There is a significant risk of psychologically harming children when biological parents are repeatedly referred to as the 'real parents'. While it may not be intended as a put-down, such terminology is invalidating to children and their foster/adoptive parents because it directly implies that that the parent-child bond is not real for foster children and adopted children." [156]

Every so often, David refers to his biological parents as his "real parents". Perhaps this adjective is a Freudian slip into his inner world as a child where he felt like his bond with his adoptive parents was less than real. Maybe he learnt that terminology from teachers, neighbors, and adoptive family members who unwittingly reinforced the notion that the Berkowitz' adoptive clan was less legitimate than the family of origin. If that were true, David's struggle to bond with his adoptive parents after they told him he was adopted becomes even more comprehensible. How do you bond with parents that you perceive as less than real?

Facts are, the Berkowitz' were two remarkable people whose realism was not authenticated by blood but by constant labors of love. Every adoptee whose been raised by wonderful adoptive parents should know that blood might be thicker than water, but love is thicker than blood.

---

[156] *Lee Dalphonse, in-person interview by Michael Caparrelli, Cranston, RI, July 10, 2023.*

Though I didn't recognize how blessed I was as a kid to have my adoptive parents, I do now. God was so good to me to give me Nat and Pearl, dad and mom.

Only 2% of readers can relate to David as being an adoptee. However, adoption is not the only trauma that disrupts the bond between child and caretaker. Similar traumas include the neglect of a child's needs. Austrian psychologist, Renee Spitz, presented compelling research in the 1950s on babies who developed physical and emotional maladies from not being held enough by guardians. Other traumas include being physically and/or sexually abused. In all cases of bond disruption, the baby's soul is torn from its initial source, compromising its adhesion to bond with anyone else. Insecure attachment styles sprout from all sorts of bond disruptions.[157]

To lighten a heavy moment, I query a teary-eyed David about his favorite song growing up, the kind of 45 record he'd played out until the needle scratched.

The Beatles but not their earlier corny hits.

Of course, tunes like *All You Need is Love* only teased younger David with pie-in-the-sky notions of something he couldn't comprehend. What if love was nowhere to be found?

I preferred The Beatles, Long and Winding Road.

I certainly see why David would chime along to that tune. In a NYPD photograph of his Yonkers apartment post-

---

[157] R. A. Spitz, No and Yes: On the Genesis of Human Communication (New York: International Universities Press, 1957).

arrest, you'll spot a few records on the messy floor.[158] I wonder if this Beatles record was one of the records. The lyrics, supposedly written by Paul McCartney about the band falling apart, poignantly convey Berkowitz's struggles with bonding. The prose captures that worn piece of tape falling off everything it tries to stick to. The lyrics capture a "long and winding road" that leads to doors that never open.[159]

ABANDONMENT TRAUMA AND DAIMONION

Daimonion targets orphans. You can learn how these imps operate by watching how their soldiers behave. For example, soldier Charles Manson learned tactics on how to hustle the fatherless in prison from fellow pimps. The pimps taught Charlie how to woo young women with "...daddy problems who'd buy into come-ons from a smooth talker."[160] Cubs are only safe from predators in the jungle when they stay within the range of the patriarchal lion's roar. Without an attachment to a patriarch, the cubs become lunch.

Jesus' pledge to believers in John 14:18 speaks volumes about protecting our welfare, "I will not leave you as orphans." [161] The Savior promised to not leave us as orphans because orphans are at risk for physical and spiritual predators.

Being an orphan is not just a reality but a mentality, a toxic

[158] Chris Harris, "Inside the Son of Sam Case," People, August 10, 2022.
[159] Joe Taysom, "The Song That Split Up the Beatles," Faroutmagazine.co.uk,,accessed April 23, 2023. https://faroutmagazine.co.uk/the-song-that-split-up-the-beatles.
[160] Jeff Guinn, Manson: The Life and Times of Charles Manson (New York: Simon and Schuster, 2013).
[161] The Holy Bible, NIV.

mindset often cemented by early childhood experiences. Realities can change for the better, yet orphans remain destitute in spirit. In fact, positive changes in reality sometimes worsen their reactions. Remember David's reaction to his nurturing adoptive parents, and later on, his birth family. The more they loved him, the more he drives them away. David shared these exact feelings with his psychiatrist on June 18, 1979,

> I dislike it when people love me too much. They become too possessive. They start to smother me. I can't breathe anymore.[162]

Anna Freud, daughter of the legendary Sigmund Freud, observed babies in an orphanage who were severed from their families during the war for their own safety. The psychoanalyst reported her findings in a manuscript entitled, *Infants without Families.* She described the infant's new geographical reality, the Hampstead War Nursery, as positive, safe, and nurturing. Yet, these scarred infants slammed their heads against floors and cribs while acting aggressively towards new caretakers. Freud stated, "all of the improvements in the child's life may dwindle down to nothing when weighed against the fact that it has to leave its family to gain them."[163]

If you suffer from an orphan mentality, how comfortable are you with people who lavish love on you uncon-ditionally? Chances are, you're cynical about every kind gesture. You think to yourself, *What's their angle?* And too much affection instigates aggression. You get angry with

---

[162] *The People vs. David Berkowitz, "Dr. David Abrahamsen-Berkowitz Letters."*
[163] *Anna Freud and Dorothy Burlingam, Infants Without Families (New York: International University Press, 1944).*

people who love you so sincerely. Maybe because, like Berkowitz, you're trying to beat them to the punch.

The most fascinating observation from Freud's findings pertains to how the orphans bonded with each other as they grew older. The bonds were so tight between the orphans that caretakers couldn't take one for a walk alone but had to invite all the others. The orphans also refused medical treatment for ailments if their peers didn't receive the same treatment. Even when disputes broke out among them, they would instantly unify and turn on any adult who tried to intervene. Freud's data established that orphans forge tribes amongst themselves.

> It was around 1975 that I met these two brothers at a party in Pelham Bay. They were bad dudes. They showed interest in what I was interested in — black magic and the occult. At the time, *The Exorcist* was popular, so we talked about it. Eventually, I was regularly meeting up with them and others at Untermyer Park in Yonkers. There, we offered sacrifices to Satan.

Data reveals that socially maladjusted kids are more likely to join cults, violent gangs, exploitative relationships, and other dastardly bands.164 Orphans are drawn to tribes where camaraderie does not entail exchanges of affection. What David found in that Satanic gathering, known as the Children, were social dynamics he related to much easier than what Nat and Pearl offered. The Children were a group of locals who engaged in satanic rituals at Untermeyer Park in Yonkers. There, he established

---

164 *Alastair Macfarlane, "Gangs and Adolescent Mental Health," Journal of Child and Adolescent Trauma 12 no. 3 (Sept. 2019).*

camaraderies where intimacy was not necessary. There, he found friends that would stand beside him (so he assumed) without needing to get inside him. He forged relationships with people that might break his back, but at least they wouldn't break his heart.

I probed the inmate, known as SOS, about his frame of mind when he was first locked up in Attica in 1978. I was curious to know if the twenty-four-year-old figured out that he was duped by daimonion.

> It took years for the truth to set in. I had this deep conviction that Satan would soon bail me out. I was committed to him, and he'd show himself committed to me. I just knew that Satan would rescue me from prison. Obviously, satan never came through. Satan abandoned me after using me.

HANDLING THE COGWHEEL

"How do you deal with goodbyes now? People coming and going?" I ask David.

In a minute or so, I'd say farewell with a fist-bump just as I ended every visit. I'd wait for the turnkey to open the steel doors, I'd head for the exit, pivot towards David for one more goodbye wave and leave my friend to himself. I wonder what becomes of David nowadays after people leave. David tells me a story that he recently shared on a website, Ariseandshine.org.

> The other night, I heard the rattle of those skateboard wheels against the concrete floor, the sound of the misery wagon. The misery wagon is what guards use to collect the belongings of inmates sick in the infirmary. For inmates, that rattle is a foreshadow of

deep heartache. The sight of that green wagon often meant that an inmate passed away. It meant, a painful goodbye. In this case, it was a friend of seventeen years battling with cancer. We were in Sullivan together, and then transferred to Shawangunk. That rattle hurt. But I didn't block it out. I grieved seeing the guard throw the last bag in the wagon.

A week after our session, I emailed David through JPay[165] to reschedule our visit on his birthday June 1. Since David has no living relatives with whom he stays in contact with, I wished to offer him company on what could be the loneliest day of the year. But I emailed him to say that I couldn't make it since my older daughter was in town.

David's response highlights the growth of a man who formerly could not tolerate relationship disappointments. Now, he handles that cogwheel of life with being funny rather than raising fury.

The only sad part is that you'll miss the birthday parade! Shawangunk put together a forty-piece marching band, a twenty-five-foot float made of cake, and one professional bowling pin juggler who can juggle sixteen pins at one time with his eyes closed. He's quite an act, and now you're gonna miss it! They will do this again on my 100th birthday, so please don't miss that.

---

[165] *https://www.jpay.com.*

CHAPTER 5

DEINDIVIDUATION

Come along with us. Let us lie in wait for innocent blood.
Let us ambush some harmless soul.
Proverbs 1:11

BELONGING

I hope you didn't wait too long?

David is short-winded, with sweat beads trickling along the brows when he asks me this question. I waited longer than the norm but relished the thirty-minute delay by people-watching in the three-ring circus, visiting room. I smirked at a plump cougar squeeze her young stud for the Polaroid® in front of that cornball Manhattan mural. I chuckled at a clash erupt between an over-bearing mommy and her inmate son. I know, I'm equally bonkers for feeding off this folly. The turnkey seated behind the desk giggles at the spectacles, too. The ground is leveled between inmates, guards, and visitors. We are all here because we are not all there.

David nearly sprinted across the facility to avoid making me wait. He cringes over the thought of being a burden to anyone. Last visit, he told me about his wish to salute the ladies in the prison mailroom and say,

I'm sorry that you have to sort through hundreds of my incoming and outgoing letters. Thank you so much for the terrific job you do.

Being a former mail-handler on 558 Grand Concourse in

the Bronx, he knew the stress of the job. God forbid, he should make their jobs difficult. David hates inconveniencing people, perhaps chronically reminiscent of how much grief he caused his family. So, I fib to spare him from cringing, "No biggie, I just got here a few minutes ago." He sighs with relief.

"Now, you said that you looked out at the skylights over Shea Stadium from your bedroom window as a kid, but were you a Yankees or a Mets fan?" I begin with a lightweight question, unaware of how much truth was jampacked into the casual subject. David pretends he's talking through a microphone like a sports announcer from a bygone era,

In right field, Roger Maris. In center field, Mickey Mantle. On the pitcher's mound, Whitey Ford. Catcher, Elston Howard.

"Ah, Yankees. The Mick is the giveaway for me." I comment.

Yea, the Yankees had great team work.

Teamwork is an underrated ingredient of success. Athletes receive accolades all the time for individual strength, speed, and stamina. Yet, the real reason behind their success is a temperament that gels well with others. Synergy, even more than ability, is the secret sauce of success.

My friends and I were a team. For instance, mountain climbing. A bunch of us kids from the inner-city joined the Appalachian Mountain Club back in the mid-60s. Just about nine miles from this prison, we'd climb the Gunks. We'd hop on a bus in the Bronx that took us all the way to Wallkill. When you drove here today, Doc, you took a right turn at the end of Rt. 300 towards Quick Road. If you took a left towards Wallkill, you'd end up where the bus dropped us off. We hiked towards the Gunks with our backpacks until a passerby gave us a lift.

"Was it the camaraderie that made you interested in mountain climbing?" I ask.

Most of my childhood pursuits were a means of connecting with my comrades. At nine years old, I didn't care about constructing forts out of sticks as much as I craved time with the friends whom I played with. Freud theorized that the Latency Stage, seven years old to twelve years old, is all about bonding with same sex peers through activities.[166] The real fun of mountain-climbing clubs and the likes wasn't just the challenges but the chumminess.

I genuinely liked the mountains. No doubt, I would have done better growing up in a small town. Rural experiences would have done me well, that's for sure. Then again, I read an ad for a Forest Ranger position in the Adirondacks after I came home from the army at twenty-one. I was interested in the job for a minute but didn't pursue it because I would have been alone. I didn't know anyone in those mountains. Being there without friends wouldn't have been the same.

---

[166] *Sigmund Freud, "Beyond the Pleasure Principle" New York: Liveright Publishers (1961).*

DEINDIVIDUATION

How much of personality is intrinsic? Deindividuation, a social phenomenon, argues that a portion of our personality is extrinsic, that is determined by the group. Deinviduation suggests that personal identity is often overridden by group identity. [167] For instance, have you ever clapped for a performance only because everyone else is applauding? Or, on the darker side, have you been in a mosh pit at a heavy metal concert? You might be gentle by virtue of disposition but act aggressively when in a crowd of slam dancers. Deindividuation suggests that our tribe shapes our vibe.

Belonging is a pivot of our personality. A preponderance of our traits spindle upon our desire to be accepted or even esteemed by our peers. For instance, you don't just like your outfit, but you wonder if others will be dazzled by it too. You use lingo that's easily grasped by your group. You even come under the influence of their values and beliefs. Monash Business School conducted research that showed friendship groups influence our political opinions; friends with similar views reinforce our positions and friends with differing views reduce our polarization.[168] All day long, you tweak yourself to fit into the tribe.

Even when you say, *I don't care what people think*, that's an inadvertent admission that you actually do care because you care that we all know that you don't care. For instance, when you post on social media, *I don't care what people think*,

[167] Jon Roeckelein, *Elsevier's Dictionary of Psychological Theories (Amsterdam: Elsevier B.V., 2006)*.
[168] Yann Algan, et.al., *"Friendship Networks and Political Opinions: A Natural Experiment Among Future French Politicians," IZA Institute of Labor and Economics, December 2020.*

you show that you care that 4,000 followers know you don't care. Selah.

It was the late 60s, Columbus High School in the Bronx, bell-bottoms, long stringy hair, protests against the Vietnam war. Those were the cool things to do, ya know. But I didn't go along with any of that. I was a patriot. I loved my country. I was joining the army soon as I graduated, and I didn't care what they thought. In fact, I left for the army the day my classmates walked across the graduation stage, June 1971. I had friends in Co-op City, a town in the North Bronx — Eddie and Lenny — who were patriots too. We talked about defending our country all the time.

Though David appeared a maverick amongst tree-huggers at Columbus High, he already had a gang of patriots waiting for him in his neighborhood. Who needs high approval ratings amongst frisbee-throwers when you already belong to a group of flag-wavers? David didn't need to fit in with the hippies because he was one of the sons of Uncle Sam. Every cub in the jungle, even the ones that roam freely, belongs to a pride. Everybody needs somebody.

I always wondered how my life would have turned out if I reconnected with childhood friends when I came home from the army. I couldn't seem to light the flame that we once shared.

THE CULT

"So, your childhood friends scatter in different directions. You're lonelier than ever, and this is the time you were introduced to the Children?" I inquire. "David, please tell me more about your introduction to this group."

It's 1975, and I show up at this party in Pelham Parkway that I was invited to. I had a joint in hand, looking for someone to smoke with. I was hoping to meet a girl, but I'd take any company.

Smoking a joint, laughing at a spoof movie, or hiking up a mountain are endeavors often done with others. Like most people, David enjoys sharing pleasures with others. He repudiates the media's depiction of him as a weird loner.

Yes, he struggled with divulging his deepest thoughts and feelings. Yes, he was a secretive person. But belonging to baseball teams, a mountain climbing club, the young firemen, auxiliary police, and the army was what he lived for. Life was always better in the company of others. Since early childhood, David lived the Hebrew adage, "A joy shared is a joy multiplied."

I meet these two brothers, Paul and Matt (pseudonyms). They seem to know more than I did about witchcraft, black magic, Satanism. They gave me answers to some of the questions about spiritual reality that I had mulled over since childhood. I mean, what I believed to be truth at that time. In fact, they even told where to go in the city to buy Anton LaVey's Satanic Bible. They mentioned this bookstore called, Magik Child.

Paul and Matt were no mavens in spiritual matters. Just a couple of rascals from Yonkers, a little older than David, with laymen's experience in the occult. Yet, they offered answers that soothed David's existential angst (a term discussed in the emptiness chapter). For nearly twenty years, David slogged over his life's purpose. He couldn't comprehend his lure to vampire flicks, Rosemary's Baby, and all the dark hideouts. Paul and Matt opened David's eyes to what appeared his true calling. For that reason, he esteemed them. The Game of Thrones saga sums it all up, "Power resides only where men believe it resides. A shadow on the wall, yet shadows can kill. And ofttimes, a very small man can cast a very large shadow."[169]

In time, they invited me to this majestic spot over-looking the Hudson in Yonkers, Untermeyer Park. There were about twenty, twenty-five others.

Doc, it looked like the scene of a horror movie inside of this particular place, Devil's cave. Satanic symbols graffitied on the walls, an altar set up for sacrifices, pitch darkness lit up by candles. Initially, I was repulsed by the sacrifice of neighborhood dogs on that altar. Contrary to what the media says, I was never a hater of animals. Annoyed by the barking, yes, but I didn't hate animals. Eventually, I was fascinated by the ceremonies they held. This was something nobody else was doing. It felt special. I felt special that I was invited into this.

"Love-bombing" is a popular recruiting tactic amongst cults. The phrase was coined by the Unification Church of the United States, also dubbed "the Moonies" after their founder Sun Myung Moon. [170] Sociologist Thomas Robbins says that love-bombing is a "sinister coercive technique" in which recruits are made to feel "special" with either affection or attention to break down their barriers. "At the early stage, resistance will be at the highest. Showing individual consideration is a perfect means to overcome it...prospective recruits are showered with

---

[169] George R. R. Martin, *A Game of Thrones* (New York: Bantam Books, 1996).
[170] James Richardson, *"Regulating Religion: Case Studies from Around Globe,"* New York City: Springer (2004).

attention. The leader wishes to seduce the new recruit into the organization's embrace, slowly habituating them to its strange rituals and complex belief systems."[171]

David was too blinded by the smoke of the love-bombing to initially discern the dangers of the cult's belief system. Love-bombing happens every day in a multiplicity of domains. Have you ever been treated "special" by some snake disguised as a Prince Charming? Or maybe a molester lavished you with gifts when you were young as part of their grooming tactics? The royal treatment floods our brains with so much dopamine that our prefrontal cortex, the logic center, disengages. We lose sight of the evil we've embraced. In some cases, we befriend perpetrators angling to destroy us. Dr. Robbins states, "There is little secret or surprise in the contention that we like people who agree with us...and would go out of their way to do things for us."[172]

"From what I've learned, and please correct me if I'm wrong, the Children were under the auspices of a much larger organization?" I ask.

Yes, our small gathering was woven into an organization known as The Process Church of the Final Judgment. And the Process gleaned their teachings from satanism and a mix of other things.

In the late 1960s, a short time after the movement was founded by a Brit by the name of Robert DeGrimston, The Process Church of the Final Judgment stretched from its

---

[171] Mark Griffiths, "Love Bombing,"Psychology Today,"last modified February 14, 2019, https://www.psychologytoday.com/us/basics/love-bombing.
[172] Griffiths, Love Bombing."

headquarters in London to twenty-two wild kids at Untermeyer Park to the Manson family in California. "Did you ever meet its founder, Robert DeGrimston?" I ask.

> Supposedly, he showed up once at Untermeyer. I was introduced to DeGrimston, but I later became doubtful if it was him. The guy didn't look like the DeGrimston I saw in pictures later on.

"What was their ultimate mission?" I ask.

> To raise anarchy much like you see with the terrorist groups oversees. Anarchy is the devil's work, and that was about our business.

Exaggerating the unrest of New York during the SOS tragedy is difficult. The OMEGA task force, 300 police officers assigned to hunt down the killer, beamed ginormous flashlights into parked cars to signal for young people to skedaddle. "No one is safe from the Son of Sam," the front page of the New York Post blared on August 1, 1977, the day after the Stacy Moskowitz shooting. Discos closed before 9 p.m., parents clung to their kids, and women even changed the color of their hair to avoid being the typical brunette target. [173] An equitable comparison from recent times would be New York City's climate in the days after two Boeing 767s struck the World Trade Center on 9/11. Like 9/11, the SOS tragedy provoked millions into a cumulative nervous breakdown. New Yorkers were falling all over themselves, trying to escape SOS.

Fear is as contagious as the common cold. Researchers from the California Institute of Technology examined

---

[173] *Harris, "Inside the Son of Sam Case."*

subject's arousal levels through a physiological-monitoring wristband when walking through a haunted house. During the thirty-minute exercise, subjects were exposed to what appeared to be the threat of suffocation, an incoming speeding car, and shots from a firing squad. Outcomes indicated a correlation between the number of friends in a group and arousal levels. Subjects walking through the haunted house in larger groups were more physiologically aroused by the threats than subjects in smaller groups.[174] As fear spreads, it spikes.

> By raising anarchy, we believed that we satisfied the appetites of the gods. We worshiped the Druid god Samhain who demanded...(David's eyes well up, his voice crackling) the sacrifice of young virgins. Samhein is where the name, Son of Sam, comes from.

"Oh, I assumed it was taken from your neighbor Sam with the barking dog?" I ask.

> The name had a double meaning. I saw my neighbor as working for the devil too.

I could never buy into such a whacky belief system, you might suppose. Experts assert that seduction into bizarre belief systems is not a matter of logical persuasion but social facilitation. Cults don't convince you with good reasons to join their activities as much as they comfort you with a good time. Instead, you'll convince yourself that black is white and up is down to lessen any cognitive dissonance you feel from being with the toxic company you enjoy.

---

[174] *Sarah M. Tashjian, et. al., "Physiological Responses to a Haunted-House Threat Experience: Distinct Tonic and Phasic Effects," Psychological Science 33 no. 2 (Feb. 2022).*

You'll rationalize away the strangest doctrines, all to fit in with the group. Soon, you'll even believe the lies you tell yourself all 3 because you crave belonging. Another way of pronouncing rationalize is "rational-lies."

An additional feature that makes a group like the Children credible is the prestige of its members. The Children were not just a ragtag band of misfits but intertwined with an elitist society. Prestigious members hosted parties at their chateaus in the Hamptons and Greenwich, Connecticut. Police officers, film producers, and doctors participated in rituals that involved animal sacrifices, sex orgies, and pornography.

"Did you know a doctor by the cult name, Molech?" I ask a question based on my research.

> Yea, we called him Dr. Palmer because he lived on Palmer Road in Yonkers. He hung out at Untermeyer Park, but I didn't know him that well. I can't even tell you his real name. He was a high priest in the cult. I heard he had children shipped to his home from Mexico or somewhere, but my first-hand knowledge is limited. This group was so secretive, ya know. Even amongst its members. Very secretive, especially with rituals criminal in nature.

The only doctor living on Palmer Road in the 1970s was Nobel Peace Prize winner, Daniel Gajdusek. Gajdusek won the award in 1976 for discovering that Kuru, a rare disease amongst the people of New Guinea, was spread through the ritualistic cannibalism of deceased relatives. [175] Gajdusek received letters from the mayor of Yonkers and

---

[175] Joe Holley, "D. Carleton Gajdusek; Controversial Scientist," *The Washington Post*, December 16, 2008.

President Gerald Ford complimenting him on his accomplishments. But even a pitch-black moon has a bright side. Gajdusek was an admitted pedophile who defended his views as natural in a documentary on YouTube, The Genius and the Boys. The doctor makes a statement that would make the most calloused criminal cringe, "Three hundred to 400 boys who had sex with me at ages eight, ten, twelve — 100 percent of them jumped into my bed asking for sex. Every boy wants a male lover."[176]

"Were these members, or any cult members, aware of SOS before it transpired?" I'm getting bolder with my questions. David nods toward my bag of spicy Cheetos.

How are those chips? I can't eat spice. My tastebuds have been conditioned to a bland diet after years of prison food.

David clasps to his privacy without buckling under the pressure of my point-blank questions. If he doesn't want to answer a question, he deflects without any apologies. He should just reply, "So, how 'bout them Yankees?" and his deflecting would not be any less blatant.

"So, the cult members played an influence on you with SOS?" I ask.

Yes.

"Were they also involved in the shootings?" I ask.

David's body tenses up like I pricked that open wound.

---

[176] "The Genius and the Boys," https://www.youtube.com/watch?v=1WF2l-d-jLM&t=65s.

I leave the subject alone, aspiring for a later opportunity to delve into the matter.

LONE GUNMAN OR MULTIPLE SHOOTERS?

David has always been reluctant to discuss the details of the group. Some speculate that he's afraid of repercussions. He stated priorly that the cult acquired facts and photos of his family, threatening to kill them if he ever disclosed secrets. Though most of his family is deceased, his adored sister and nieces are still alive. Others speculate that David lied about the cult's role in the crimes during that 1990s televised interview where he claimed that seven of the SOS shootings were committed by other cult members. I resolve to confront these discrepancies at a later date.

I should have never moved to Yonkers. I relocated to be closer to what I perceived to be my friends at that time. Bad move on my part.

DEINDIVIDUATION AND DAIMONION

How does daimonion intersect with deindividuation? As we've seen repeatedly throughout our journey, supernatural entities do not operate apart from natural phenomena. Do not think of supernatural as purely otherworldly, like little devils or angels floating above the horizons. Rather, "supernatural" means injecting the "super" into the "natural." In this case, evil injects its fatalistic power into a law of human nature known deindividuation. If evil is like the "rapids of a waterfall," as David described it priorly, then deindividuation is the actual current through which the water flows.

Deindividuation is a state of mind whereby you become so immersed in group norms that you lose your own sense of identity. David Berkowitz's adopted father, Nat, taught him to treat his neighbor with dignity. That ethos was ingrained in David, as evident in his helping hand towards that lady stranded on Lake Avenue in a snowbank, or his military service to our country.

That's not to say that David wasn't angry, all on his own, without any help from the group (Part of me believes that he could have met the Girl Scouts and still committed the crimes). Surely, he destroyed property but gunning down the defenseless was something else. Once immersed in the social norms of the Children – substance abuse, child pornography and other deviant behaviors under the guise of rituals - all of his own moral restraints were cast at the wayside. Wolves behave more ferociously when surrounded by packs than when treading the forest alone.

Deindividuation, and its horrors, are on full display during the Holocaust. A short film, *Sing a Little Louder,* offers a glimpse into how this phenomenon affected everyone in 1940s Europe. Masses of Germans fell under the spell of deindividuation as a maniacal chancellor slaughtered eleven million. Families gathered for worship in congregations across Germany while hearing the screams of children on trains zipping nearby. "Mommy, what's that sound?" a child asked momma. "Nothing. Just sing a little louder," mom replies. [177]Deindividuation is when you go along just to get along, even when others are at risk.

Social psychologists offer three reasons why deindividuation lends itself to violence. The first reason is known as diffusion of responsibility, a mindset whereby individuals

---

[177] *"Sing a little louder,' Short film, Kingdom Works, 2015.*

pass the buck of responsibility. You presume that someone else will take responsibility for any crimes committed.[178]

Interestingly enough, David spoke priorly about a "rift" between himself and the two brothers that introduced him to the cult. He claimed that the rift happened during SOS. Though David didn't detail the feud, he said that he felt "used" by the brothers. What David meant exactly by "used" is unclear. Perhaps severance from the group occurred when David realized he was left alone on the hook for the crimes. Diffusion of responsibility was no longer possible.

The second reason is anonymity — a delusional mindset whereby you perceive yourself as unidentifiable in the crowd. In 1969, orchestrator of the legendary Stanford prison experiment, Philip Zimbardo, dressed female students in lab coats for an experiment on anonymity and behavior. Half of the participants wore identity-concealing hoods, while others were hoodless with name tags. Zimbardo instructed the participants to administer an electric shock to a confederate (a supporter of slavery). The hooded participants were two times more likely to shock the confederate than the hoodless.[179] Anonymity clearly emboldened their bad behavior. Well, a crowd works just like a hood. A crowd, or a group of rascals hanging at Untermeyer, offers a sense of anonymity that unshackles our inner animal without the fear of being identified.

---

[178] Feldman, R.S., Rosen, F.P. Diffusion of responsibility in crime, punishment, and other adversity. Law Human behavior. 2, (1978).

[179] Philip G. Zimbardo, "The Human Choice: Individuation, Reason, and Order Versus Deindividuation, Impulse, and Chaos," in the Nebraska Symposium on Motivation, ed. W. D. Arnold and D. Levine (Lincoln, NE: University of Nebraska, 1969).

The last factor is known as synergy, defined as "the cooperation of two or more agents that produce a combined effect greater than the sum of their separate parts."[180] Synergy is not about addition but multiplication. For instance, Joshua 23:10 doesn't say, *One puts a thousand to flight. Two puts two thousand to flight.* Instead, it says, "One puts a thousand to flight. Two puts ten thousand to flight."[181] The verse illustrates the exponential effects of synergy, a principle that can work for both the positive and negative. Genesis 19:1-13 chronicles a mob of Sodomites that surrounded Lot's home, demanding sexual favors from Lot's guests. Genesis 19:9 shows how the mob motivated each other to break down Lot's front door.[182] As the mob unifies, power synergistically intensifies.

Evil synergy is also evident during the infamous blackout of 1977, the same year as the SOS tragedy. At 9:37 p.m. on July 13, 1977, the largest generator in New York City, nicknamed the "Big Allis," shut down after power lines were overtaxed. Nearly every neighborhood in the five Burroughs went black. For the next twenty-six hours, 1,616 stores were looted – most notably, seventy-five marts on a five-block stretch in Crown Heights were set ablaze by covetous neighbors. Dozens of Pontiacs were snatched from a Bronx dealership and 550 intervening police officers were assaulted as citizens morphed into animals. The looters fed off of each other's energy.[183]

Have you ever seen televised footage of Hitler's speeches? Notice the energy level of the Nazis when

---

[180] *Merriam Webster, s.v. "synergy," accessed July 20, 2023, https://www.merriam-webster.com/dictionary/synergy.*

[181] *The Holy Bible, NIV.*

[182] *The Holy Bible, NIV.*

[183] *"New York Blackout II, 1977 Year in Review,".Upi.com, https://www.upi.com/Archives/Audio/Events-of-1977/New-York-Blackout-II.*

they rally together around Hitler. That collective passion is almost electrifying. When we'd chant to Satan at Untermeyer Park together as one group out in the middle of nowhere, that's what it felt like. It was electrifying, just like the crowd of Nazis hailing Hitler. You could feel this superpower flowing through you.

"What scripture verse comes to mind when you think of how demons capitalize on social influences?" I ask David. What David and I have in common, besides our adoration for New York City, love of lasagna, and affinity for a good laugh, is our reverence for the sacred scriptures. We posture ourselves before that ancient manuscript like a student sits at the feet of his Rabbi. Without delay, David replies,

Proverbs 1:11 says it all about how Satan manipulates social forces. "Come let us" – the key word is "us" – "let us lie in wait for blood. Let us ambush the innocent without cause." Satan works through evil alliances, ya know.

Once again, when David recites this verse, is he applying it to the slaughter of animals? Carcasses of German Shepherds were supposedly found in the water aqueducts of the Untermeyer Park area, according to 1976 police reports.[184] The existence of a cult, and it's influence upon David, was not far-fetched by any means. But how involved was this cult in SOS? Does David just mean that he and the cult ambushed innocent dogs?

---

[184] Megan Roberts, "Satanic Panic in America's Greatest Forgotten Garden," *Atlas Obscura*, last modified August 30, 2022, https://www.atlasobscura.com/articles/son-of-sam-satanic-panic-untermyer-park.

Or does David mean that cult members were also hands-on involved in the SOS tragedies? His televised statements in the early 1990s suggested multiple shooters. Honestly, the jury, in my mind, hasn't arrived at a verdict yet simply because David offered conflicted accounts in the past and remains evasive within our sessions about the "crimes."

Either way, the deinviduation phenomenon helps us understand how David felt so invincible during the shooting spree. Even if group members were uninvolved in the shootings, a subculture that celebrates slaughter, revels in mass hysteria and canonizes Satan left its mark on David's psyche.

Deindividuation greets the members of the Children, not only in life, but also in death. Nearly all of the Untermeyer wretches died in mysterious ways within a short time frame. A brother that introduced David to the Children was found shot to death in Minot, North Dakota, less than a year after David's arrest. The other brother was killed in a fatal, one-vehicle crash on the West Side Highway in Manhattan. Murders, drug overdoses, and suicides marked the fates of others. When one domino falls, they all fall.

> If the Lord had not been on my side, I would have suffered the same fate as the rest of them. Don't forget, I was stabbed in the neck at the same time as the other cult members died horribly.

With a low-key glance over David's head, I read the clock — 11:30 a.m. is a timely departure to scoop my daughter from her bus stop, and two minutes remain.

"David, I'm sorry to end before lunch, but my daughter needs a ride in just a few hours," I say.

No worries.

We exchange parting words, fist bump, and I gesture for the turnkey to electronically unbolt the door.

"Sorry, it's countdown time. You can't go anywhere until countdown is over," the turnkey states with a firm tongue.

"But can't you just do the count amongst the people in the visiting room, then let me go?" I ask, annoyed.

"Nope. The count involves the entire facility," he says unapologetically. The culture of Shawangunk Correctional Facility ranks low on individualism. No one is counted until everyone is counted.

I apologize. I should have told you that countdown is at 11:30 a.m. It'll probably take about fifteen minutes or so.

"No fault of your own. You didn't know I had to leave at that time," I respond.

For nearly twenty minutes, we awkwardly shoot the breeze as I'm on the edge of my seat. I pretend to be engaged in David's thoughts about recent news stories in the Ukraine, but I'm really thinking about picking up my daughter on time. I know how to go along to get along too. Finally, the turnkey signals me. The barred door opens electronically and I'm on my way.

With a heavy paw on the pedal, I head to Rhode Island. I have no choice but to suddenly halt behind two cars at a red light in a small, Normal Rockwell town. The traffic signal takes so long to flash green that I could watch the entire *Godfather* trilogy. Perhaps the two drivers in front of me picked up on my hurried vibe because they blow the traffic stop, one right after the other.

Because I'm a dutiful Christian, I park for a moment at the red light. Because I'm a flawed man, I ponder, "How would a cop be able to stop all three of us for blowing the light?" Far from my finest moment, I blow the light too. Like I said, deindividuation.

David Berkowitz at James M. Kieran High School.

CHAPTER 6

HEAD TRAUMA
& PRENATAL PROGRAMMING

It (demon) often throws him into fire or water to kill him.
Mark 9:22

MISOPHONIA

The visiting room at Shawangunk gets rowdy sometimes.
Inmates, when back in the cellblocks, keep their feelings
bottled up. Belly-laughing makes you look pathetic
amongst thugs with Satanic symbols billboarded on their
beefy torsos. Outbursts of anger might get you into a
scuffle with someone who has more screws loose than you.
Tears make you look like easy prey. So, all week long,
you're capping your sensitivity. But, in the visiting room,
a face-to-face with your sweetheart pops open the lid on
that bottle. Hence, emotions flying everywhere makes a
riotous environment.

With the rowdiness comes the manhandling of furniture.
Seated behind us, chair legs scrape against the floor as an
inmate reaches over to smooch his lady. The grating
against the linoleum distracts me for a second, but I have a
brawny ignore muscle. I tune out the high-pitched
scratching sounds. I effortlessly block out the cacophony
of chewing and chitchatting. But not David. He puckers his
face like the chair legs scraped across his corneas. Certain
sounds get underneath his skin.

Please keep me in your prayers. The cellblocks have
been so noisy since the recent shakedown. Every so

often, the guards search our cells for any restricted items. It could be as simple as having an excessive amount of clothes, hygiene products, or what have you. Some inmates didn't pass the test, so to speak. Since the shakedown, so much racket.

Misophonia plagued David since his days in the Bronx, a disorder affecting twenty percent of the general population in which particular sounds trigger emotional reactions sometimes to the point of rage.[185] His half-sister Roslyn talked about a phone call conversation with him a year before his arrest when David complained about the super's two big canines in the backyard that barked all the time (David shot one of the canines but was never caught).

Do you hear that? Do you hear those dogs? They're driving me crazy. Sometimes, I think they're doing it just for spite, just to get me. When I come home, and they know I have to sleep, they start barking.

Perhaps no noise drove a spike up his spine like the barking of his neighbor Sam Carr's black Labrador, Harvey. Initially, David vented in a threatening letter on April 19, 1977:

Samuel Carr, I have asked you kindly to stop that dog from howling all day long, yet he continues to do so. I pleaded with you. I told you how it is destroying my family. We have no peace, no rest....my life is destroyed now. I have nothing to lose anymore. I can see that there shall be no peace in my life and my family's life until I end yours.

---

[185] *Arjan Schröder, et al., "Misophonia Is Associated with Altered Brain Activity in the Auditory Cortex and Salience Network," Scientific Reports 9 no. 1 (May 2019): 7542.*

The letter was signed at the bottom, "A citizen."[186] Ten days later, David shot the dog (Fortunately, Harvey did recover from the gunshot wound, living many years).

Even after his arrest, while confined to Attica, he wrote a letter to Dr. David Abrahamsen on January 10, 1981, that reveals his agony over particular noises. The letter states as follows,

> Gum cracking, the filthy disgusting, wretched habit of clicking one's chewing gum in her mouth, is, I believe, a crime to be punished only by death. Nothing, but nothing, enrages me more than to see a man or woman making constant cracking noises with chewing gum. I have gotten off buses, sometimes a half a mile from my apartment, when a person was on a city bus and was cracking gum...and once I was planning on going from corner to corner in NYC so that I may shoot and kill people who crack their chewing gum in public places, I would have done it in broad daylight and without the slightest fear. This is how much I hate this callous criminal action.[187]

HEAD INJURIES

"David, did you experience any head injuries as a child?" I inquire. A good portion of psychology derives from biology. If David had biological injuries, particularly within the brain, it might explain some psychological maladies such as misophonia and the resultant madness. Sounds initially pass through the ear canal but are processed within the brain. Damage to the brain could

---

186 *Abrahamsen, Confessions.*
187 *The People vs. David Berkowitz, "Dr. David Abrahamsen-Berkowitz Letters."*

result in sound irritation. David gestures the number two with his fingers in response to my question.

> My first head injury, I was about six or seven-years-old playing with friends outside my apartment on Stratford Avenue. I think it might have been summertime. Neighbors were outside, mainly middle-aged to elderly, seated in their lawn chairs, chatting about current events, while we kids played stickball in the streets. My grandmother was one of the ladies. Out of nowhere, a rusty pipe about two feet long came flying at me. I don't remember who threw it. I just remember it was an accident, and I bled profusely. My grandmother, Helen, took me inside, bandaged my forehead, and laid me down. Several days later, my parents took me to Dr. Edward Liss for a treatment of fresh gauze, re-bandaging, and a tetanus shot. I still have the bump over sixty years later, see?

I notice an indentation on his forehead, nearly the length of a crayon. Behind the forehead, the focal point of the pipe injury is the frontal lobe. Any damage to that region of the brain could result in personality changes, a hard time managing emotions, impaired judgment, depression, and auditory detection problems.[188] Regarding auditory detection problems, imagine someone suddenly raising the volume of your flatscreen to its max. You are startled by the loud noise to the point of screaming at them, *Turn that TV down!* Lucky is such a person for not being too close lest you slap them. That's what it's like living with damage to the auditory region of the brain.

---

[188] *Daniel Amen, Email to the author, August 2, 2022.*

My second head injury is so typical to me. I hated elementary school so much that I'd sit at the edge of my seat, waiting for the bell to ring. I'd nestle my textbooks under my arms like a football, and as soon as the bell rang, dash out the door like I was running for the end zone. I make it to the corner of Manor and Westchester, where a crossing guard was there to help us cross the street. Ya know how busy the Bronx streets are? Me being me, I didn't even see the crossing guard because I was running so fast. Bam! A midsized vehicle struck me, and I went flying into the air. The driver, a middle-aged lady, was so distraught that she remained at the scene for a bit. Believe it or not, I was fine after that injury. No blood or anything. An ambulance took me to Jacobi Hospital, but they didn't do much. It appeared to be no big deal.

Unbeknownst to David, not all brain injuries are detectable to the naked eye. Traumatic brain injury (TBI) happens when the brain bounces in the skull after an accident, leading to the rupture of brain cells or blood vessels as well as significant chemical changes. But all that damage happens underneath the surface. When you consider that the brain is the consistency of soft butter encased in a shell with many thorny ridges, you take seriously seemingly mild accidents.[189] Only a brain scan unveils if the stick of butter stays in shape after being tackled on a football field, karate chopped to the head, or in the case of David, whacked by a pipe and a car.

On my way home from Shawangunk, I listened to a

---

[189] Daniel Amen, "Most Important Lesson from 83,000 Brain Scans," TEDxOrangeCoast, last modified October 16, 2013, https://www.youtube.com/watch?v=esPRsT-lmw8.

YouTube video by Dr. Daniel Amen entitled, *The Most Important Lesson from 83,000 Brain Scans.*[190] Dr. Amen is the go-to shrink for Hollywood celebrities at the verge of a breakdown, practicing as both a psychiatrist and brain trauma specialist. I pulled over on the side of a rural Hudson Valley Road to send his office an email. I knew that the only chance of him responding would be a bodacious phrase in the subject box. My subject box read, "David Berkowitz needs your help, Doc," with a list of questions inside the email. If anyone knows how brain traumas contribute to deranged acts of violence, it's the doctor with over 180,000 brain scans from 155 nations in his database relating to human behavior.[153]

Dr. Amen responded within hours to my email, "Sound sensitivity is often the result of frontal lobe damage. The frontal lobes cannot properly inhibit extraneous noise, leaving the subject chronically stressed and irritated. David's accidents could have changed the trajectory of his life, especially if it affected the left side of his brain. I often say that the number one thing I have learned from our brain imaging work is that mild traumatic head injuries ruin people's lives, and no one knows because most psychiatrists never look at the organ they treat.

"Regarding David's violence, I think of all behavior, happening in four circles: biological (head injury, infection, toxin, genetic issues, etc.), psychological (negative thinking patterns or childhood stress), social (modeling), and spiritual (lack of clear guidelines or morals or harsh morals). How many circles does David have?[191]"

Dr. Amen's email adds a whole new meaning to that

---

[190] Amen, *"Most Important Lesson."*
[191] *Daniel Amen, Email to the author, August 2, 2022.*

statement we've all heard from someone dismissing our mental health struggles, *This is all in your head, Mike*. I feel like replying, Y*ea, my problem is in my head. It's quite possibly in my brain.* Battles with mental health issues are not just cognitive cobwebs that I disentangle through therapy. But there's a physiology behind these battles that often requires medical treatment like remedying a broken ankle or diabetes. The brain is the most pivotal organ of the body. If that organ becomes sick, the entire organism is sick.

David is not the only inmate at Shawangunk with brain injuries. Data clearly establishes a correlation between traumatic brain injury (TBI) and violent crimes. A few years ago, a study was performed in Sweden on a cohort of 269 violent offenders, aged eighteen to twenty-five in Sweden. The results indicated that 77.5% of these violent offenders reported at least one TBI in their lifetime with criminalistic tendencies subsequent to their head trauma. That's nine times the amount of head injuries than the general population, of which only 8.5% suffered a TBI.[192]

I asked Dr. Amen in a follow-up email if we could administer a Brain Spect (a sophisticated brain scan) on David. Brain Spect offers a 3-D glimpse of altered blood flow in the brain, signaling any damage resulting from head trauma. I knew that the average cost was $3,500, but I'd be willing to fund it myself if it were possible. Having studied countless criminal brains, Dr. Amen quickly responded with, "QEEG (a method of analyzing brain waves) would be your best study that could be done in

[192] Samuel Katzin, et. al., "Exploring Traumatic Brain Injuries and Aggressive Antisocial Behaviors in Young Male Violent Offenders," Frontiers in Psychiatry 11 (Oct. 2020): https://www.frontiersin.org/articles/10.3389/fpsyt.2020.507196/full.

prison."[193]My next visit with David, I told him about the QEEG. Not wanting to be a nuisance to the higher-ups at Shawangunk, David declined.

PRENATAL PROGRAMMING

Ya know, my physical injuries began long before those two head traumas. My mother's pregnancy with me was a difficult one. Her and my birth father, Joseph Kleinman, got into big blowouts about my birth. My mother, Betty, insisted on keeping me. My birth father, who I never knew, demanded she give me up for adoption or else he would financially deprive her.

My poor mother had no financial means to raise me. Anyway, they would fight. My mom told me how she jumped on top of him with closed fists, pounding on him. All the while, she was pregnant with me. I always wondered what kind of effect that fighting had on my development.

David instinctually knows what researchers like Annie Murphy Paul and Dr. Catherine Monk are discovering through scientific method about prenatal programming. Prenatal programming is an ever-expanding body of research on how mental and physical health lifespan trajectories are influenced by experiences in the womb.[194] David understood that his learning began not on the first day of kindergarten, or even in his tiny living space on 1105

---

[193] Daniel Amen, Email to the author, August 12, 2022.
[194] M. Camille Hoffman, "Stress, the Placenta, and Fetal Programming of Behavior: Genes' First Encounter with the Environment," The American Journal of Psychiatry 173 no. 7 (July 2016): 655-657.

Stratford Avenue in the Bronx, but inside the prenatal chambers of Betty Broder Falco.

Annie Murphy Paul, an acclaimed science journalist, describes the environmental cues that a fetus receives from the mother's world as "Biological Postcards."[195] A postcard is a memo from one world to another, letting the recipient know how to prepare for their arrival into that new world. A postcard might tell you by its glossy image, *Dress warm! It's cold here!* or *Brace yourself! Lots of danger here.*

Similarly, environmental cues tell the fetus that the world he/she is about to enter is safe or dangerous, warm or cold, pleasurable or painful, etc. From October 1952 to June 1953, a fetus named David received biological postcards that cautioned him for his arrival into a world of constant warfare. No surprise that David was an aggressive baby from a very early age despite the safety of the Berkowitz home. Prenatal postcards from Betty's contentious world primed him for battle.

In 2000, Dr. Catherine Monk and colleagues revealed through experiment that Annie Murphy Paul's explanation is more than a metaphor. The experiment's results indicated fetuses of anxious mothers possess a higher heart rate than non-anxious mothers.[196] An elevated heart rate is the fetus' way of non-verbally telling us, *I'm feeling overwhelmed.* Relating to David's prenatal development, Betty Falco Broder was described by her cousin Susan Sugar as a "irrationally super-sensitive type" and a

---

[195] *Annie Murphy Paul, "What We Learn Before We're Born," TEDTalk, last modified November 29, 2011,*
https://www.youtube.com/watch?v=stngBN4hp14&t=864s.
[196] *Michael T. Kinsella and Catherine Monk, "Impact of Maternal Stress, Depression and Anxiety on Fetal Neurobehavioral Development," Clinical Obstetrics and Gynecology 52 no. 3 (Sept. 2009):425-40.*

"neurotic." David said about his own mother in a letter that she was always anxiously hovering over her granddaughters, Lynn and Wendy.[197] Add to her high-strung temperament the scuffles with deadbeat Joseph when she was pregnant. David's heart rate while in the womb must have beat like drums at a heavy metal concert.

Furthermore, Humphrey and colleagues performed studies on the infants of stressed mothers during the prenatal stage. The data revealed brain damage beyond the womb — decreased functional connectivity between the amygdala and the medial prefrontal cortex at the five-week point of infancy.[198] The amygdala is the alarm system of the body; it rings loudly whenever it detects a possible threat. The medial prefrontal cortex is the regulation center of the body; it discerns the legitimacy of all threats. When there is no connectivity between the amygdala and the medial prefrontal cortex, the brain is incapable of monitoring every alarm that sounds. That was David's reality all throughout childhood and young adulthood — false alarms constantly ringing in his head. An analysis of his letters during his mid-20s shows a young man constantly alarmed by neighbors, relatives, and friends.

PRENATAL PROGRAMMING AND DAIMONION

Daimonion are like sharks attracted to wounded fish. From a distance of 1/3 mile, a shark discerns a droplet of blood and trails that drop back to its source. The sharks chow down on the afflicted sea creature as soon as they find it.

---

[197] The People vs. David Berkowitz, "Dr. David Abrahamsen-Berkowitz Letters."
[198] Kathryn L. Humphreys, M.C. Camacho, Marissa C. Roth, Elizabeth C. Estes, "Prenatal Stress Exposure and Multimodal Assessment of Amygdala-Medial Prefrontal Cortex Connectivity in Infants," Developmental Cognitive Neuroscience 46 no. (Dec. 2020).

In the same manner, daimonion target wounded people. Moses describes how Amalek, an Old Testament type of Satan, preys upon "the feeble" amongst a tribe of believers in Deuteronomy 25:18.[199] Watch how this reality plays out in the life of David Berkowitz from the time of conception. David's soul is wounded from the womb, making him a target for blood-thirsty daimonion.

Let's begin with prenatal wounds. To understand how spiritual entities weasel into the womb, consider the case of John the Baptist. Take note that the prophet was "filled with the Spirit" during his prenatal development, according to Luke 1:15.[200] Imagine, a fetus that worships God! How does this happen? Luke 1:41 tells us that his mother, Elizabeth, was filled with the Spirit.[201] She was probably praying, singing, and reciting the Torah all while carrying her baby. Think about how these biological postcards shape the spiritual makeup of baby Johnny. In short, John the Baptist's spirituality was influenced by his carrier, Elizabeth's, spirituality. Of course, the spirit of God filled John supernaturally, but through the medium of his mother's body.

Now, if a fetus can be positively impacted by the mother's spirituality, then it stands to reason that the fetus can be negatively influenced. Consider Betty's spiritual condition when she bore her baby. According to David's recollecttions of his mother, along with letters written by her cousin Susan Sugar, indicate she was a highly neurotic personality. In David's letter to Dr. Abrahamsen on August 2, 1979, describing his mother, he wrote,

---

[199] *The Holy Bible, KJV.*
[200] *The Holy Bible, KJV.*
[201] *The Holy Bible, KJV.*

She is a woman who is scared of her own shadow...All she does all day is beg, plead, and constantly apologize. What she apologizes for, I do not know. If my sister sends the kids to Carvel, she becomes semi-hysterical, almost to the point of breaking down. My nieces walk two blocks from the house before my mother starts running after them down the street. She escorts my mature nieces everywhere and while she's doing this, she's continually lecturing them on safety and about sex perverts.[202]

Betty was harassed by what the Apostle Paul calls in II Timothy 1:7, a "spirit of fear."[203] Betty's fear was not just transactional, that is, between her and others, but trans-generational. She transmits that toxic energy to her fetus. David was involuntarily drafted into a battle with a spirit of fear long before he even knew the alphabet. Fear was hardwired into his disposition through pre-natal programming. David tells me about his childhood,

I was a scared kid from as early as I can recall. I would sleep in my parents' bed all the time because of constant terror.

Now, fear is a doorway for demonic attack. Before Joshua faces enemies, God commands him, "Be not afraid."[204] Enemies pounce upon us when we exhibit signs of feeling threatened.

Author Neil T. Anderson illustrates this principle that demons are drawn to fearful dispositions with an anecdote from his childhood. Anderson describes a neighborhood

[202]*The People vs. David Berkowitz, "Dr. David Abrahamsen-Berkowitz Letters."*
[203] *The Holy Bible, KJV.*
[204] *The Holy Bible, KJV.*

dog that barked at him and his brothers when they were kids. The dog chased only him down while dismissing his siblings. Why him? Because he was the only kid that ran scared from the hound. As soon as he started running, that fearful action provoked the hound to hunt him down.[205] Similarly, daimonion aggressively pursues the fearful.

How does fear escalate to violence? Daimonion whips up our fear into violence through our fight/flight instincts. Some who are scared take flight. Others who are scared fight. Most vacillate between flight and fight, depending upon the situation. Take for instance, the startled animal that behaves viciously when frightened. From a neurological perspective, the same neurotransmitters behind fear also prompt rage. [206] Carried away by a mix of neurotransmitters and paranormal energy, the scared become scary.

Ishmael was a scared baby that grew into a hostile man. In Genesis 16:12, Ishmael is portrayed as "a wild donkey of a man; his hand will be against everyone and everyone's hand against him. He will live in hostility towards all his brothers."[207] How did Ishmael become such a pugnacious personality? What made him so hostile? Let's trace his development back to the prenatal period.

Genesis 16:4 tells us that Hagar was despised during her pregnancy with Ishmael by Abraham's wife, Sarah. [208]

---

205 Neil T. Anderson, "This Is the War We're Facing," last modified October 23, 2013,
https://www.youtube.com/watch?v=2FBC4G1hU90&list=PLVtGS2qilLGV2oN1JIJx
u-kz6v-edF_8w.
206 Fushun Wang, et al., "Neurotransmitters and Emotions," Frontiers in Psychology 11 (Jan. 2020): https://www.frontiersin.org/articles/10.3389/fpsyg.2020.00021/full.
207 The Holy Bible, NIV.
208 The Holy Bible, NIV.

Hagar was caught in a stressful love triangle between Abraham and Sarah. Hagar is subjected to contention with Sarah, all while carrying Ishmael inside of her. Biological postcards with memos that said, *The world you are about to enter is a contentious place* were sent from Hagar's central nervous system to her unborn baby. Like David Berkowitz, Ishmael arrives into the world as a fearful baby that grows into a pugnacious personality.

HEAD INJURIES AND DAIMONION

Now, let's talk brain trauma. In Mark 9:18, we encounter a young man seized by an evil spirit that throws him to the ground. In addition, "the boy foams at the mouth, gnashes his teeth, and becomes rigid."[209] Critics claim that this passage accentuates the inaccuracy of the Bible. They say that the Bible shows itself outdated by attributing the boy's behavior to demons when we now know that these seizures are the symptoms of epilepsy. What these biased critics fail to consider is that such seizures are also the result of brain trauma. Being regularly thrown to the ground by an evil spirit would undoubtedly fracture the brain, causing all kinds of unusual behaviors. A survey of 2,500 retired NFL players indicated that football players are permitted no more than three concussions in their lifetime without lifelong consequences.[210] This boy was "often" thrown to the ground. What would be the physical consequences of such regular head trauma?

Why would daimonion assault the brain? As discussed, a traumatized brain equates to a higher sensitivity to sudden

---

209 *The Holy Bible, NIV.*
210 Kevin Guskiewicz, et.al., *"Recurrent Concussion and Risk of Depression in Retired Professional Football Players,"* Medicine and Science in Sports and Exercise *39 no. 6 (June 2007): 903-909.*

sounds. Also, a limited ability to regulate feelings induced by these sudden sounds is evident. Hence, a buildup of stress occurs. David's letter to his psychiatrist on August 2, 1979, cracks open the psyche of a man with limited stress management faculties. His words reveal a man who killed not just for reward but for relief.

> I am the killer. True. But I didn't do it for the sake of gallivanting. I didn't kill for "the hell of it" or a joke...But my actions were a result of an intense amount of pressure and frustration that developed around and inside of me.[211]

David perceived his neighbor Sam Carr's dog, Harvey, as both auditory torture as well as a supernatural tormentor. On some occasions, David describes Harvey as a howling animal that drove him mad. Other times, the dog is a 2,000-year-old demon driving him to kill. This dual perception is not contradictory; rather, a complete picture of how the diabolical channels biological nuisances into violence. David elucidates on the torment in a letter to his psychiatrist while still under that awful spell from hell.

> But please don't forget one negative factor in my life which nearly drove me to madness — barking dogs and extremely loud television sets....Sam Carr certainly lacked concern for others. I pleaded. I warned. I threatened. I finally shot at his dog. He was lucky because I was waiting for him. I hid in the bushes behind his house in order to kill him with my rifle. But I finally fired on the dog instead. He never showed. [212]

---

[211] *The People vs. David Berkowitz*, "*Dr. David Abrahamsen-Berkowitz Letters.*"
[212] *The People vs. David Berkowitz*, "*Dr. David Abrahamsen-Berkowitz Letters.*"

GOD SILENCES THE STORM

Pandemonium in the visiting room escalates. David and I rely on the coping strategy he learned back in 1988 when he knelt bedside with a Gideon Bible opened to Psalm 34:6 — the tactic of prayer. We close our eyes to block out distractions. I pray for Jesus to silence the storm. David backs me up with a couple of "Amens" as I petition God for a change in the atmosphere. "Jesus, please give us peace," I pray.

Following the prayer, the racket recommences. Hardly anything changes in the environment. The dude behind me is still grating his chair against the floor. The chewing and chitchatting resume. I won't try to sound spiritual. I doubt for at least a moment the authority of our prayers.

I look over at David, expecting strain in his face. Yet, David smiles amidst the sounds without any facial contortions; instead, dimples on display with happy eyes. Sometimes, prayer changes circumstances. In this case, prayer changed the man. Sometimes, God takes you out of the storm. In this case, God took the storm out of David.

CHAPTER 7

EMPTINESS

When it (demon) arrives, it finds the house empty, swept
clean and put in order. Then it goes and takes with it
seven other spirits more wicked than itself,
and they go in and live there.
Matthew 12:44-45

EXISTENTIAL SORROW

The visiting room at Shawangunk is unusually chilly.
Though late September brings a breeze, I don't spot any
windows open. The state of New York will not dish out
money for air conditioners this time of year, so the draft is
not manufactured. I snuggle my hands between my legs to
keep warm while awaiting David's entrance. Surveying the
inmate's faces, I learn that the draft is more impressionistic
than actual. No smiles. No hugs and kisses. No intimate
chats with lovers. Blank expressions from stoic men chill
the atmosphere like a mausoleum with open caskets.

David arrives with hungry eyes. He subtlety leans into me
from his chair like he's in need of something. I offer him a
raspberry iced tea from the vending machine or the bag of
Fritos® he usually prefers amongst all the artificial chips,
but he possesses no such appetite. His soul, not his
stomach, grumbles for something good other than
goodies.

Do you have any reports to share with me, doc?
Testimonies, answered prayers. Sometimes, it gets
so gloomy here that I'm desperate for good news.

I'm tempted to uplift David with pie-in-the-sky. Maybe telling him that some big New York City publishing company might be interested in our project will spark a mile. Perhaps notifying him that a faith-based recovery program known as Adult & Teen Challenge Center might be willing to host him if he should ever make parole will perk him up. But knowing David, these circumstantial blessings won't satisfy his soul. In fact, giving lifers an optimistic forecast only fuels their disappointment. Inmates who've been locked away for decades are cynical of hope since the flip side is pain. By arousing their hope, you simultaneously awaken their hurt. So, I stick to the frigid facts, "Not much happening. How about you?"

> Just feeling a little empty lately. I always had this void inside my heart. I mean, since I was a young kid. Of course, Christ filled that void many years ago. But I still feel it sometimes. I'm a believer but I'm human.

Existential sorrow, a feeling familiar to everyone but understood by only a few, is the void that David references. The philosopher Soren Kierkegaard described existential sorrow as a meaninglessness we all experience at some point, a sensation rooted in the reality of physical and spiritual death. "When people realize that they are alive and will one day die — and there is no meaning to cling to — that person is in an existential crisis and would feel a sense of dread or angst."[213] King Solomon describes this same existential sorrow in Ecclesiastes 1:14 when he says, "All of it is meaningless, a chasing after the wind."[214]

But there was a difference between Solomon and David.

---

[213] *Sören Kierkegaard, The Sickness unto Death (Princeton, NJ: Princeton University Press, 1983).*
[214] *The Holy Bible, NIV.*

Solomon learned about his void after exhausting himself on 700 wives and 300 concubines, along with acquiring so many assets that archeologists are still digging up his gold. Solomon scaled to the top of many mountains, only to find nothing at the summit. David, on the other hand, knew life was empty since early childhood; a reality so gloomy that he pondered a death-plunge from his 6th floor fire escape. For some folks, emptiness manifests through boredom, lifeless routines, and bereavement. For David, he'd sit at the edge of that rusty egress, dangling his feet, with the thought of kissing concrete.

At five years old, I felt empty, and I was simultaneously allured by the mysterious. My gramma Helen and grandpa Harry lived in this apartment on 940 Kelly Street in the Bronx. The apartment had this dumb waiter, one of those devices hooked to a rope that made its way from the apartment into the basement. My gramma sticks her head into the darkness and yells at the Super, "Mr. Tessler, please send the dumbwaiter up." A minute later, the dumb waiter emerges. She puts her trash inside of it, and it disappears into the darkness. I'd look down into that murky tunnel, wondering what was on the other side. Who was this man at the bottom of that tunnel? My imagination ran wild. I was drawn to what's on the other side, ya know?

David echoes the cry of every empty soul, a feeling captured by the barren soul, Jim Morrison, in his song "Break on Through to the Other Side."[215] Poets throughout the centuries plagued by that feeling of melancholy wrote about visions of another realm. Individuals with

---

[215] Max Bell, "The 20 Best Songs by The Doors" Loudersound.com, last modified August 2, 2021, https://www.loudersound.com/features/the-20-best-doors-songs.

emptiness are more prone to seek fulfillment from beyond the natural sphere.

For instance, a survey conducted on 122 respondents from an urban mental health clinic confirmed a relationship between depression and spiritual beliefs. 81% of the depressed considered themselves religious.[216] The results infer that you approach the beginning of eternity only after you come to the end of your humanity. Jesus states this principle in Matthew 9:12, "It is not the healthy who need a doctor but the sick."[217] If you're down, look at the bright side — being flat on your back is the best vantage point to look but up.

NEGATIVE RELIGIOUS COPING

Even when I attended church on the army base in Kentucky, I was fascinated by the pastor's teachings on eternity. After the service, I'd visit the church bookstore. I'd read that Hal Lindsay book. I think it was called, *The* Late Great Planet Earth. All about the apocalypse, God's judgment, and the end of time. The pastor preached a great deal on that subject too.

For many folks, religious experiences close that existential gap. I now feel complete since surrendering my life to Christ, many testify. Others, like David, fall into a trap known as negative religious coping. Negative religious coping (NRC) entails a chronic state of conflict with a divine entity that punishes bad decisions and rewards good

---

[216] *Benjamin R. Doolittle and Michael Farrell, "The Association Between Spirituality and Depression in an Urban Clinic," Primary Care Companion to the Journal of Clinical Psychiatry 6 no. 3 (June 2004): 114-118.*
[217] *The Holy Bible, NIV.*

behaviors. [218] David's statement to Dr. Abrahamsen in 1979 qualifies him as a candidate of negative religious coping when he attended that church in the army,

> When I worshipped God, it was out of terror. When I didn't behave, He would put a curse on me. Maybe He'd even kill me.[219]

NRC temporarily massages the soul with the deception, *If I'm a bad boy, I'll suffer bad consequences. But if I'm a good boy, I'll avoid punishment and receive rewards.* NRC is called a coping skill because it offers a sense of control over our fate, albeit an illusion. Yet, data shows that NRC backfires by diminishing the quality of mental health over the course of time[220] because rascals like David learn that they can never be good enough. Anxiety plagues NRC practitioners who can't always get it right and dread God's response. So, the void resumes, except it becomes more like the hollow center of a tornado.

"Evidently, your religious experiences in the army didn't fill the void. What other types of things do you pursue to plug the hole?" I ask.

> I was born with this exploratory nature. My pals and I rode our bicycles throughout the Bronx, but I always rode further than everyone else. My friends weren't comfortable with venturing out far as I did. So, I'd ended up riding my bike alone. I

[218] Janusz Surzykiewicz Sebastian BinyaminSkalski, Małgorzata Niesiobędzka,Karol Konaszewski, "Exploring the mediating effects of negative and positive religious coping between resilience and mental well-being," *Frontiers in Behavioral Neuroscience* 16 (Oct. 2022): doi: 10.3389/fnbeh.2022.954382.

[219] *The people vs. David Berkowitz,* "Dr. David Abrahamsen-Berkowitz Letters."

[220] Surzykiewicz et. al., "Exploring the Mediating Effects."

actually made it to Cos Cob in Connecticut, like twenty-two miles from my home. Also, I would rummage through tenement basements in the city, looking for something. Not sure exactly of what I was looking for, but always exploring. Like I was trying to find something I lost.

Though exploration is integral to healthy development, David's hunt becomes less and less satisfying. C.S. Lewis describes this trap in his book, *Screwtape Letters*, where the satanic being says that his goal is to arouse within humanity a never-ending chase. "An ever-increasing craving for an ever-diminishing pleasure is the formula," Uncle Screwtape tells his nephew, Wormwood.[221]

CAN VIOLENCE BE AN ADDICTION?

David exhibited an addictive personality, a common outgrowth of emptiness.

> I guess I was trying to fill that void inside my heart. But I'd get bored with everything quick. I'd play with some toy, then break it after a few days. I was an avid collector of baseball cards. In those days, we would stash them inside shoe boxes. Then, I got tired of baseball cards. And I was an adrenaline junkie. Always doing dangerous things. Jumping subway trains, climbing mountains, lighting fires. But even that rush only lasted a short time.

I wonder if the SOS crimes were addictive too. Was David hitched to homicide like a man hooked to heroine? Did the pulling of a trigger offer him a rush that kept him coming back for more? I'm reluctant to pose these questions

---

[221] C. S. Lewis, *The Screwtape Letters* (London: William Collins, 2012).

because I've priorly witnessed how much grief David suffers when discussing the crime spree. Be that as it may, I propound the question since David's feedback might benefit some reader stuck in the addiction to violence. "Was SOS addictive?" I ask.

I think I will have a drink. But not raspberry iced tea. I get sick of the same old thing. How about a cherry cola?

Approaching the vending machine, I notice a sign, "Credit Card Reader Broken." Dozens of cherry colas, along with other sizzling sodas, tease me with glossy containers. The sodas seductively whisper, *You can look, but you can't touch.* The irony of how this broken vending machine relates to my chat with David doesn't elude me. The vending machine, similar to the nature of life, showcases a host of pleasures in view but out of reach. All of humanity chases after something in this life that flashes before their eyes — happiness, peace, etc. — but cannot be fully obtained. And for David, every pleasure he sought only teased him to no end.

Returning with water instead of cola, I ask the question again, "Was SOS a kind of addiction?" A vein bulges above his eyebrows like a man deadlifting 300 pounds, not so subtly revealing the density of the subject. Even decades later, the enormous weight of his crimes still isn't any lighter. Many mornings, David awakens with a heavy heart from the thought of his victims and their families. The closer I get to discussing the actual SOS tragedies, the harder it becomes for David to talk.

I told you before that I was doing the devil's work.

"Yes, but the devil has no power over us without our

desires. Isn't that what James 1:15 tells us? Desire gives birth to sin, and sin is what allows Satan access into us. So there had to be some kind of desire behind the crimes." I reference the scriptures knowing David's reverence for God's word. Yet, the weight of his crimes is still too much for him to bear. His eyes pool with tears. No easy thing for David to concur with having had a desire to kill. It is much easier to say that Satan possessed him than a desire overtook him.

With a gentle tone, I frame the question another way, "Wouldn't you agree that Satan makes slaves out of us?" David nods since Satan is an agreeable topic. "Well, slavery and compulsion are synonyms. Did you have compulsions to commit these crimes?" I ask.

> Urges, yes. I'd sit on a bench at Ferry Point Park, searching for serenity. Or, I'd park my car many nights at Orchard Beach, hoping to escape the urges. Sometimes, I'd wrestle with those urges all night in my car. Roll the windows up and down, tossing to and fro, searching for a comfortable position. Just couldn't get comfortable. Couldn't shake the urges.

A key feature of addiction is compulsion. A compulsion is when you can't get away from the stimulus, yet you can't get enough of it. A conflict exists within your soul between a demand to experience the stimulus and a desire to escape it. I want away from it, yet I want more of it, is the tug-of-war that every addict engages in. The apostle Paul alludes to this addictive component in Romans 7 when he confesses, "For what I want to do, I do not do. But what I hate to do, I do." I humorously label this chapter, "the doo-doo chapter" for anyone that's ever been stuck in some doo-doo. I don't do what I want to do, but I do do what I don't want to do.

"How about obsessive thinking? Was there any obsessive thinking?" I ask. David suspires with deep sorrow and admits:

> I spent so much money on gasoline. Money that I didn't have to spend, ya know... driving around the city for hours after I'd get out of work. I worked until midnight, punch out of the post office and head to my car. The gun was in the glove compartment waiting for me. I'd drive and drive. I was living hand to mouth because so much of my income was consumed by this mission. So, yea, obsession is a fitting word.

Like all addictions, SOS cost David more than he ever wanted to spend. Another key characteristic of addiction is a broken calculator. The prefrontal cortex, the center of the brain that calculates the assets and liabilities of every decision, malfunctions when a person becomes obsessed.[222] At the apex of addiction, some folks sell their automobiles in exchange for a nanosecond of euphoria.

"Did you derive any pleasure from SOS, even if it was just brief?" I ask. Of course, all addictive behaviors are reinforced by a desirable carrot waved in front of the frantic bunny rabbit.

> Like I said, I was demonized. The demon depleted David's personality from my body.

"Let me rephrase the question. Did the demon inside you derive any pleasure?" I ask. I keep the emphasis upon the

---

[222] Linda J. Porrino and David Lyons, "Orbital and Medial Prefrontal Cortex and Psychostimulant Abuse: Studies in Animal Models," Cerebral Cortex 10 no. 3(March 2000).

demon rather than David. Of course, I believe he was demonized but not at the expense of his own desires. Highlighting the demon rather than David affords him some breathing room inside that air-tight cell of shame.

I guess you could say that.

You don't typically find violence listed as an addiction. Cocaine, alcohol, gambling, food, and even sex make the list, but hardly any books or websites mention violence. Facts are, great pleasure can be found in the power that ensues violence, especially when emptiness is your baseline (a neurological explanation is provided later in this chapter). Give an empty soul a title or a position, a badge or a uniform, and they quickly morph into Mussolini. Power might be the most intoxicating, non-pharmaceutical narcotic known to mankind. Acid trips aren't nearly as mind-altering as the power trip.

As a teenager, I felt hollow as a drum, a melancholy that stalked me even into adulthood. My younger cousin visited my home during that bleak era. We were alone in my basement bedroom when I decided that we should wrestle. I applied an aggressive full nelson, a maneuver where you master your opponent from behind while he squealed like a mouse stomped on by an elephant. Dopamine surged through my blood-stream as I held his life in my hands. Ashamedly, I derived pleasure from that moment of power. Fortunately, my aunt interrupted our wrestling match by barging into the room. Thankfully, my taste for violence never evolved into an appetite.

David stares off into yonder like a man exhausted from toiling all day under a hot sun. The conversation sapped him of all his strength. The sight of his fatigue inspires me to steer the talk towards downhill pathways. We spend the rest of the session chitchatting about prison reform, recidivism factors, and the likelihood of his own release. David's future is much easier to discuss than the past.

EMPTINESS AND DAIMONION

How do demons interact with emptiness? First, let's establish the fact that people with blank stares and empty souls are demon's pick of the litter. Proverbs 16:27 states that, "Idle hands are the devil's workshop."[223] St. Jerome derived inspiration from this proverb in the 4th century when he wrote, "Engage in some occupation so that the devil may always find that you're busy." [224] Many of men were twiddling their thumbs the moment they were mandated by a demon to raise ruckus on earth.

Jesus describes a demon's interest in an empty house in Matthew 12:44, a metaphor signifying a barren soul. Jesus states in Matthew 12:45, "Then it goes and takes with it seven other spirits more wicked than itself, and they go and live in there."[225] Demons target folks with a hollowness that accommodates their hellish presence. Empty people save space inside of themselves for paranormal influences.

How does daimonion maneuver emptiness? A demon prefers that our emptiness is a notion we believe as real, not just something we feel. We all feel empty at one point or another. But we don't all buy into a worldview that asserts: Life is empty. Nothing matters. Everything is meaningless.

---

[223] The Holy Bible, The Living Bible.
[224] Madeline Kalu, "What Is the Origin of 'Idle Hands Are the Devil's Workshop'?, Christianity.com, last modified May 17, 2022, https://www.christianity.com/wiki/sin/what-is-the-origin-of-idle-hands-are-the-devils-workshop.
[225] The Holy Bible, NIV.

When daimonion connive you into a nothingness worldview, you can become an easy mark for all kinds of suggestions. G.K. Chesterton summarized the greasy slope into moral depravity after rejecting the meaningful, "When a man stops believing in God (the source of all meaning), he doesn't believe in nothing but believes in anything."[226] You're down for anything when you believe in nothing.

When I peer into twenty-four-year-old David's vacant eyes, the mugshot captured by NYPD on August 11, 1977, I recognize the nothingness. I'm reminiscent of my own empty youth that paved the way for destruction. When I was invited to my first porn movie, I asked myself, Why not? When friends suggested we rob a car, I asked myself, Why not? When I pondered hanging myself from a rubber cord coiled around the basement pipe, I asked myself, Why not? I was an eager candidate for a host of hell's suggestions for one simple reason — hollow containers are the easiest to fill.

NIHILISM

Nihilism, a theory conceptualized by the philosopher Frederick Nietzsche, states that everything means nothing. This worldview rejects all values, principles, and absolutes other than the notion that life is utterly meaningless. [227]Nihilism is the common fate of anyone whose emotional emptiness persists for too long. In the case of David Berkowitz, he felt empty for nearly twenty years before nihilism caught up to him.

[226] Dale Ahlquist, "Believing in Anything," Faithandculture.com, accessed May 29, 2019, https://www.faithandculture.com/home/2019/5/29-believing-in-anything .
[227] Gilles Deleuze, Nietzsche and Philosophy,trans.Hugh Tomlinson (London: The Athlone Press, 1983).

With nihilism often emerges an impulse to destroy. Columbine shooter, Eric Harris, rails against despicable humanity in journal entries but only after confessing his nihilistic convictions. Harris scribbles, "I just love Hobbes and Nietzsche," and "Anything and everything that happens in our world is just that, a happening. We try to have a universal law or code of good and bad, but that isn't #$%@ correct!" [228] Harris and a host of other school shooters are the children of Nietzsche. Nietzsche was reported to be a mild-mannered man, but his ideas bore rippling effects larger than the pebble itself. Nietzsche's ideological children set out to destroy what their father only devalued.[229]

Thomas Hibbs, professor of philosophy at Boston College, explains the relationship between nihilism and violence in popular culture, particularly movies and television shows over the past twenty-five years, and how that relates to the rise of admirable, emotionally indifferent anti-heroes.[230]

For instance, Dr. Hannibal Lecter from Silence of the Lambs flaunts his freedom from all moral restraints and exhibits his ultimate disregard for human life through a witty, suave style by saying, "I'm having an old friend for dinner" (a reference to his act of cannibalism). Audience members chuckle about the one-liner, admiring that Lector is so liberated from morality. Or, closer to home, Travis Bickle, who made violence look easy by gesturing a trigger as he sits in a pool of blood after shooting several people. Such nihilistic flicks invite youngsters into a belief

---

[228] *Eric Harris and Dylan Klebold, The Journals of Dylan Klebold and Eric Harris (Independently published, 2019).*

[229] *Deleuze, Nietzsche and Philosophy,*

[230] *Thomas Hibbs, Shows About Nothing: Nihilism in Popular Culture from The Exorcist to Seinfeld (Mc Lean, VA: Spence Publishing, 2000).*

in nothing that emboldens them to do anything. Stop caring so much, and you can become as cool and cruel as Lector and Bickle is the subliminal message.

David's reply to Dr. Abrahamsen's letter from his Attica cell in 1979 reveals at least a tinge of nihilism within his worldview. A tinge like a subtle dosage of fentanyl, small enough to go unnoticed but potent enough to kill an elephant. David, though a Satanist at the time of the letter, also possessed the convictions of a nihilist. From this Nietzsche vantage point, wasting human life was as easy as stomping upon a dead leaf. David reveals his nihilism to Dr. Abrahamsen by saying,

Value? You mean human life has value?[231]

Let's discuss emptiness from a biological point of view. The data shows that depression, a sibling of emptiness, is closely linked to fits of rage. [232] How so? Depression weakens the serotonin system of the brain, a chemical that enables someone to regulate intense emotions such as anger. Serotonin is often described as the body's natural mood stabilizer. 233 Think of serotonin like the brake system within a car. Imagine discovering that your brake pads are gone after gunning an automobile to a high speed. This illustrates a depressed person's attempt to cool down after being fired up from a heated argument or an altercation. Serotonin is not present to regulate your heated emotions. For this reason, people with no handle

[231] The people vs. David Berkowitz, "Dr. David Abrahamsen-Berkowitz Letters."
[232] Kate Kelland, "Feeling Angry? Blame It on Low Serotonin," ABC Science, September 16, 2011,
https://www.abc.net.au/science/articles/2011/09/16/3319463.htm.
[233] D. Saldanha, et.al., "Serum Serotonin Abnormality in Depression," Medical Journal Armed Forces India65 no.2 (Apr. 2009): 108-112.

on sadness are more likely to fly off the handle with madness.

David elaborates on his state of unmanageable rage to Dr. Abrahamsen in a letter from June 1979. He describes how the outbursts were impossible to manage in the moments of the shootings.

> Repressed within the deep recesses of my mind for so very long, it [rage] came forth in a sudden burst.

Once the aggression-switch is flipped, an addictive cycle is potentially set in motion. A person can be addicted to aggression just like a binge eater craves chicken wings. Researchers at Vanderbilt University in Nashville discovered that the same reward pathway of the brain that lights up with feel-good substances is also triggered by aggression. A positive feedback loop occurs when acting aggressively that keeps people enslaved to their own passion. [234] Hence, the reason that Solomon says in Proverbs 13:2, "...the treacherous have an appetite for violence."

Furthermore, researchers performed a study with rodents that shed light on several eye-opening realities–aggression is highly motivating, and the behavior will persist even in the face of punishment. Rodents kept returning to aggressive behaviors despite any agony inflicted upon them.[235] Like the rodents, SOS was willing to pay a high price for a low life. SOS was ready to face the

[234] Maria Couppis and Craig Kennedy, "The Rewarding Effect of Aggression Is Reduced by Nucleus Accubems Dopamine Receptor Antagonism in Mice," Psychopharmacology 197 no. 3 (Apr. 2008:449–456.

[235] Sam A Golden, Michelle Jin, and Yavin Shaham, "Animal Models of (or for) Aggression Reward, Addiction, and Relapse: Behavior and Circuits," The Journal of Neuroscience 39 no. 21 (May 2019): 3996-4008.

ultimate consequences, as evident by the chilling letter left beside the bodies of Alexander Esau and Valentina Suriani.[236] The letter read:

...TO STOP ME, YOU MUST KILL ME.

WINNING SOULS, NOT WASTING SOULS

"Ah, I know what I want to share with you," I suddenly recall news that would be dully received by a lady anxious to win the lottery or an amorous dude hoping to get lucky with a curvy blonde on a date. The delight of this news is an acquired taste that only few possess. "You asked me earlier if I had any good news, so here it is," I state.

I knew that David would revel in this report. "A young suicidal man responded to the altar call at a church where I shared snippets of your story. I prayed with him, and he accepted Christ as Lord and Savior," I say. David sparkles like a Christmas tree. His droopy eyes pop open while his frown sprouts up like a flower after winter. He whoops,

That's fantastic. So amazing! Ya know, that reminds me of this letter I received. Many years ago, I started praying for this Native American tribe in Nova Scotia that never heard the gospel. They're called the Mic Mac. I mailed out my testimony booklet, *Son of Sam, Son of Hope* to members of that tribe. Well, I received a letter from a sister in the faith that a guy named Alwyn gave his life to Christ. The first convert of the Mic Mac in history! The tribe actually kept my letter, after all these years. Imagine, God chose a convict like me to plant the first seed of salvation in that area!

---

[236] *David Berkowitz,*
https://www.crimelibrary.org/serial_killers/notorious/berkowitz/letter.

David smiles like he won a platinum trophy. In 1977, David addressed a letter under the spell of the SOS to the NYPD Chief of Detectives, Joseph Borelli; a blood-stained memorandum found between two bodies slumped over in a parked car. In that letter, he spooked the city that never sleeps. Decades later, David mails an epistle to another chief and his followers with an entirely different agenda. The first letter aroused fear, the second letter awakened faith.

For David, hearing the news of a life liberated by his story is more fulfilling than any fire ever lit or mountain ever scaled. The report of a suicidal kid touched by his testimony uplifts his soul more than any crime he ever committed. Such a testimony fills the void within his heart more than cherry Pepsis® or White Castle burgers. David quotes a verse that captures the plugging of his soul-hole, "Jesus said to his disciples in John 4:32, 'I have food to eat that you know nothing about...My food is to do the will of Him who sent me and finish His work.'"[237] In this second chapter of David's life, working for God plugs his hole. Sharing his story soothes all existential sorrow. The old David plugged the hole within by wasting souls. The new David fills the void by winning souls.

---

[237] *The Holy Bible, NIV.*

CHAPTER 8

COGNITIVE DISTORTIONS

When he lies, he speaks his native language, for he is
a liar, and the father of lies. John 8:44

CLEARING THE AIR

I fidget with my sterling silver, chain-linked bracelet while
awaiting David's entrance. I hastened to meet David after
receiving an email last night that expressed his disappointment about my recent post on Facebook. News whizzed to
him from friends on the outside that I posted content
about his family. Violating his trust weighs heavily upon
me so I twiddle with the bracelet, a practice that releases
my neurotic energy. I'm anxious to clear the air.

David edges into the visit room, eyebrows crossed with
confusion. Inching his way towards me, he glances back at
the guard as if to ask, Do you know what this is about? My
visit is unscheduled, and it's 8:30 a.m. All of our previous
sessions were penciled on David's calendar and usually
after 9:30 a.m. David prefers his days to be orderly and
predictable. If he could schedule his sneezes, he would. He
sits down slowly, unsure of what to expect from this
impromptu session.

"David, I'm sorry. I didn't know it would be a problem to
post your sister's name. I figured that since you were
letting me use her name in the book, it would be okay on
social media," I say.

Mike, my sister, and my nieces might be on social media.
I would never want to do anything to alarm

them, shame them, or whatever. Even though we haven't spoken for over forty-five years, they are so close to my heart, ya see. The media hounded them for years, and now I want them to have their privacy.

"I understand. How about I just describe her as your sister without mentioning any name?" I ask. David replies,

I don't know. Let me think on it.

"Okay. In the meantime, I won't post anything without you reading it first," I respond. David nods. We both take a deep breath simultaneously as the air freshens between us. Clearing the air gives Satan, the prince of the air, no place between us.

"Since I'm here, do you mind if I ask you a few questions?" David settles into the chair like a man ready to eat a holiday dinner. "You once told me that if you could talk sense to your younger self, you'd say, 'David, these are lies you're believing.' What were the earliest lies you believed?" I'm hoping to gather more insights into the twisted mentality behind SOS reality. All horrific realities begin as slowly, brewing mentalities.

Early psychiatrist's reports indicate David as suffering from a delusional personality disorder. Behaviors surrounding the SOS tragedy were undoubtedly delusional — such as his conviction that a 5,000 year old demon spoke to him through his neighbor's Labrador Retriever, Harvey. Also, David was convinced that Craig Glassman, a neighbor beneath him at 35 Pine Street, was a messenger of satan tinkering with his brain. Glassman's blasting television from unit 6E was equivalent to satanic howls making their way through the ceiling into David's apartment. Craig Glassman's name is mentioned in a SOS letter, "Because Craig is Craig, so must the streets be filled with Craig (death)."[238]

COGNITIVE DISTORTIONS

But long before the delusions, David's mind was infested with some basic human distortions. A cognitive distortion is a jaded view of reality,[239] a common phenomenon that affects everyone at some point. We might not all have delusions, but we can all grasp distortions. Cognitive distortions plagued David like a chronic eye ailment since early childhood. David helps me trace these cognitive distortions from six years old all the way up until the present day.

Like I said before, believing at five or six years old that I killed my biological mother at the hour of birth. Actually, believing that I must have kicked her too hard when coming out of her womb. I mean, I really believed that craziness.

David's perception at that age, though a contortion of reality, was consistent with his stage of development. Jean Piaget, a developmental psychological, conceptualized that during the pre-operational stage (toddler to seven years old), kids perceive themselves as the center of the universe. Therefore, kids easily misjudge themselves as the cause of all things, good and bad.[240] Today's adoption

---

[238] Ronald Smothers, "Neighbor Who Got Threat Letter Was at Arrest Sight," New York Times, August 12, 1977.

[239] Petra Helmond, Geertjan Overbeek,, Daniel Brugman, and John C. Gibbs, "A Meta-Analysis on Cognitive Distortions and Externalizing Problem Behavior," Criminal Justice and Behavior 42 no. 3 (March 2015): 245-262.

[240] Jean Piaget, The Psychology of Intelligence (Totowa, NJ: Littlefield Adam Publisher, 1981).

experts, more informed than the 1960s specialists, suggests telling young kids the basics rather than explicit details about their adoption.[241]

Presuming that oneself is the cause behind all outcomes does not evaporate after the pre-operational stage. Personalizations, a cognitive distortion where people assign blame to themselves for events outside their control, continues into adulthood.[242] For instance, do you presume your spouse is upset with you when she's in a bad mood? Right away, you ask, *What did I do wrong?* despite the fact that she had a rough day at work. That's personalizations at its best. She responds, *Not everything is about you, so get over yourself.*

> Then, of course, I misinterpreted statements that my adoptive mom made when she tucked me in at night. Pearl would say, "God be with you, Angels watch over you, pleasant dreams," before I went to bed every night. She meant it innocently, but man, oh man, I took that statement as angels reporting back to God about my every move (David motions like he's writing on an invisible pad). I believed angels jotted down every mischievous deed and snitched back to God, who would punish me in some mysterious way for those misdeeds.

---

[241] Nancy Lovering, "How to Tell Your Child They're Adopted," Psychcentral.com, last modified January 25, 2022, https://psychcentral.com/lib/how-to-tell-your-child-theyre-adopted.

[242] Toni Bernhard, "It's Time to Stop Taking Things Personally," Psychologytoday.com, last modified August 28, 2018, https://www.psychologytoday.com/ca/blog/turning-straw-gold/201808/its-time-stop-taking-things-personally.

JUST WORLD FALLACY

Personalizations are greasy slopes into another cognitive distortion known as Just World Fallacy (JWF). JWF, conceptualized by social psychologist Melvin Lerner in the 1960s, emphasizes a divine entity, or a karma-driven universe, that punishes earthlings for every wrong and prizes them for every right. JWF links every outcome with a prior decision we made. [243] JWF pervades our culture through urban memes such as, *What goes around comes around* or country adages such as *the chickens come home to roost.* Even biblical truths such as the law of reaping and sowing is fanatically interpreted as meaning every affliction you suffer derives from a bad decision.

JWF shows up all over the Bible. Job's frenemies spewed this nonsense to him about the death of his kids at the hour of his grief in Job 8:4, "When your children sinned against Him, He gave them over to the penalty of their sin." [244] Jesus' disciples exhibited this cognitive distortion when they asked the Savior in John 9:2, "Who sinned that this man was born blind?" Jesus shattered JWF with the reply, "Neither this man nor his parents sinned." [245] JWF surfaces all throughout the scriptures because it's a common plague of humanity.

JWF is easy to welcome with open arms because of our soul's longing to believe that existence is safe. *If I'm good, then only good things will happen,* helps us cope with the capricious nature of life, even though it flies in the face of

---

[243] Melvin J. Lerner and Leo Montada, *"An Overview: Advances in Belief in a Just World Theory and Methods,"* in Responses to Victimizations and Belief in a Just World (New York: Plenum Press, 1998).
[244] The Holy Bible, NIV.
[245] The Holy Bible, NIV.

a Bible that teaches "time and chance happen to all men," as stated in Ecclesiastes 9:11.[246] JWF offers us a sense of control over our future, albeit a false sense. JWF is especially tantalizing to people who prefer a formularized universe where life is predictable, such as inmates frazzled by guests who show up unexpectedly. Hint, hint.

On one hand, JWF alleviates the anxiety of the morally fastidious. *I fear no harm descending upon my home since I'm so compliant.* On the other hand, JWF exacerbates the nervousness of rascals. *I fear God storming my home like a thief in the night since I'm so defiant.* Given the fact that David was a rascal who couldn't get his act together, JWF only rattled his nerves.

CRUEL GOD THEOLOGY

When I stubbed my toe, which was frequent because of clumsiness, I presumed God was punishing me. When I heard lightning strike, I thought that God was upset with me. Every bang of my elbow, stub of my toe, every accident, I interpreted all of these happenstances as God 's vengeance towards my shenanigans from the day before.

Many were the mallets that hammered into David's impressionable psyche the notion that God was mad because he was bad. Teachers branded him a *naughty boy* by positioning his desk at the center of the class. *Now, everyone can see what a bad boy you are, David.* A neighbor yanked him by his collar with harsh words, *You rotten kid* after David stuck his tongue out at the neighbor's wife. Older bullies, mostly Italian kids, made it clear that Jews were despicable.

---

[246] *The Holy Bible, NIV*

Or, most devastatingly, members of the extended Berkowitz family, cerebral card players who battled wits at the dinner table on a Sunday afternoon, bickered about the hyperactive nuisance racing near their feet. Little David frolicked under the table like a mouse looking for cheese. *What the heck is wrong with him?* one relative asked another. David overheard these nasty remarks, internalizing the insults as an accurate gauge of his character.

And, of course, there was Hebrew training. David perceived all of those Old Testament stories of God's explosive wrath as glimpses into his inevitable fate. Pearl's mysterious ceremonies — Shabbat, Passover, Hanukkah, and Rosh Hashanah — heightened the suspense of God's fury. Staring into the flames of her religious candles illuminating the dimly lit apartment, David saw God's blazing anger.

"How did this radical view of God affect your life?" I ask.

It's like, I craved punishment or something. I'd break the toys my parents gave me like I didn't deserve them. When they replaced that toy with a new toy, which they often did, I broke the new toy too. I subconsciously wanted them to punish me for being a bad boy. I'd even pick fights with older, bigger kids in school, unconsciously looking for a beating.

David fetishizes punishment like a man who cuddles with fanged wolves for merriment. A masochistic personality slowly takes shape throughout his childhood, whereby pain rather than pleasure stimulates the striatum, the reward center of the brain. Nobody could understand, not even David, why he preferred scoldings over hugs. Underneath it all, punishment seemed more sensible because he was so naughty, and God was so angry.

And if my parents doted on me too much, I'd misbehave even more.

David's father, Nat, baffled over his son rejecting his affection. How could this child whom he rescued from a damsel in distress on a Brooklyn hospital stoop push him away? One evening, when a ten-year-old David walked by Nat with a death-stare, Nat bolted himself in the bathroom to sob. Pearl banged on the door with concern that her husband might harm himself. She was a witness to Nat's ceaseless, unreciprocated gestures of love. She saw him often hand David a dollar bill for school lunch, an exorbitant amount of money in 1960. Inside that itty-bitty tenement bathroom, Nat tortured himself with the question, *Why won't my son receive my love?*

I couldn't handle being rewarded or loved. I was too bad for that.

Sabotaging a good thing is a sure sign that one feels undeserving. How many adulterous affairs, plummets into addiction, and other self-destructive escapades occur during blissful times? Perhaps because the person throwing it all away is more terrified of fortune than misfortune. Fortune feels like a trophy they didn't earn. Yesteryear comedian Jack Benny had the same inner turmoil when receiving an award at a ceremony until he had an epiphany, "I don't deserve this award, but I'll take it because I have arthritis and don't deserve that either."[247] Maturity means realizing that fortunes and misfortunes do not always match your merit. Rain falls on the just and the unjust alike. David was still a long distance from Jack Benny's epiphany.

---

[247] Herbert L. Fred, *"On Getting What We Deserve," The Texas Heart Institute Journal 38 no. 2 (2011): 106–107.*

My head got really twisted from fourteen years old onward. My parents head out to eat on a Saturday night at a Chinese restaurant. After they leave, I raid the fridge and watch horror movies all night. Not sure when I fell asleep, but I wake up the next morning to find an empty house. A light flickers above their bed with the sheets still tucked in. I called some relatives looking for them, but nobody knew anything. Then, the phone rings. It's dad telling me mom collapsed the night before at the restaurant. "Doctors are taking care of her at James Ewing Hospital in Manhattan, trying to figure out what's wrong," he says.

Mom's peck on his forehead would be the last smooch he ever received from the lady who cherished him since he was four days old. Back in the 1940s, Pearl Berkowitz lost the privilege of bearing babies from a medical procedure that rectified her cancer. When Mrs. Miller, a liaison between the Berkowitz family and Betty Falco, phoned her back in 1953 with the thrilling news, "A Jewish baby boy will be available for adoption in Brooklyn, if you and Nat are interested", Pearl called her back without delay. She was over the moon to be a mom. She raised David with iron-pressed outfits, cupboards filled with snacks, and the latest toys.

A short time before Pearl's collapse, David made his Bar Mitzvah at the Temple Adath Israel on 169th Grand Concourse and the Grand Concourse in the Bronx. This accomplishment was all due to mom's proddings. Later that day, cheering family and friends encircled Pearl and her thirteen-year-old boy dancing to Chubby Checker's *The Twist*. A new chapter entitled "Happiness" unfolded for the Berkowitz family as David's grades improved along with matriculation into manhood via the Jewish passageway. Pearl was so happy to see David mature from a bad boy into a good man.

In June 1966, Pearl completed an application for Co-Op City, a new housing project engineered by banker Abraham Kazan who believed that affordable, spacious abodes would solve the social problems confronting New Yorkers.[248] Pearl shared the dream of most residents from the wedged-tight South Bronx — a safer, middle-class environment within the newly designed thirty-five buildings located in the North Bronx. Pearl's wish to relocate was motivated by one thing — David. She hand-wrote neatly on the application, "We are most anxious to move into co-op city. It would be a fine place to raise my son."[249]

> There she was, my beloved mom, who gave me so much, swollen from the treatment to remedy the cancer. Her skin was grey, her head nearly bald with some patches of white hair. I guess the disease returned with a vengeance. She had breast cancer that spread throughout her body, ya know. Before all of that, she was my beautiful mother.

Pearl's shapely figure withered into a skeleton inside that hospital bed, too sickly to ever return home. According to young David, Pearl's deterioration was all because of those nosey angels ratting him out to God. Like every lightning bolt, stub of the toe, bang of the elbow, and that head-on collision with a car, Pearl's death was another well-deserved penalty for his mischief.

---

[248] Abraham E. Kazan, "Cooperative Housing in the United States", Annals of the American Academy of Political and Social Science 191, (May 1937): 137–143.
[249] John Hamill, "Meet the Boy Next Door Who Grew Up to Be the Son of Sam," Daily News, August 12, 1977.

I couldn't stay too long in the hospital room, so I'd leave my dad by her bedside and go for long angry walks in the city. It was too painful for me to see her like that. She never returned home again. After a couple of months, she was transferred to the terminally ill ward and passed thereafter. She died October 5, 1967, and I was so angry with God.

Tragedies disrupt the formative years by altering the way we perceive the world. For instance, the death, imprisonment, or abandonment of a parent shakes our foundation, making earth feel like an unsafe place. From the catastrophe onward, God is perceived as deadbeat at best, *God, where are you!* or dastardly at worst, *God, you're so cruel!* The tragedies we go through aren't nearly as poisonous as the resultant ideologies that go through us.

On one hand, her death made sense because it felt like I deserved it. Another punishment from God, ya see. On the other hand, I hated God. How could he take my mother, a saint, and not take me, a rebel? I deserved to die, not her. On one hand, her death felt just. On other hand, it felt so unjust.

Years later, after David returned from the army, he lends an ear to the teachings of Process Church. The Process Church taught that Satan and Jesus were brothers feuding but would reconcile after the great Armageddon. David and others were mandated to pave the way into Armageddon by inciting anarchy across American soil. Slaughtering innocent people brought the world one step closer to a harmonious end. A just world was possible, not by God protecting man, but by man playing God. God proved himself to be unqualified to make the world right, so the torch was passed to David and friends.

Do I believe these cognitive distortions were the crux behind David's crimes? I'd venture to say that the distortions rationalized, not energized, the crimes. Cognitive distortions were the mental justifications that made shedding blood easier for his conscience. What energized the crimes were matters of the heart - such as anger, shame and rejection - whipped up by demonic forces. The heart of the matter is always a matter of the heart.

I was on an unstoppable mission. Like my destiny was fixed.

Fixed Mindset, the opposite of a Growth Mindset, is a cognitive distortion where a person believes that his/her traits are immutable. A fixed mindset is a hopeless outlook where you feel like any efforts to change your character are futile, so why even bother trying. David Yeager, an associate professor of developmental psychology, created a training program to reduce bullying within schools by instilling a Growth Mindset. A Growth Mindset asserts *I don't have to be a bully, but I can become a kinder person.* Applying his training program, students were two to three times more likely to engage in pro-social behaviors than bullying. [250] David never had such training, hence believing that he was predetermined to be satan's tool. David's mind was not in flux but set in stone.

On August 10, 1977, outside of his Yonkers apartment at 35 Pine Street, David's cognitive distortions – JWF, Cruel God Theology, Fixed Mindset – finally got the best of him.

---

[250] Kristen Villanueva, "Reduce Bullying by Cultivating Growth Mindsets," Mindsetworks.com, November 21, 2017, https://blog.mindsetworks.com/entry/reduce-bullying-by-cultivating-growth-mindsets.

Here's how Detective Philip Fehr depicts the events that led to David's capture.

"Berkowitz was not easy to catch. The NYPD pulled out all of the stops. Nearly every cop was invested in some level in finding Son of Sam. I did roadblocks at the Whitestone bridge. We knew the killer lived in another borough because criminals hardly play in their own backyard. So, after the UNSUB killed a girl in Queens, we formed roadblocks at the bridge, scanning cars that passed through, looking for a male that fit the description – chubby with curly hair and firearms. With all of our efforts, the silliest thing got him caught. A stupid parking ticket did him in!"[251]

What does Detective Fehr mean, a parking ticket?

On August 9, 1977, a few days after the slaying of Stacy Moskowitz, Brooklyn Detective James Justus rummaged through parking summons from the night of the murder. He hoped to find someone who saw something in the area of the shooting. A ticket neatly penned by Officer Michael Cataneo snatched his attention. *Perhaps the owner of a 1970 Ford Galaxie from Yonkers who parked in front of a fire hydrant on 290 Bay 17th Street has helpful information. Wait a minute! What was a Yonkers resident doing in Bath Beach, Brooklyn after midnight?* Cataneo's question inspired investigators to pursue David Berkowitz, not as merely a potential witness, but a suspect.[252] Imagine, a $35 summons amidst thousands of tickets slapped on violators' windshields ended the yearlong bedlam called Son of Sam.

---

[251] *Philip Fehr, telephone interview. April 25, 2023.*
[252] *James Barron, "How a Son of Sam Detective Realized, 'This has got to be our guy,'" New York Times, August. 6, 2017.*

David suspects that his carelessness of parking next to a fire hydrant not far from Stacy's murder was a subconscious move to sabotage himself. The sensation of relief he felt at his arrest awakened him to that subconscious drive. The parking summons was more than a silly coincidence but another manifestation of David's masochistic personality. Furthermore, NYPD later realized that David even left two of his fingerprints on an SOS letter. Being a first-hand witness of David's meticulous nature, I find it unfathomable that the prints were mishaps. If God would not judge fairly, then David would snatch the gavel from his hands and judge himself.

> I was so out of touch with reality at my arrest. I was living in the devil's playground – my own head.

Sergeant Joseph Coffee, an NYPD detective who worked feverishly on capturing the SOS, confirmed that David was a disturbed young man in his statement to the *New York Post* in 2007. "When I entered the room on the 13th floor, I wanted to pick up Berkowitz and throw him out the window. But when he started talking about getting messages from a dog, I realized I was not dealing with a mob killer, but a psycho, a sick man." Coffey said that talking to Berkowitz was like dialoguing with a "head of lettuce in a supermarket."[253]

COGNITIVE DISTORTIONS AND DAIMONION

Cognitive distortions are how daimonion ambushes humanity. Spiritual warfare is not like ancient mythology, or even contemporary cartoons, where we wrestle with fairies (a fairy is the ancient word for evil creatures with

---

[253] *Sam Roberts, "Joseph Coffey at 77; Detective Took Son of Sam Confession," Boston Globe, October 7, 2015.*

magical powers). That's how a dispute with the devil plays out within these silly tales - you fling a ghoulish fairy into the air, and march over the dismantled creature triumphantly.

The Apostle Paul describes spiritual warfare in II Corinthians 10:5, in which he urges believers to "cast down every argument." [254] The term argument in Greek, logismous, means speculative thoughts. Logismous means persuasive but poisonous lines of reasoning.[255] Logismous' are cognitive distortions, the crevices where demons hide. The Apostle enlightens us about spiritual warfare within II Corinthians 10 - *In your battle with evil, don't worry about fairies. Instead, pay careful attention to your theories.*

In the case of David Berkowitz, Personalization, Just World Fallacy, the Fixed Mindset, and a Cruel God Theology were all head-games that Daimonion employed to overtake him. These whacky theories cemented a pathway of terror that resulted in six deaths and seven injuries. David mentioned a few times within the sessions, as well as a statement made within one of the SOS letters, that he was "programmed to kill." The programming entails these whacky theories.

Out of all these theories, the Cruel God Theology is most pivotal. Mankind's first temptation, recorded in Genesis 3, was allurement into believing that God was cruel. First, the serpent said to Eve, "Did God really say that you must not eat from any tree in the garden?" The serpent insinuates that Eve will starve to death under God's capricious regime even though she obeys Him. Second, the serpent said to

---

[254] *The Holy Bible, NKJV.*
[255] *"logismos," Bible hub, https://biblehub.com/greek/3053.htm.*

Eve, "You will not certainly die," [256] about Eve being punished if she violates the command. The serpent suggests that God does not punish wrongdoing. Simply stated, Eve is duped into believing God punishes the good and pardons the bad.

The writings of mass shooters indicate obsessions with an upside-down world. Nikolas Cruz, the twenty-three-year-old who opened fire at a Parkland, Florida high school on Valentines Day 2008, left a note on his cell phone in which he described life as "unfair."[257] Eric Harris spewed in his diary on April 10, 1998, "God, everything is so corrupt...this isn't a world anymore. It's HOE (abbreviation for Hell O\on Earth), and no one knows it."[258] The Virginia Tech shooter perceived his campus as inequitably governed by "rich kids" who acted as "deceptive charlatans".[259] Lastly, David believed that God's world was unjust since a guy like him existed while his virtuous mother perished.

Continuing with the Genesis account, Eve is now tempted to play God herself. In Genesis 3:5, the serpent tells Eve, if she eats the fruit, "you will be like God." [260] Such an appealing offer to a woman who feels that God is derelict in his duties. Isn't it most tempting to usurp leadership when leadership isn't doing their job? Simply stated, Eve plays God because she believes that God hasn't adequately performed His own role.

Likewise, mass shooters manifest their wannabe-God

[256] The Holy Bible, NIV.
[257] Curt Anderson and Terry Spencer, "Sheriff: Parkland Shooter Assaulted Jail Officer," The Florida Times Union, last modified November 14, 2018.
[258] Harris and Klebold, The Journals of Dylan Klebold and Eric Harris.
[259] Adam Geller, Killer Railed Against 'Rich Kids,' 'Debauchery' and 'Deceitful Charlatans,' Metro West Daily News, April 17, 2007.
[260] The Holy Bible, NIV.

wishes. Eric Harris stated in his diary on April 12, 1998, "I feel like god, and how I wish I was!" After purchasing his weapons, he wrote on November 22, 1998, "I feel more confident, stronger, more god-like."[261] Eliot Rodgers, the twenty-two-year-old British son of an assistant director on the film *Hunger Games*, boasted before the Isla Vista killings, "I am Elliot Rodger...Magnificent, glorious, supreme, eminent ... Divine! I am the closest thing there is to a living god."[262]

Behavioral science demonstrates a connection between belief in a cruel God and subsequent aggressive behaviors. An experiment conducted by Brigham Young University and Vrije University showed that reading passages about God's violent acts outside of its redemptive context boosts aggression levels. In the study, participants blasted a noise at losing participants much louder after being exposed to a capricious portrayal of the Almighty.[263] Theology is at the core of psychology - the God we see heavily influences the person we shall be. No wonder why Jesus asks the apostle Peter in Matthew 16:15, "Who do you say I am?"[264]

And these crazy thoughts about life weren't just in my head. They were being reinforced by everything around me. Like, everything I was seeing confirmed what was in my head.

---

[261] *Harris and, Klebold, The Journals of Dylan Klebold and Eric Harris.*
[262] *Linda Massarella, Sophia Rosenbaum, and Leonard Green, "The Vile Manifesto of a Killer," New York Post, July 14, 2023.*
[263] *Ed Stoddard, "Violent Scripture May Increase Aggression – study," Reuters,.Last modified March 6, 2007, https://www.reuters.com/article/idUSN06403213.*
[264] *The Holy Bible, NIV.*

MEDIA, MUSIC AND MOVIES

All of David's cognitive distortions were deep-dyed through media, music and movies. All of these forms of entertainment reinforced the lies that David believed. Take, for instance, the media. David indulged on news channels from early childhood, often spellbound by race riots, explosions in Vietnam, and the assignations of John F. Kennedy, Robert F. Kennedy, and Martin Luther King, Jr.

> It was the late 60s, and there was this collective sense that the world was in trouble. Like, death was knocking at all of our doors. What I watched really got trapped in my mind, ya know. I felt that death was inevitable.

Or, how about music? David bows his head almost reverently and recites the lyrics to the song that he listened to all the time before and during SOS - Barry McGuire's *Eve of Destruction*. David's song is quietly reverent, like a catholic caroling hymns at midnight mass. The song evokes imagery from Red China, hostile Selma, Alabama, and bodies floating in the Jordan River.[265]

> I listened to Eve of Destruction all the time. Over fifty years later, I still remember every lyric. In fact, I put the song on my tablet recently. That song made me feel like the end was near for all of us.

Freud theorized that humans possess a life instinct known as "Eros" and a death instinct known as "Thanatos." In cushioned times, Eros is cultivated — a desire to dwell in the land, procreate, and live long, happy lives. In crazy

---

[265] *Barry McGuire, "Eve of Destruction," BarryMcGuire.com.*

times, Thanatos is awakened — an eagerness to meet the end as a passageway into a better existence.[266] Hence, the reason that jihadists who fly planes into buildings typically grow up within nations in crisis. Within those tumultuous territories, Thanatos is constantly fed. A daily diet of televised disasters helped mold David into a jihadist of sorts.

And, of course, movies. Nothing reinforced David's cognitive distortions in one shot like the film, *Taxi Driver*.[267] David recalls a line from the movie right before Travis Bickle unleashes his wrath on NYC's filth. The statement made by Bickle encapsulates the Fixed Mindset that David himself possessed.

> I identified with Travis Bickle. He says, "My whole life was pointed in one direction. There was never any choice for me." That's how I felt about my mission with SOS.

Taxi Driver also paints the picture of a world where evil must be punished. The hoodlums that profit off the sexuality of a twelve-year-old girl are executed, while the henchman is rewarded with fame. *Taxi Driver* trumpets the message that a Just World is not possible with passive men but only with indignant men who rise up and take their place. The ancient truth, "Vengeance is mine" is usurped with "Vengeance is thine."

> I know this will be hard to swallow for some people, but I actually believed that the crimes were a service to humanity. My mind was so twisted back then, I know. But I believed that these crimes satiated the

---

266 Freud, *"Beyond the Pleasure Principle."*
267 Scorsese, *Taxi Driver*.

appetite of the demons, preventing worldwide destruction.

Tuning into David's tale, I think to myself, I'm too strong-minded for this nonsense. I couldn't be so easily seduced. Then, I take notice of my bracelet that I've been tinkering with throughout the session. To my surprise, I pretzeled the silver wristband into a complicated knot. The bracelet is almost as snarled as the psyche behind SOS. A metaphor emerges about how easy it is to get something twisted. Cognitive distortions are not the traits of a few madmen but the traps of all mortals.

NAT AND NEYSA

Cognitive distortions infect the vicious as well as their victims. Neysa Moskowitz, the mother of the vivacious Stacy Moskowitz (last victim of Son of Sam), perceived the world through a jaded lens until her breakthrough in the latter years of life. Neysa forgave David, and that experience felt like scales fell off her eyes. She told her Miami neighbor after her head cleared, "Don't let anger eat you up."[268] Both the vicious and the victims get their heads twisted pretty easily.

And, of course, Nat Berkowitz plodded under a heavy fog for decades until he transitioned into eternal bliss at 101 years old. David told me that his father felt deep regret, questioning if he made detrimental mistakes in parenting. In 1975, a sixty-four-year-old Nat left his son and elderly mother in NYC for a Floridian retirement with his new wife, a move that he second guessed after David's arrest. *What would have happened if I stayed?* Nat's head was in knots for many years.

---

[268] *Peyser, "A Mom Dies."*

After our session, I composed the following poem that captured Nat's long tunnel of confusion in the days after SOS. I emailed David a copy of the poem, to which he expresses his gratitude.

A Father 's Confusion
Son, where did I go wrong?
Toiled at Berk's hardware,
Lavished you with fine things,
Were my workdays too long?

Son, what did I miss?
Noticed you distressed,
Sessions with Mrs. Sosnoff,
Perhaps another therapist?

Son, why cringe at my touch?
Hid in the bathroom,
Soaked towels with tears,
Was my affection too much?

Son, recall happy times?
Camping, swimming, fishing.
Our last drive to Mount Washington.
Tell me, am I complicit in your crimes?

Son, the world sees you vile.
Son of Sam, wicked king Wicker,
.44 caliber killer.
Tell me, are you still my child?

Son, thank you for sharing Christ.
Even if I'm guilty of something,
Even if I failed miserably.
I'm grateful that He paid the price.)

A few minutes before wrapping up our visit, David replies to what I asked earlier in the session.

Regarding what you said earlier about social media, you don't have to check back with me on what you post. I trust you. Just please use wisdom.

"Thanks. Was there any particular event that straightened out your view of God?" I ask.

Back in winter 1988, I'd take these long walks by myself in the prison yard. It's like ten degrees outside, and this younger Latino named Rick approaches me, "God sent me here to be your friend." Initially, I thought this was crazy... especially when he told me that God forgives me. I replied, "God doesn't like me very much, believe me. I've done too many awful things for him to forgive me." But this guy, Rick, kept telling me about God's love. He didn't badger me, just kept planting seeds. He'd meet me in the prison yard day after day. Then, he gives me a Gideon Bible, and after six weeks of reading that Bible late in my cell, the scales fell of my eyes.

SPARE PARTS

That chronic eye ailment, a.k.a. cognitive distortions, plaguing him since childhood was supernaturally remedied. David was once blind, but now he could see. David grins ear to ear when mulling over the shift in his perspective about God since his arrest decades ago.

On December 8, 2017, I developed a strange discomfort around my left shoulder with this tightness in my upper chest. Shortness of breath, too, ya know. The officer in charge of my housing area called the infirmary. There, I was checked out by the doctor, who ordered an EKG. After seeing the results, he immediately had the nurse call for an ambulance.

At St. Luke's in Newburgh, the head cardiologist came into the little waiting room I was confined to, still shackled with chains and locks and stuck on an uncomfortable gurney, the doctor told the three correctional officers guarding me that I had to go to a hospital with a cardio unit. It was a toss-up between Westchester County Medical Center, which is where I was arrested, or Albany Medical Center in Albany. Westchester quickly responded that they had no bed space, thank God! No Westchester nightmares for me.

At Albany's Cardio Unit, one of the best in the country, I got a quadruple bypass. The doctor explained to me that they took some arteries out of my leg to replace the arteries from my heart. I replied, "God is amazing!" The doctor asked, "Why do you say that?" I replied, "God knew I would screw up my arteries, so he made me with spare parts."

David Berkowitz, Pasco Manzo (President of New England and New Jersey Adult & Teen Challenge) and myself.

CHAPTER 9

DEFENSE MECHANISMS

"When I kept silent, my bones wasted away..."
Psalm 32:3[269]

TOO MUCH TO CARRY

"Nino's Pizza on Gun Hill Road", I greet David on the phone after accepting charges from Shawangunk Correctional Facility. In my greeting, I throw in a reference to the Bronx boulevard where David's father, Nat, owned his hardware store back in the 60s and 70s – Gun Hill Road. Nostalgia is a bitter-sweet taste to a man whose present circumstances range from bland to acidic. I'm comforting David with one of the few amenities he has left – memories.

Hey Nino, I'll take a large pizza with everything but anchovies.

David plays along with an over-the-top New York accent that sounds like the character *Roseannadanna* from 1970s Saturday Night Live. We both learned over the last 15 months that humor anesthetizes the agony of dark subjects such as mental illness, demonic oppression and murder. If you're gonna survive life, you have to find the funny in whatever comes your way. Solomon said it right in Proverbs 17:22, "A cheerful heart is good medicine."[270]

All kidding aside, I need to talk with you about some things. I've been under such heaviness for a long

---

[269] *The Holy Bible, NIV.*
[270] *The Holy Bible, NIV.*

time. I'm so exhausted, ya know. It's just too much to carry.

"What are we talking about David?" I ask. I am 75% sure of what he means but I want him to say it. The last thing I want to do is jam words into his mouth. From David's own self-assessment, he has a long history of being suggestible to overbearing shrinks, cops, and pressmen.

I'm talking about my crimes.

When David describes the SOS shootings, he doesn't dub them as killings or murders. Both those graphic descriptors would be agonizing reminders about the brutality of SOS. Instead, he places the tragedies under a more generic label known as "crimes." In this sense, his usage of the term "crimes" is a defense mechanism that eases his conscience from guilt and shame. All defense mechanisms, which there are many, help us to dodge pain. [271] More specifically, "crimes" is a specific defense mechanism known as a euphemism – soft language that lessens the harshness of a brutal reality. [272]

I've been in denial about some things.

I awake at 4:30am to a full moon seemingly levitating above the New England landscape. A full moon typically connotes ominous activity – werewolves, vampires, and the walking dead. A full moon is when the monsters come out.

---

[271] Uwe Hentschel,, Juris G. Draguns,,Wolfram Ehlers,and Gudmund Smith, eds., "Defense Mechanisms: Current Approaches to Research and Measurement," in Defense Mechanisms: Theoretical, Research and Clinical Perspectives, ed. Hentschel, G. Smith, J. G. Draguns, & W. Ehlers (Amsterdam: Elsevier, 2004).
[272] Merriam Webster, s.v. "euphemism," https://www.merriam-webster.com/dictionary/euphemism.

For me, this spectacle that manifests every 29 days simply signifies full transparency. The waning crescent is when the moon is least transparent, resembling a toenail in the sky. The last quarter is when the moon is nearly half of its shape. A full moon, on the other hand, bellows, "Here I am! All of me without any hiding!". How sacred that the Creator billboards the significance of this monumental day across the sky. Today is the day that David offers me a full-moon confession.

FOUR KINDS OF DENIAL

During my 3-hour commute to Shawangunk, I mull over the term that David used over the phone – "denial." Data indicates four kinds of denial – denial of facts, denial of impact, denial of responsibility and denial of hope. All four denials insulate our fragile psyches from feeling the pangs of reality. Denial of facts shields you from facing a mess. Denial of responsibility shields you from your role in the mess. Denial of impact shields you from how the mess you made affected others. Lastly, denial of hope shields you from the work of cleaning the mess up.[273] C.S. Lewis sums it all up by saying, "Denial is a shock absorber for the soul."[274]

When Hagar hides from her baby Ishmael in the desert in Genesis 21:15, saying "I cannot watch my baby die," she's in denial about the facts. When Peter says that he's not a follower of Christ in Matthew 26:70, he's in denial about his responsibility. When Amnon demands that his half-sister, Tamar, leave his presence after sexually assaulting her in II Samuel 13:17, and then orders his servant to bolt

---

[273] Bill Herring, "The Four Denials of Responsibility," Last modified February 7, 2010, https://www.billherring.com/article/four-denials-responsibility.
[274] Lewis, Mere Christianity.

the door shut, he's in denial over the impact of what he did. Lastly, when Judas Iscariot hangs himself in Matthew 27:5, he's in denial about hope.[275]

David Berkowitz will be the first to tell you that he carefully coated his psyche with all four denials during SOS. First, the denial of facts. David arrived punctually for his 4:30pm shift at the post office as if the prior evening of bloody mayhem was a movie he saw on television. He escorted female colleagues to their car after work saying, "Be careful. The Son of Sam is at large". Contrary to popular opinion, these gestures were not a sadistic game. Rather, the behaviors of a man rambling through a false reality where the light of yesterday flickered for just a few seconds while sorting through thousands of stamped envelopes.

Second, the denial of responsibility. David admitted within interviews at Attica that he felt comfortable explaining his crimes as workings of the devil because the description helped him evade feelings of culpability. Yes, David used the devil like the ancients exploited scapegoats in order to shift their blame onto the animals. (However, that admission does not mean the devil did not also use him. We return to a clearer understanding of this paradox in the final chapter).

Third, the denial of impact. David Berkowitz' choice of weapon was a .44 caliber bulldog – what he considered the swiftest method of execution. He would later say, "I didn't want to hurt them. Just kill them." David persuaded himself that the shootings were innocuous. If the deaths were impactful, it was not the abrupt ending of innocent lives. Rather, the propitiation of Samhain's appetite for blood

---

[275] *The Holy Bible, KJV.*

so that the prince of darkness wouldn't stir up worldwide calamity.

Lastly, the denial of hope. On August 6, 1977, a few days before his arrest, David loaded up all of his weapons, jammed them into a duffel bag and drove over two hours to the Hamptons. When he arrived, he sat on a beach outside of a club. There, he envisaged a mass shooting that would end suicide-by-cop. At this point, the demons were nearly finished with him, and life felt over. The prospect of mending his wrongs did not exist. Like Judas, he believed he passed the point of no return. Fortunately for everyone, sudden hail intercepted the plan.

I could dissect David's denial all day long. But I'd be a hypocrite since I have my own story of delicate self-deceptions. Well, let's discuss that a little later.

David and I arrive simultaneously within the visiting room. All prior visits, I showed up first with an average waiting time of 15 minutes. Clearly, we are both eager to uncover a wound that's been concealed too long.

David, with heavy eyes, settles into the chair.

> I haven't been able to sleep well, ya know. Like I said on the phone, just so much heaviness.

"Dave, I hate to rub it in, but I sleep like a baby. That's not to say that I'm any more holy than you. Two reasons why a person sleeps well – a clear conscience and a bad memory. It's a little of each for me," I reply.

We both half-heartedly chuckle.

"You wanted to talk with me about your past? In particular,

the crimes," I shift gears from gaiety to empathy.

I just wish I could erase all that's happened. Pastors tell me that I should just forget the past.

"And how is that working out for you?" I pose that question a therapist asks to gently snap someone out of a dazed state. Facts are, forgetting is impossible since we don't live in the past as much as the past lives in us.

David offers no reply.

RUNNING FROM YOUR PAST

Running from your past is like that lady in the horror flicks running from the monster. As she dashes out of some creepy house into the middle of a cornfield, she assumes she's making headway from that hellish creature. That monster seems so far off in the distance. An expression of relief appears on her face as she slows down to take a breath. Thankfully, the monster is way behind her. But, out of nowhere, the monster behind her pops up before her.

That's exactly what happens when you run from your past. For example, studies show that people who suppress trauma are more frequently triggered by present circumstances.[276] A trigger invokes flashbacks from the past, high levels of anxiety or potent negative emotions such as disgust, anger, fear, or grief. Keep running, and the triggers keep happening. Facts are, whatever you run from will run you.

---

[276] Ashley Borders, "Beliefs, Traits and Motivations Underlying Rumination," In Rumination and Related Constructs, (London: Academic press, 2020).

Pastors have told me, "David, why do you make an effort to remember your past when God has forgotten it?"

"Dave, I've heard you say that many times. I'm not so sure that God's forgetting is amnesia. If that's the case, why does His word remind us of Moses murdering an Egyptian, King David's affair with Bathsheba and the Apostle Paul's genocide of the early church. If God forgot, then how did He remember to jot these facts down in His word? Forget is an anthropomorphic term to highlight the fact that God doesn't fixate on our sins like people do," I say.

Again, David stays silent.

"Of course, clergyman reference Philippians 3:13[277] as the basis for forgetting the past. You know, where Paul says, "Forgetting those things which are behind." But a closer look at the context shows that Paul meant specifically the accolades that made him conceited – being a 'Pharisee among Pharisees'." I hardly ever get preachy with David, but our long journey paved the way for this moment. "Forgetting everything would discredit the testimony of God's restorative power. He took chicken poop and made chicken soup" I say facetiously.

This time, David offers a boyish smile like he heard an amusing wisecrack from the kid next to him on the school bus.

"Dave, I read the parole transcript you gave me. You know, your last parole hearing? Here is what it says, 'The parole board commends your personal growth, programmatic achievements and productive use of time.... Yet, the parole

---

[277] *The Holy Bible, NIV.*

board is also concerned that you remain dissociated from the crimes you committed and the terror you inflicted on New York City and beyond. Parole denied."[278] This time, I look directly at David for more than just silence.

I don't disagree. So much trauma, ya know. I live in denial about what I did. It's hard for me to face my crimes.

Here we go again with the euphemisms. "You mean, shootings. Murders." I reply firmly.

Yes, the shootings.

The vein that bugles across David's forehead like he's deadlifting a thousand pounds returns. The weight of the SOS tragedies becomes the heaviest when defense mechanisms fall at the wayside.

EUPHEMISMS

Before I push any harder, I'm reminded of the humanness of euphemisms. I used a euphemism yesterday when I depicted a falsehood I told as a *half-truth*. Facts are, a *half-truth* is a whole lie no matter how you cut it. But I preferred the phrase *half-truth* because it's easier on my fragile psyche.

Before you crucify David, take note to some of your own euphemisms. *I'm going to the gentleman's club tonight* – oh you mean, that place where some guy's daughter takes her clothes off for your money. *I was let go from work* – oh you mean, you were fired for being a slouch. *Me and Mrs. Jones are friends with benefits* – oh, you mean you're having an

---

[278] *"New York State Parole Board Transcript, David Berkowitz," May 2022.*

affair with the neighbor's wife. Hypocrisy is holding a PhD in David Berkowitz' crimes, but you still haven't graduated kindergarten with your own misdeeds.

"Dave, you know there's no need to revisit the gory details of the crimes. But one detail awaits our attention. One detail, I believe you want to discuss. That one detail - who pulled the trigger in all of the shootings?" I ask.

David drops his head like he's ducking a jab to the nose. David ducked the truth since childhood. When mom inquired about his charred windowsill from setting toys on fire, he played dumb. When Miss Sosnoff probed about the basis of his anger, he shrugged his shoulders in silence. When dad pled with him to open up about his troubles, he hid inside his bedroom with the music cranked up. Years later, when his sister Roslyn voiced her concerns about his masochistic behaviors, such as punching himself in the head, he drove her away. David could sidestep being cornered in by a sumo wrestler if necessary.

That's why I wanted to meet. Time for me to fess up.

Confession is no painless matter. Actor Robert Downey Jr. once described his admission of being an addict as tantamount to hugging a cactus. Downey says that confessing the ugly parts of yourself, rather than hiding them, is like opening your arms wide to that prickly plant. The outcome of such an experience leaves you humble. *Hugging the cactus was the prerequisite for my transformation*, Downey says.[279]

I'm reminded of that moment in Genesis 32 when the

[279] Sarah Ann Hughes, "Robert Downey Jr: Hollywood Should Forgive Mel Gibson," *Washington Post*, October 15, 2011.

angel asked Jacob the question, "What is your name?" The name, Jacob, meant a person who supplants, deceives, and hustles others. By answering that angel's question, Jacob would be admitting who he was. "Jacob," he replies. After Jacob admits who he is, the angel changes his name to a more noble moniker, *Israel*. Transformation only begins when denial ends.[280]

"The facts don't add up, Dave. You avowed in a 1990s interview that the crimes were cultic, and that a handful of the shootings were pulled off by other members while you were present. Yet, you told me that you went on the hunt for victims after you punched out from the post-office job around midnight. Cruising for hours throughout the streets of New York for the ultimate sacrifice was your nightly tradition. Such a scenario doesn't sound like teamwork, Dave? Sounds like you were alone." I ask.

With his head still bowed, David appears to be praying for strength. Prayer is an amazing coping mechanism. Though some psychologists use *Defense Mechanisms* and *Coping Mechanisms* interchangeably, I do not teach it that way in my psychology courses at the colleges. A defense mechanism, like euphemisms and denial, enable you to block the pain. A coping mechanism, like prayer, enables you to bear the pain.

SHOCKING CONFESSIONS

David is done with defense mechanisms. Coping mechanisms is what he relies upon. David is done with blocking the pain. Jesus' mandate, *Pick up your cross*, means bear

---

[280] *The Holy Bible, NIV.*

the pain. David looks up and fixes his gaze on my face.

I did all the shootings.

I sit speechless while witnessing a man hug a cactus tightly. My jaw drops while watching a man answer the angel's confrontational question. *Yes, I am Jacob, the heel-grabber, the hustler, the deceiver.*

> I wanted to tell Mrs. Moskowitz the truth before she passed but we never had the opportunity to meet. I wanted to tell her, face to face, that I did it. Nobody else. I did it. (A heavy pause) I shot her beautiful daughter, Stacy.

No waxing crescent moon appears in the sky. No last quarter moon hangs in that sky either. Just a full moon on display for the world to behold.

> I lied in that 1990s interview. I felt so much pressure from certain entities. I was in heavy denial. The trauma that I inflicted on others, and myself, was so deep. I'm so sorry I did that interview. I can't live in denial any longer.

David's full moon confession does not draw out the werewolves, vampires, and the walking dead. Nope, it is not a call to awaken the monsters. Rather, this full moon summons all broken men.

"Dave, I'm touched by your confession. I feel like the bright lamp above your head just swung in my direction," I say.

Confession is a church sacrament that bears cathartic benefits for the confessor. Slepian and colleagues (2017) conducted a study that featured 38 areas of life where people are likely to keep a secret. The results showed that 97% of people are withholding secrets, and the average person keeps a secret within 13 of those categories.[281] The data also shows a prevalence of mental health problems such as depression and anxiety. Could we be suffering within our world from a lack of confession? As they say in the halls of Alcoholics Anonymous, *you're only as sick as your secrets.*

"Dave, do you remember when I told you that I resigned from pastoring because of my heart attacks? Well, that's not entirely true. Facts are, I was divorced after 18 years of marriage," I confess.

David, still under immense contrition, gives me a slightly confused look.

"Why didn't I tell you that? The church esteems marriage, and rightly so. But that value system lends itself to divorce being perceived as the unpardonable sin. Especially as a clergyman, divorce feels like a scarlet letter that you can't escape. A good handful of church people, I mean like close friends, suddenly ghosted me because of the divorce a few years back. So, I don't talk about it. I guess, I got my own secrets to reckon with." I confess.

Certainly, the most despised man in 1970s New York City knows what it means to be standing solo against the world. Hardly anyone, other than a few friends and the saintly Nat Berkowitz, walked in when the rest of the world stormed out.

---

[281] Michael Slepian and Katharine H. Greenaway, "The Benefits and Burdens of Keeping Others' Secrets," Journal of Experimental Social Psychology78 (Sept. 2018): 220-232.

"Also, divorce for me means that I failed. And, I did fail. I prioritized the needs of the church, and career ambitions over my wife at the time", I admit with a hoarse throat. "Thankfully, God was merciful to me. And blessed me with a new chapter of life, and a woman named Alicia whom I adore. But the failure still sometimes feels like sticky tar", I add.

Of course, my divorce sounds petty compared to David's heinous acts. However, from a Christian standpoint, our iniquities are not assessed like being graded on a bell curve. Instead, our iniquities are judged against the standard of God's perfection. From that vantage point, the difference between David's crimes and my crimes is tiny. Let me say it this way. If two men engage in a leaping contest, and the first contestant jumps a few feet ahead of the second contestant, a few feet is a big difference. But, if the finish line is China, the difference of a few feet is inconsequential. In light of God's infinitely high standard, the disparity between divorce and murder is minuscule.

David clasps my hands as we pray together. The gap between monster and man is bridged. The line between psychopath and person diminishes. At the foot of the cross, all have sinned and fallen short of the glory of God.

THE SOFTEST PILLOW

The morning after our visit, I am settled into an armchair with a book at hand when my cellphone notifies me of an incoming call from Shawangunk Correctional. After accepting the charges, I'm greeted without delay by a chipper voice.

Brother Mike, how's it going this morning?

"Dave, is that you? You sound great. You must have just finished that large pizza with everything on it." I reply.

Everything but anchovies. I'm just relieved today, ya know. I slept last night like God lifted a huge boulder from my chest during our talk.

I reply, "Thrilled to hear, David. I'm sleeping better myself. I'm sleeping better, not from a bad memory, but a clear conscience. A clear conscience is a much more comfortable pillow."

Then, I acknowledged my sin to you,
and did not cover up my iniquity....
And you forgave the guilt of my sin.
Psalm 32:3-5[282]

---

[282] *The Holy Bible, NIV.*

Nat Berkowitz, David's adoptive father,
who died at 101 years old in 2012.

CHAPTER 10

JUST BABIES

Surely, I was brought forth in inquiry.
I was sinful when my mother conceived me.
Psalm 51:5

For You created my inmost being.
You knit me together in my mother's womb.
Psalm 139:13.

A HERO OR A SKUNK

Before David arrives, I notice a young mom sparing no effort to keep her rambunctious toddler occupied. The ginger-haired tot points at the vending machine for a candy bar. Mom's forbiddance only makes the delicacy more desirable. So, she redirects the boy's zeal towards a mini puzzle fished out of her purse. Thankfully, the boy's interest piques in the harlequin cardboard cutouts instead of the eye candy.

From an itty-bitty age, we all show a leaning towards forbidden things, yet simultaneously wishing for better things. Psalm 51:5 and Psalm 139:13 paint a paradox of what happens in the womb — we were shaped by iniquity (Psalm 51:5) yet knit together by divinity (Psalm 139:13). That ginger tot, like all of us, exhibits early evidence of being a sinner and a winner. Oswald Chambers said it best, "In every man, there lies a potential hero and a potential skunk."[283]

---

[283] *Oswald Chambers, The Quotable Oswald Chambers, (Grand Rapids, MI: Discovery House, 2008).*

250

Dad, a princely inmate who just appeared, caught a glimpse of his toddler eyeballing the Hershey® bar just as mom pulled out the puzzle. As dad takes his seat, he signals his prodigy towards a bill dangling from mom's purse. Now, the tot is torn between the brainteaser or the tongue-tickler, the puzzle or a bill to buy the Hershey bar. With a wink from dad, the tot pushes aside the puzzle and reaches for the bill. Which would you reach for? As a child, I'd pick the Hershey bar over the puzzle any day of the week. More often than not, Psalm 51:5 triumphs over Psalm 139:13, the Adamic nature over the *Imago Dei* (the image of God).

MAD, BAD, OR BEEN HAD?

David arrives short-winded from scurrying across the facility. I hit him with a heavy question early into our session. After thirty-four sessions, the logs of trust are warm enough to start a fire right away. "Do you believe that you were born evil? I mean, like Rosemary's baby?"

This inquiry stems from the endless debate, not only surrounding David Berkowitz but every slayer of innocent blood. The opinions on the SOS and other serial murderers' nature are vast — psychopathic, psychotic, or possessed? After reading this book, you've probably formed an opinion too. Psychopathic means that David was *bad*, psychotic means he was *mad* (like wacko), and possessed means he'd been *had* (like possessed).

Cops, clinicians, and clergy spew opinions about David that align with their seats of expertise. Cops consider SOS as psychopathic, deserving of the guillotine. Clinicians empathize with such killers as acting out of neurosis or psychosis. Clergy are likely to incriminate Satan and sin for the killings. Where you stand on the issue all depends upon where you sit on the issue. I've had the tension of sitting in two seats — a clergyman who believes in the supernatural and a researcher of human behavior who grasps the psyche. David speaks:

> I believe that I was demonized, to some level, since I was a child. Ya know, like the boy in Mark 9. The Bible says that the evil spirit threw the boy into the fire. I also had urges to throw myself in front of subway trains at six-years-old. I'd pin myself against the wall of the station so that I wouldn't succumb to the urge. I wrestled with urges to throw myself in front of moving traffic in the Bronx. Those urges, just like the Bible describes, were demons. And the demons increased in quantity and potency as I grew older.

"Do you still have those same urges to hurt yourself? Or urges to hurt others?" I ask the question because if the urges are gone, it's imperative to understand what stopped them.

Whatever eradicated David's urges reveals the nature of what stimulated them. If psychotropics purged the violent urges, then psychosis was behind the crimes. If positive support systems flushed them out, then social maladjustment was behind them. If therapy made the difference, then emotional problems were behind them. As we've seen throughout our journey, all of these factors played supporting roles in the 1970s tragedy. Once again, only a fool presumes the last block in Jenga caused the tower's collapse.

However, every supporting cast has a leading antagonist. What or who was the leading antagonist in the horror story entitled SOS?

No, I haven't had those urges in a long time. Urges to hurt myself and hurt people? Gone for many, many years. Do I get in bad moods? Yea, of course. Mike, you used a good word to describe the moods. You once used the term funks. Yes, I get into funks. But urges to hurt myself or others — no.

"Psychiatric medication? What are you on, if any at all?" I ask.

I had to rule out the possibility that psychotropics were his real savior. For instance, a drug like Thorazine is an antipsychotic that blocks the flow of dopamine in a brain overloaded with it. Too much dopamine results in psychotic symptoms such as delusions and hallucinations, sometimes the basis behind violent crimes. Thorazine shuts down the psychotic symptoms behind delusion-based crimes by disrupting dopamine.[284] If psychotropics were David's savior, then it stands to reason that psychosis was David's villain.

Funny you ask me that because Larry King posed the same question, "Are you on any psych meds?" when he interviewed me in 1999 for his evening show.[285] I think he was surprised at how calm and lucid I was during the interview. So, I'll tell you what I told him. No, I'm not on any psych medication.

In 1978, a few months after David's arrest, King's County Hospital heavily drugged the unhinged detainee. Subdual, by whatever means necessary, has always been the

---

[284] Krutika Chokhawala and Lee Stevens, *Antipsychotic Medications* (Treasure Island, FL: Statpearls Publishing, 2023).
[285] "*The Son of Sam on Larry King Weekend,*" interview with David Berkowitz, 1999, https://youtu.be/gCGF6W_NAV8.

way society handles its madmen. Back in Bible days, a demoniac man caused commotion in a town called the Gadarenes. The inhabitants of that town chained the man, hand and foot. [286] Today, metallic shackles are not as common as chemical shackles. Like the doctors at King's County, the default position of handling madmen is to restrain them with psychotropics. Since the world doesn't know how to save a madman, the only other option is to subdue that madman.

> Up until my conversion in 1988, I dwelt in darkness. I practiced Satanic rituals back in my cell. I was still lonely, suicidal, angry. I got so angry one day that I severely beat another inmate after he harassed me. The guards threw me in the "box" for 90 days over that incident.

While medications are sometimes necessary, pills accomplished little for David. And David is not alone with his testimony about impotent drugs. Reports allege that Eric Harris ingested his daily Luvox at the time of the Columbine shooting [287] while his partner, Dylan Klebold, was seen taking antidepressants. [288] Not only were these medications ineffectual in saving the killers, but they proved impotent in subduing them. Similarly, the demoniac from the Gadarenes in Mark 5 broke the chains off his hands and feet because nothing "was strong enough to subdue him." [289]

I've witnessed medication bear good results many times in

---

[286] *The Holy Bible, KJV.*

[287] Steve Salvatore, *"Columbine Shooter Was Prescribed Anti-depressant," CNN.com, April 29, 1999, http://www.cnn.com/HEALTH/9904/29/luvox.explainer/.*

[288] Sue Klebold, *A Mother's Reckoning: Living in the Aftermath of Tragedy* (New York: Crown Publishers, 2016).

[289] *The Holy Bible, NIV.*

my pastoral ministry. But, society makes a grave mistake by crowning pills as a savior. No pills are strong enough to subdue the evil that carries humans away.

"Some perceive you as a psychopath. What's your take on that term?" I ask.

Anti-Social Disorder, the clinical descriptor for psychopaths, would not be treated with medication. Anti-socials, or psychopaths, make hardly any headway with therapy that treats their unconventional personality traits — risky behaviors, aggressive proclivities, and a chilling fearlessness.[290]

> For many years, I saw myself as bad. I guess you could say a psychopath. I swallowed the FBI and Dr. David Abrahamsen's assessment of me. I believed these assessments, ya know. These were the experts, so I figured they knew what they were talking about.

Locked away in Attica from 1978-82, David wrestled with the etiology of his evil. For a while, he went along with Dr. Abrahamsen's assessment — a pure psychopath. In those days, he feasted on Seattle serial killer Ted Bundy's televised trial while identifying deeply with the prolific killer's antisocial tendencies. He devoured the Co-Ed Killer, Ed Kemper's biography, calling it "a mirror" into his own mind. If you probed twenty-six-year-old David about his self-concept, he'd tell you what he wrote his girlfriend during that era:

> I believe I know Bundy, his personality and mind, better than most people because I am what he is — a

---

[290] *Diagnostic and Statistical Manual of Mental Disorders, American Psychiatric Association, 5th ed. (2013), "s.v. Antisocial Disorder."*

MICHAEL A. CAPARRELLI, PhD

psychopathic personality. This is not one who is crazy but one who is clever, cunning, and mischievous. I am this type of person, but I am also trying to change.[291]

Maybe David was biologically ingrained as a psychopath. In 2014, a Kansas University professor performed a genetic analysis of eighty-nine inmates who committed violent and nonviolent crimes. Inmates with the MAOA -L gene were more likely to have committed violence. MAOA-L is dubbed, "the warrior gene," because of its link with aggressive, risky behavior by disrupting the flow of serotonin. This is the supposed gene behind psychopathy.[292]

No doubt, David was an aggressive high-roller his entire life. He lit fires, vandalized property, joined the army during war, engaged in occult activity, and shot fifteen people. He loved the idea of jumping out of helicopters in the army like he saw in the commercials (in addition to his deep patriotism). He was eager to leave the army after a few months of monotony in South Korea. He was promised a transfer to the tumultuous Vietnam but was disappointed when it never happened. Anecdotal evidence suggest that David was genetically hardwired as "a warrior."

But even if that diagnosis is accurate, is that an adequate explanation for the evil David committed? Not all psychopaths reign terror over people.

---

[291] *The People vs. David Berkowitz, "Dr. David Abrahamsen-Berkowitz Letters."*.
[292] *Philip Hunter, "The Psycho Gene," EMBO Reports 11 no. 9 (Sept. 11, 2010): 667-669.*

For instance, James Fallon is a neuroscientist who stumbled upon a startling realization when examining the brains of violent offenders — his own brain scan displayed the same psychopathic characteristics. He later discovered that he also had the MAOA-L gene and that there were at least eight murderers within his family tree. He says that his psychopathic tendencies — risky actions, unconventional thinking, aggressive behaviors — were channeled towards making ground-breaking contributions in medical science. Fallon is a family man and an award-winning scientist. He labels himself "a pro-social psychopath."[293] Psychopathy is like a scalpel, capable of maiming or mending someone. Evil pertains to the one holding the blade.

Mike, I've come back to my original story. The very first report I gave the police back in 1977, just after I was arrested. The story I told those detectives before the shrinks and the media got in my head. It's the story I gave that parole board last May. The truth is, I was demonized.

Most Americans dismiss demonology as an archaic practice. We are so left brained that our heads tilt when standing upright. Yet, demonology remains a common approach when treating deranged behavior in Eastern countries and over 2/3rds of the world.

In a prior session, I invited my psychology student, Edward, from Northpoint Bible College to Shawangunk. Edward, a foreign exchange student from Kenya, challenged the rationalism of America during our commute to visit David. "Dr. Caparrelli, if the American approach to

---

[293] "The Moth: Confessions of a Pro-social Psychopath - James Fallon," Youtube, June 4, 2011, https://Youtu.be/fzqn6z_Iss0.

treating mentally sick people is superior to Africa, then why are there significantly more serial killings in America than Africa? Why is America leading the way in child sex trafficking and a host of other crimes?" my much younger but equally wise student asks. To Edward's point, America not only leads the way in serial killings and sex trafficking but also depression and anxiety.[294]

Some interpret David's belief that he was Satanically targeted as symptomatic of narcissism, a disorder characterized by thinking of oneself as special. Some construe David's stories about being handpicked by hell as exaggerated self-importance. I, myself, admittedly considered narcissism in our earlier sessions. But as I mentioned in the introduction, I bracketed these clinical labels in previous chapters so that I could identify with David as a man rather than a monster.

After spending many hours with David, I do not detect narcissism (that probably wouldn't have been the case forty years ago). Instead, he exhibits humility by regularly mentioning people he cares about. "Please keep my friend Chuck in prayer," David asks.

Or "Please pray that this Muslim inmate shows up at our chapel this week. I gave him a Bible, sealed in an envelope, so he wouldn't get harassed by other inmates."

C.S. Lewis' words justly depict the man that David has become, "Humble people don't think less of themselves. Humble people think of themselves less."[295] More than likely, he was narcissistic in his youth, but cataclysmic changes have undoubtedly occurred.

---

[294] *Edward Mburur, conversation with the author, October 2, 2022.*
[295] *C.S. Lewis, Mere Christianity (London: Macmillan Publishers, 1952).*

DAVID'S CONVERSION STORY

What I know for sure is the demons left me in 1988 when I surrendered my life to Christ.

Now, this is a story we all want to hear. David Berkowitzis exorcised of the demons that drove him to commit the SOS tragedy. I imagine his head spinning like Linda Blair, or foam frothing out of his mouth, or his eyes rolling like numbers in a slot machine. I envision a cinematic showdown between the forces of good and evil. Of course, that's how the movies portray such phenomena.

"Tell me what happened in that moment you were saved and delivered from demons? Where were you? What were you doing? Did anything unusual transpire?" I ask, wishing I had a bag of popcorn. Before David shares his encounter, I envision the mattress within his tiny cell levitating from the ground. I'm expecting this story to be as cinematic as *The Exorcist.*

I was alone in my cell reading Psalm 34:6, "This poor man cried, and the Lord heard him, and saved him from his trouble."[296] Everything hit me at once — the guilt of what I'd done, the shame of who I'd become. I fell to my knees in that cold cell, sobbed in repentance for a good while, and went to sleep. I woke up the next morning, and I felt 100 pounds lighter. It was the most quiet and peaceful day, and I sensed that it was the beginning of a new life.

That's it? Initially, I was flabbergasted by the lack of

---

[296] *The Holy Bible, NIV.*

pandemonium in David's exorcism. After further reflection, his noiseless salvation taught me something about demons and the divine.

The quietness of David's deliverance was proof that the darkness was no match for the light. If you flick the light switch in a dingy room, the light instantly dispels the darkness without any tussle. David's life for the first three decades was pitch black, and he turned on heaven's light with a heartfelt prayer. Christ instantly expelled the powers of darkness as easy as the flick of a light switch. Before Christ, daimonion barged through the front door of David's life with racket and commotion. After Christ, daimonion cowardly tiptoed out the back door, never to be seen again.

Based on David's conversion story, and the thirty-five years of fruits that followed, the leading antagonist in the SOS tragedy was not biological or psychological but diabolical. How do we know this? If anti-psychotic meds purged the violent urges from David, then it stands to reason that psychosis drove the urges. If the Savior delivered David from the urges, then it stands to reason that Satan drove the urges. The Savior's mission, accomplished in David's cell at the hour of his conversion, is clearly stated in I John 3:8, "For this purpose, the Son of God was manifested that He might destroy the works of the devil."[297]

I posed the question within the introduction, *Did David use the devil?* Over the last 100 hours, we learned that David applies defense mechanisms to block intense feelings of guilt and shame over his intolerable deeds. Certainly, David held satan liable on certain occasions when he

---

[297] *The Holy Bible, NIV.*

probably should have just fessed up, "I'm the man." So yes, David used the devil during and after his killing spree. At various points, the devil was a defense mechanism.

But does that mean the devil didn't use David? Let's face it, all toxic relationships consist of two parties who exploit one another. The pimp exploits the prostitute for profit, but in many cases, the prostitute also uses the pimp for protection. Satan and our sinful-self engage in a blood-sucking affair like the pimp and the prostitute or like two tics and no dog. Yes, David used the devil while the devil exploited David.

Of course, demonic activity is viewed by most shrinks as psychotic breaks. Even the *Rite of Exorcism*, published by Paul V in 1614, cautions clergymen to distinguish between demon possession and melancholy (a catchall term for mental sickness) since they resemble one another.[298] But Richard Gallagher, an Ivy League psychiatrist who teaches at New York Medical College, is a believer in demons after witnessing the demonized speak Latin without any foreknowledge and reveal the deepest secrets of people in their company along with sacred objects chucked from shelves. Gallagher once participated in an exorcism where a ninety-pound woman flung a 200-pound Lutheran deacon across the room.

"That's not psychiatry. That's beyond psychiatry," Gallagher said.[299]

"So, why you? Out of all your friends growing up — Eddie, Lenny — why were you targeted by Satan?" I ask. My research shows that David's childhood friends grew up to

---

[298] Paul V, "Rite of Exorcism," Roman Catholic Church, 1614.
[299] John Blake, "When Exorcists Need Help, They Call Him," CNN, August 4, 2017.

be police officers, firemen, and even doctors. Of course, those careers don't negate the possibility of demonization. The devil has many costumes. But none grew up to be SOS.

Remember that lion we talked about during our first session. The Apostle Peter describes Satan as "like a lion." Lions prey upon the weakest animals in the herd or the flock. I was that weak animal, that sickly gazelle. I must have given off the scent of vulnerability.

Evil preys upon folks with risk factors. A risk factor is a vulnerability that increases the likelihood of contracting a disorder. Just as risk factors exist with mental sickness, they also exist with spiritual sickness. Loneliness, shame, anger, abandonment, trauma, and the other conditions discussed in this book are the vulnerabilities, or risk factors, that lay out the welcome mat for hell's henchmen.

As I mentioned many times, I acted defiantly from a young age. The angry outbursts, smashing my toys, the fires, disobeying my parents. So, I'm sure, all of those rebellious decisions gave Satan something to work with too.

Noticing David's passion when breaking down the scriptures, I'm suddenly awakened to the flip side of why daimonion preyed upon his weakness. Weakness is useful to the Divine. The apostle Paul tells us in I Corinthians 1:27 that God prefers the weak things over the strong things of this world.[300] God actually chooses the weak as his vessels.

Ironically, being vulnerable is what makes us so valuable to God. Satan preys upon weakness, whereas the spirit

---

[300] *The Holy Bible, NIV.*

prays through our weakness. Vulnerability is both an entry point for daimonion and an opportunity for the Divine. How precious is human weakness that both the Savior and Satan wage war over it?

"David, maybe Satan chased you because God chose you?' I ask.

> You know what's crazy? Around the same time that I started sensing evil, about five or six years old, I heard the audible voice of God call my name. I heard it twice, actually. The first time, I heard it tenderly — "David." The second time, I was up to no good. Ya know, childhood shenanigans. The second time, I heard the voice sternly — "David." I believe that God had a call on my life from a young age, and Satan knew that. But I made some bad choices that played into Satan's plot rather than God's plan.

David's calling is blatant when you audit the minutes of his average day over the last few decades. On the streets, David lived under a compulsion to please the god, Samhain. He wrote to Captain Borelli,

> I DON'T WANT TO KILL ANYMORE. NO, SIR, NO MORE. BUT I MUST HONOUR THY FATHER.[301]

Now, he lives at the behest of Jesus. David preps himself for regular Bible studies, disciples other inmates in the precious faith, and responds to worldwide mail with his testimony. In this second era of life, David still gets carried away. David is still "possessed," only this time by the divine rather than daimonion.

---

[301] Ivins, "Second Letter from .44 Slayer."

IS DAVID'S CONVERSION REAL?

"What do you say to those who label your experience with Christ a 'jailhouse conversion?'" I ask. I knew I didn't need to clarify the meaning of the derogatory phrase, jailhouse conversion. The phrase is popularly used to describe cons with "testiphonies" rather than testimonies, who spout religion to hustle a parole board.

Data shows that religious conversions behind bars alone make little impact on recidivism rates. But let's not forget the well-known inmates who converted to religion in prison and lived altruistically after their release, such as Nixon's Watergate henchman, Chuck Colson [302] or Jack Murphy, who stole the largest sapphire in 1964.[303]Shall we dismiss these bona fide conversions? Only an idiot throws away a real dollar bill because of the innumerable counterfeits in circulation.

David replies to my question,

> People who doubt jailhouse conversions don't understand life behind bars. Becoming a Christian in prison is not the easy path. I've known inmates who were mocked by the gangs they broke allegiance with because of their conversion. Some inmates were even beaten or stabbed. A jailhouse conversion means something more than the general public realizes because of the courage behind the decision.

I'm often asked, *Do you believe David's conversion is real?* I typically reply, *What's the litmus test for a man's character?*

---

[302] *Chuck Colson Born-again (Minneapolis, MN: Chosen Books, 1976).*
[303] *Colson, Born-again.*

Usually, the answer I receive is *actions*. I then explain that a person can fake actions too. Shakespeare said it right, "All the world is a stage" where people are like thespians putting on a show with pretentious actions.

The real hard thing to fake is reactions. With that said, I beheld David's reactions to an inmate who offended him, recollections that disturbed him, conflicts that rubbed him the wrong way, and most astonishingly, a shocking confession of his solo role in SOS. Reactions are behaviors under pressure in real time, nearly impossible to disguise with phony virtue. Reactions, not actions, are the best evidence of character.

Is David perfect? If perfection is what I observed, I'd be skeptical towards his conversion. Instead, I witnessed a man who works through many imperfections – anger, shame, denial. If you ask a gemologist how to discern the difference between a real and a fake diamond, you'll be told to look for the flaws. If the stone has no flaws, it's a fake like a cubic zirconia. If the stone exhibits imperfections, it just might be a diamond. Likewise, David's flaws rather than his flairs verify that he's the real deal.

Another clincher that David's testimony is genuine is the absence of evil for thirty-five years. No man escapes the hounds of hell, a team he once played on, for that long apart from an encounter with the Almighty. In thirty-five years, the prison record of Inmate #78A1976 – once arsonist, vandal, cult member, serial murderer – documents two harmless infractions based on misunderstandings. The first infraction logs David as not being in a certain location at an expected time. The second write-up shows David gifting a Bible to another inmate without permission from a turnkey. No other violations occurred in thirty-five years since his conversion. Pandora holds a better shot of shoving evil back into its box than David resigning from wickedness. An ancient Spanish proverb says, "The tiger that has once tasted blood is never sated with the taste of it."[304] Only God could endow the tiger with a new appetite.

I am not the only believer in David's testimony. Frank DeGennaro, a close friend of David for over thirty years, receives flak from the general public about his fondness towards the infamous inmate. Friendship with David can be like standing under a sign that says, "Drop Zone: Watch your head for falling rocks." Frank says, "People run their mouths about how his behavior is a show for the parole board. What they don't know is that David didn't even show up for many of his parole hearings. In 2002, he even wrote a letter to then New York governor George Pataki saying that he does not deserve parole."[305]

"David, what would you do with your life if the State of New York ever released you from Shawangunk?" I ask.

I pose the hypothetical to a man locked up since his twenty-fourth birthday, forty-five years ago. Could he even survive the alterations of the American landscape? A recent trip to the dentist in Westchester County opened David's eyes to a whole new world. Guards escorted him shackled through a college town amongst yuppy students with no idea they brushed up against the one known in the media as SOS. David stood shocked when spotting men and women exiting from the same gender-neutral bathrooms. *Toto, I got a feeling we're not in the 1970s Bronx anymore.*

[304] *Kalima quotes, https://kalimaquotes.com/quotes/31112/the-tiger-that-has-once.*
[305] *Frank Degenarro, email correspondence with author, April 2, 2023.*

Well, first of all, the parole board told me that if I ever was released, I'd be placed in a shelter in New York City. I'd never survive in New York City. I just wouldn't. It would have to be a more rural setting. I'd prefer life as it is now in Shawangunk Correctional to a shelter in New York City. God knows what's best for me, and I accept His will, whatever it is.

In Psalm 16:6, David the psalmist makes a similar statement to David the prisoner. The psalmist sings to God, "Your boundary lines have fallen in pleasant places."[306]

Do you believe that David Berkowitz would kill again if ever released? is a question I've been asked many times since the onset of this case study.

After 100 hours of data collection, I don't believe that David could hurt even a moth if released. Nonetheless, mental breakdowns of all different types could happen to anyone without the proper placement and provisions. David Berkowitz would agree with me that if he were ever released, he'd pray for God's lines to fall in pleasant places.

Nat Berkowitz pinned his hopes on David's release until March 2012, when he passaged into eternity at a creased 101 years old. Initially, Nat felt his son was too disturbed to be on the loose. But, over the years, David demonstrated a metamorphosis into the stalwart man that Nat always aspired him to become. Nat even hoped for his son's release. Nat's anticipation of a parole board's approval endued him with the will to survive for over a century.

A bittersweet moment for me, to say the least, was talking with my father over the phone in his final

---

[306] *The Holy Bible, NIV.*

moments. It was just before he died when I shared Christ with him. He couldn't verbally respond, he was too sick, but a friend at his bedside told me that he affirmatively gestured at my invitation to the Cross (David swallows a lump of tears protruding from his neck like a golf ball). I hope I see a proud look on his face in heaven when noticing me like, "That's my boy." I brought him much shame my first chapter of life, I want to honor him this chapter.

The New York State parole board upholds a less-than-par opinion of Inmate #78A1976, an assessment not exactly aligned with dad's perspective. A short time after evaluating David on May 19, 2022, officials responded with a denial. Pastor Don Wilkerson, cofounder of Teen Challenge (a faith-based substance abuse inpatient treatment center), disagrees with the parole board. He has known David for several decades and believes in his transformation. Pastor Don states, "Were David ever free, I'd ask him to be our in-house teacher at Brooklyn Teen Challenge. He is truly a miracle."[307]

Just before our session closes, I overhear that young mom say to her little rascal with Hershey smeared across his upper lip, "No more chocolate for you. We got a Halloween party to attend tomorrow with lots of candy."

I'm reminded that the night of witches and warlocks awaits us. In my own home, my wife and young adult kids will probably want to watch *Silence of the Lambs* or some other hair-raising flick. I'm not into horror films, but I appreciate a good suspense equally as much as any other movie buff. Off the cuff, I ask David, "Why do you suppose people are so fascinated with horror movies?"

---

[307] *Rev. Don Wilkerson, interview with the author, March 2, 2023.*

Have you seen that episode of the TV show, I think it's called, *The Purge*? I don't watch that stuff. I mean, when I was a kid, I was all about Dracula and vampires. Now, that stuff disturbs my spirit, ya know. Anyway, a friend told me that the characters were wearing masks of the Manson family and SOS. It's just crazy how people get carried away with evil. To answer your question, I think people like horror movies because it's a reflection of what's inside their hearts. The Bible says, "the heart of man is wicked and deceitful above all things".

David quotes Jeremiah 17:9 [308], an indictment from the mouth of the weeping prophet against the entire human race. The verse squares off with humanism, the predominant worldview of our era that teaches mankind is inherently good. Conversely, the verse suggests that we are ALL bent towards bad.

Raising children will convince you of the reality behind Jeremiah 17:9. You don't have to educate kids to be possessive; contrarily, you have to teach kids to share. You don't have to teach kids to lie; contrarily, you have to teach kids to tell the truth. You don't have to teach kids to be aggressive; contrarily, you have to teach kids to be gentle. Sin manifests effortlessly in children just as weeds grow naturally in a garden. Good character, like a rose, must be cultivated. Deception, aggression, and all other forms of iniquity grow naturally like weeds.

Regarding murder specifically, Jesus' legendary Sermon on the Mount prosecutes all of humanity as murderers when he says, "But I tell you that anyone who is angry

---

[308] *The Holy Bible, KJV.*

(hates) with a brother or sister will be subject to judgment (the penalty of a murderer)." [309] The hater has no right to look down on the murderer since the only factors preventing him from the brutal act is law, order, and circumstances.

Data corroborates the ancient claims of Jesus that we all harbor murderous impulses. Researchers from Arizona State University conducted a survey in 1993 that revealed 79% of men and 58% of women admitted to homicidal fantasies. [310] Our hands might not commit murderous deeds, but our hearts harbor murderous seeds. From the moment of birth, we're all potential monsters in the making.

"So, you believe that we are all capable of becoming monsters? Of course, providing certain risk factors," I ask.

> Doesn't it seem like FBI's criminal profiles keep expanding? With every incident, we learn about another kid who nobody expected to shoot up a mall or a school. Yes, demonization can happen to almost anyone with the risk factors we discussed over the last year or so.

The convict with the camera bids David and I for our customary photo just as we're brushing crumbs of lunch into a napkin. Posing in front of Shawangunk's latest Manhattan mural, slightly more lifelike than the last spoof, Dave flaunts his dimples and sparkling pearly whites. Being tired, I give a death stare. I was too tired to flex my facial muscles. After reviewing the Polaroid, I tell   David,

---

[309] *The Holy Bible, NIV.*

[310] Douglas Kenrick, "Homicidal Fantasies," *Ethology and Sociobiology 14 no.4 (July 1993): 231-246.*

"You look like a nice guy. Show this photo to the parole board, and they'll go easy on you next time."

David replies with his signature wit:

You, on the other hand, look like a convict.

I offer no rebuttal to his funny observation. Facts are, I could have easily gone down the path of deviance. There, but for the grace of God, go I.

JUST BABIES

After a farewell fist bump with my friend, I set sail from Shawangunk to lower Manhattan for an on-foot crime tour of America's most notorious city. I booked the tour that morning. My fascination is not with gory crime scenes but the anecdotes of ordinary people who commit deranged deeds. Spare me the details of how the victims died. Just tell me how the perpetrators lived — the brownstone-crammed streets they strolled, play-grounds frequented with their tots, diners where they chowed down on a cream-cheese smothered bagel. I'm spellbound when I hear any detail that makes me think, *Me too!*

I arrive in Greenwich Village to meet a group of nut jobs taking refuge under umbrellas from the day's drizzle. The tour guide is an aficionado who garners facts about New York City's bloody history, like an old lady collects fridge magnets in her high-rise apartment. I discern that he's more invested in the facts than outlandish myths by the way he stops to read the plaques on the brownstones. He's not as whacky as the crowd paying him for the tour.

Right away, the annoyances begin.

"That's the house of horrors where that devil beat his six-year-old daughter to death," a whacky lady points her finger across the street.

"He was a monster," his pal replies.

"I heard he had wild sex parties in the home with perverts from around the neighborhood," another chimes in.

The ivy-leagued tour guide looks away to hide the eyes he can't help but roll.

A lady who resembles the eccentric Mrs. Peacock from *Clue* pipes up, "So, any monsters born on this street?"

Other wackos look over in suspense for any ghoulish details that the tour guide might divulge about the dungy West 10th Street. Admittedly, my antennas poke upward. Maybe an infamous mob boss was born in this area. My Bronx-native stepfather told me endless stories about the ruthless mafiosos of New York City.

The tour guide's poignant comeback captures everything I've learned about monsters in 100 hours with David Berkowitz. The tour guide's reply: "No monsters born on this street. Just babies."

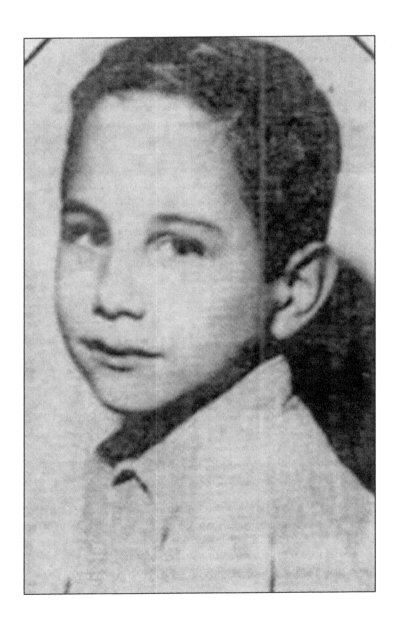

BIBLIOGRAPHY

Abrahamsen, David. "Confessions of Son of Sam." *Columbia University*, 1985.

Abrams, David B. et al. *Attachment Theory*. New York, NY: Springer New York: Encyclopedia of Behavioral Medicine, 2013.

Abrams, David B. "Attachment Theory." *Encyclopedia of Behavioral Medicine*, 2013.

Ackerman, Courtney. "19 Best Narrative Therapy Techniques & Worksheets." PositivePsychology.com. Last modified June 18, 2017.

Adoptee Reasons. "Top 5 Reasons Adoptees Search for Birth Family Members." Adoption.com. Last modified 2016. https://adoption.com/top-5-reasons-adoptees-search-for-birth-family-members/.

Ahlquist, Dale. "Believing in Anything." *Faith and Culture*, May 2019.

Algan, Yann, Nicolò Dalvit, Quoc-Anh Do, Alexis L. Chapelain, and Yves Zenou. "Friendship Networks and Political Opinions: A Natural Experiment among Future French Politicians." *Monash Business School*, December 2020.

Amen, Daniel. "Email Correspondence." Last modified August 12, 2022.

Amen, Daniel. "Email Correspondence." Last modified August 2, 2022.

Amen, Daniel. "Understanding the Relationship between Survivor's Guilt and PTSD." Mental Healthcare Clinic Focusing On Your Brain Health | Dr. Amen. Last modified March 1, 2021. https://www.amenclinics.com/blog/understanding-the-relationship-between-survivors-guilt-and-ptsd/.

American Psychiatric Association. *The Diagnostic and Statistical Manual of Mental Disorders*, 5th ed. American Psychiatric Association, 2013.

Anderson, Neil T. "Neil T Anderson on Spiritual Warfare: "This is the War We're Facing"." YouTube. Last modified October 23, 2013. https://www.youtube.com/watch?v=2FBC4G1hU90&list=PLVtGS2qi lLGV2oNlJIJxu-kz6v-edF_8W.

Ariseanshine.org. The Official Website of David Berkowitz.

Associated Press. "Sheriff: Parkland Shooting Suspect Assaulted Jail Officer." AP News/The Florida Times Union. Last modified November 14, 2018. https://apnews.com/article/8eb5491626b245038a34c14a8f1571c4.

Barclay, William. *The Gospel of Mark*. Westminster Press, 1975.

Baron-Cohen, S. *The Science of Evil: On Empathy and the Origins of Cruelty. Basic Books*. New York, New York.2011.

Barron, James. "How a Son of Sam Detective Realized 'This Has Got to Be the Guy'." The New York Times. Last modified August 6, 2017.

Bell, Max. "The 20 Best Songs by the Doors." Louder Sound. Last modified August 2, 2021.

Bernhard, Toni. "It's Time to Stop Taking Things Personally." Psychology Today. Last modified August 18, 2018.

Bible Hub. "Index of /lexicon/revelation." Bible Hub: Search, Read, Study the Bible in Many Languages. n.d. https://biblehub.com/lexicon/revelation/.

Bible Lexicon. "Strong's #5117 - τόπος - Old & New Testament Greek Lexical Dictionary - StudyLight.org." StudyLight.org. Last modified 2015. https://www.studylight.org/lexicons/eng/greek/5117.html.

Blake, John. "When Exorcists Need Help, They Call Him." CNN. Last modified August 4, 2017.

Bllim, Howard. "Re-examination of Berkowitz Files Offers New In." The New York Times. Last modified May 17, 1978.

Bono, Sal. "40 Years After 'Son of Sam' Arrest, Detective Reveals How Cops Finally Ended His Reign of Terror." Inside Edition. Last modified August 1, 2017.

Borders, Ashley. *Beliefs, Traits, and Motivations Underlying Rumination. Rumination and Related Constructs.* Academic Press, 2020.

Buder, Leonard. "Inquiry Reported into New Theory On 'son of Sam' (Published 1979)." The New York Times. Last modified October 19, 1979.

Böckler, Nils, Thorsten Seeger, Peter Sitzer, and Wilhelm Heitmeyer. "School Shootings: Conceptual Framework and International Empirical Trends." *School shootings: International research, case studies, and concepts for prevention*, 2013. Springer, New York, NY.

Chambers, Oswald. *The Quotable Oswald Chambers.* Discovery House, 2008.

Chokhawala, Krutika. "Antipsychotic Medications." StatPearls Publishing. Last modified January 2023.

Colson, Chuck. *Born-again.* Chosen Books, 1976.

Cornell Research Program on Self-Injury and Recovery. https://www.selfinjury.bctr.cornell.edu/perch/resources/how-does-self-injury-change-feelings-5.pdf.

Couppis, Maria, and Craig Kennedy. "The Rewarding Effect of Aggression is Reduced by Nucleus Accumbens Dopamine Receptor Antagonism in Mice." Psychopharmacology. Last modified 2008. 197:449–456

Cullen, Dave. *Columbine.* London, England: riverrun, 2019.

Dahmer, Jeffrey. "Inside Edition interview with Dahmer." n.d. https://www.youtube.com/watch?v=iWjYsxaBjBI.

Dalphonse, Lee. "Interview." Cranston, Rhode Island. Last modified July 10, 2023. https://www.selfinjury.bctr.cornell.edu/perch/resources/how-does-self-injury-change-feelings-5.pdf.

Davila, Andrea. "Son of Sam Shoots and Kills Couple Sitting in Parked Car in the Bronx." Daily News. Last modified April 18, 1977.

De Palma, B. *Scarface*. Universal Pictures, 1983.

Degenarro, Frank. "Email Correspondence." Last modified April 2, 2023.

Delbanco, Andrew. *The Death of Satan*. Create Space Publishing, 2013.

Deleuze, Gilles. *Nietzsche and Philosophy*. Translated by Hugh Tomlinson. London: The Athlone Press, 1962. Published 1983

Diagnostic and Statistical Manual of Mental Disorders. American psychiatric Association, 2013.

Dockrill, Peter. "Being an Only Child can Actually Change Structure of Brain." Science Alert. Last modified May 17, 2017.

Fallon, James. "The Confessions of a Pro-Social Psychopath." n.d. https://www.youtu.be/fzqn6z_Iss0.

Farrelly, Peter. *Green Book*. Universal Pictures, 2008.

Fatherhood Stats. https://www.fatherhood.org/father-absence-statistic.

Fehr, Philip. "Interview over Telephone." The Cornell Research Program on Self-Injury and Recovery. Last modified April 25, 2023.

Ferreira, C., M. Moura-Ramos, Marcela Matos, and Ana Galhardo. "A new measure to assess external and internal shame: development, factor structure and psychometric properties of the External and Internal Shame Scale." *Current Psychology* 41 (2022), 1892-1901.

Fowler, Leanne, and David Berkowitz. "Son of Sam." *Radford University* (n.d.). http://maamodt.asp.radford.edu/Psyc%20405.

Franklin, Joe. "How Does Self-Injury Change Feelings?" The Cornell Research Program on Self-Injury and Recovery. Last modified 2014. https://www.selfinjury.bctr.cornell.edu/perch/resources/how-does-self-injury-change-feelings-5.pdf.

Fred, Herbert. "On Getting What We Deserve." *The Texas Heart Institute Journal* 38, no. 2 (2011), 106-107.

Freud, Anna, and Dorothy Burlingam. *Infants without Families.* New York: International University Press, 1944.

Freud, Sigmund. *Beyond the Pleasure Principle.* New York: Liveright Publishers, 1961.

Freud, Sigmund. *The Interpretation of Dreams.* Translated by A. A. Brill. Wordsworth Editions, 1997.

Geller, Adam. "Killer railed against 'rich kids,' 'debauchery' and 'deceitful charlatans'." Metro West Daily News. Last modified April 17, 2007.

George R.R., Marting. *A Game of Thrones.* New York: Bantam Books, 1996.

Gilbert, Alicia. "The psychology behind getting drunk and saying hurtful things." Soberish.com. Last modified May 23, 2023.

Gilligan, James. "Shame, Guilt, and Violence." *Social Research* 70, no. 4 (2003), 1149–80.

Ginsberg, Arthur. "The Iceman and the Psychiatrist." Home Box Office (HBO). Last modified 2003.

Global Sales of Psych Drugs. GlobalData. Last modified April 6, 2020. https://www.globaldata.com/media/pharma/global-sales-of-psychiatric-drugs-could-reach-more-than-40bn-by-2025-due-to-coronavirus-says-globaldata/.

Golden, Sam A., MIchelle Jin, and Yavin Shaham. "Animal Models of (or for) Aggression Reward, Addiction, and Relapse: Behavior and Circuits." *The Journal of Neuroscience* 39 (2019), 3996-4008.

Gonzalez, David. "How Fire Defined the Bronx and Us." New York Times. Last modified January 20, 2022.

Good Reads. https://www.goodreads.com/quotes/101973-nothing-makes-us-so-lonely-as-our-secrets

Grasso, Matteao, Larissa Albantakis, Jonathan P. Lang, and Giulio Tononi. "Causal Reductionism and Causal Structures." National Neuroscience. Last modified October 2021.

Griffiths, Mark. "Love Bombing." Psychology Today. Last modified February 14, 2019.

Guinn, Jeff. *Manson: The Life and Times of Charles Manson*. Simon and Schuster, n.d.

Gun violence archive. "Gun Violence Archive: Mass Shooting in 2023." Last modified 2023. https://www.gunviolencearchive.org/reports/mass-shooting.

Gunther, Anna. "Younger Generations are Lonelier and Social Media Doesn't Help." Cbsnews.com. Last modified January 22, 2020.

Guskiewicz, Kevin. "Recurrent concussion and risk of depression in retired professional football players. Medical science sports exercise." June 2007.

Haberman, Clyde. "For Shame: A Brief History of the Perp Walk." New York Times. Last modified December 2, 2018.

Hamill, John. "Meet the boy next door who grew up to be the Son of Sam." Daily News. Last modified August 12, 1977.

Harris, Chris. "Inside the Son of Sam Case." People. Last modified August 10, 2022.

Harris, Eric, and Dylan Klebold. *The Journals of Dylan Klebold and Eric Harris*. Independently Published, 2019.

Helmond, Petra, Geertjan Overbek, Daniel Brugman, and John C. Gibbs. "A Meta-Analysis on Cognitive Distortions and Externalizing Problem Behavior." *Criminal Justice and Behavior*, 2015.

Hentschel, U., J. G. Draguns, W. Ehlers, and G. Smith. *Defense mechanisms: Current approaches to research and measurement.* in U. Hentschel, G. Smith, J. G. Draguns, & W. Ehlers (Eds.), Defense Mechanisms: Theoretical, Research and Clinical Perspectives, 2004.

Hepper, P. G., D. Scott, and S. Shahidullah. "Newborn and Fetal Response to Maternal Voice." *Journal of Reproductive and Infant Psychology* 11, no. 3 (1993), 147.

Herring, Bill. "The Four Denials of Responsibility." 2010. https://www.billherring.com/article/four-denials-responsibility.

Hill, Taryn. "Survey Says 1 in 5 People are keeping a Major Secret from Spouse." HuffPost.com. Last modified August 1, 2014.

Hoffman, MC. "Stress, the Placenta, and Fetal Programming of Behavior: Genes' First Encounter with the Environment." The American Journal of Psychiatry. Last modified July 2016. 173.

Holley, Joe. "D. Carleton Gajdusek; Controversial Scientist." The Washington Post. Last modified December 16, 2008.

Hostage to the devil Podcast. "Episode 4, Son of Sam." (n.d.). https://youtu.be/ep9KcYwMXm.

Hughes, Sarah. "Robert Downey Jr: Hollywood should forgive Mel Gibson." October 2011.

Humphreys, KL, MC Camacho, MC Roth, and EC Estes. "Prenatal Stress Exposure and Multimodal Assessment of Amygdala-Medial Prefrontal Cortex Connectivity in Infants." *Dev Cogn Neurosci* 46 (December 2020).

Hunter, Phillip. "The Psycho Gene." EMBO Reports. Last modified September 11, 2010.

Inside Edition. https://www.youtube.com/watch?v=PIMHQ4Y_EzQ&t=699s.

Ivins, Molly. "Second letter from .44 Slayer has Police Chasing Four Nicknames." New York Times. Last modified June 7, 1977. p. 28.

Jenner, H. "The Pygmalion Effect." *Alcoholism Treatment Quarterly.* 7(2), 1990.

JPay. JPay | Your Home for Corrections Services. n.d. https://www.jpay.com.

Kalima Quotes. https://kalimaquotes.com/quotes/31112/the-tiger-that-has-once.

Kalu, Madeline. "What is the Meaning of, Idle Hands?" Christianity.com. Last modified May 17, 2022.

Kanikowska, Dominika. "Stress Hormones Spike as Temperature Rises." American Psychological Society. Last modified April 25, 2018.

Katzin, S., P. Andiné, B. Hofvander, E. Billstedt, and M. Wallinius. "Exploring Traumatic Brain Injuries and Aggressive Antisocial Behaviors in Young Male Violent Offenders." *Front Psychiatry* 11 (October 2020).

Kawamoto, Taisha, Keiichi Onoda, Ken'ichiro Nakashima, Hiroshi Nittono, Shuhei Yamaguchi, and Mitsuhiro Ura. "Is Dorsal Anterior Cingulate Cortex Activation in Response to Social Exclusion Due to Expectancy Violation?" Frontiers in Evolutionary Neuroscience. Last modified July 27, 2012.

Kazan, Abraham. "Cooperative Housing in the United States/",, Annals of the American Academy of Political and Social Science." *Consumers' Cooperation* 191 (May 1937), 137–143.

Kelland, Kate. "Feeling angry? Blame it on Low Serotonin." *ABC Science*, September 2011.

Keller, Tim. "Sermon, Spiritual Warfare." (n.d.). https://m.youtube.com/watch?v=JcPlfM7w-ZE&feature=youtu.be.

Kenrick, Douglas. "Homicidal Fantasies." *Ethology and Sociobiology* 14 (1993).

Kierkegaard, S. "The Sickness unto Death." *Princeton University*, 1983.

Kilgannon, Corey. "Yes, Son of Sam Slept Sere." The New York Times. Last modified February 15, 2007.

King, Larry. "Interview with David Berkowitz." n.d. https://youtu.be/gCGF6W_NAV8.

Kinsella, MT, and C. Monk. "Impact of Maternal Stress, Depression and Anxiety on Fetal Neurobehavioral Development." *Clin Obstet Gynecol* 52, no. 3 (September 2009), 425-40.

Kirschner, David. "Adoption Forensics: The Connection between Adoption and Forensics." Crime Magazine. Last modified October 13, 2009.

Klebold, Sue. "A Mother's Reckoning: Living in the Aftermath Of tragedy." *Crown Publishers*, 2016.

Lawrenz, Mel. "The Ten Commandments and Our Relationships with Others." Last modified April 23, 2018.

Leibelt, Jm. "Culture Post: Modern Family – Average Parent Spends Just 5 Hours Face-To-Face With Their Kids per Week." HomeWord. Last modified February 7, 2020.

Lerner, Melvin J., and Leo Montada. *An Overview: Advances in Belief in a Just World Theory and Methods.* New York: Plenum: Critical Issues in Social Justice, 1998.

Lescase, Lee. "Yelling I'd kill them all again' Berkowitz Derails Sentencing." Washington Post. Last modified May 23, 1978.

Lewinsky, Monica. "Ted Talk. The Price of Shame." n.d. https://youtu.be/H_8y0WLm78U.

Lewis, C. S. "Mere Christianity." Macmillan Publishers. Last modified 1952.

Lidge, E. F. "Perp Walks and Prosecutorial Ethics." *Nevada Law Journal, Fall,* 2006.

Lindquist, B. "The Genius and the Boys." (n.d.). https://www.youtube.com/watch?v=1WF2l-d-jLM&t=65s.

Lombroso, C. *Criminal Man.* Putnam Press1911.

Long-Crowell, Erin. "The Halo Effect: Definition, Advantages & Disadvantages." Psychology 104: Social Psychology. Last modified 2021. study.com.

Lovering, Nancy. "How To Tell Your Child they're Adopted." Psychcentral. Last modified January 25, 2022.

Lupis, S. B., N. J. Sabik, and J. M. Wolf. "Role of Shame and Body Esteem in Cortisol Stress Responses." *J Behav Med* 39 (2016), 262-275.

Macfarlane, A. "Gangs and Adolescent Mental Health. Journal of Child and Adolescent Trauma." Last modified September 12, 2019.

Magnus, Edie. "Radar Blames X-factor." NBCnews.com. Last modified August 12, 2005.

Mark Twain's quote. https://www.grainy quote.com/quotes/mark_twain.

Massarella, Linda, Sophia Rosenbaum, and Leonard Green. "The Vile Manifesto of a Killer." New York Post. Last modified July 14, 2023.

Mayfield, Marvin. "A Half Century After Attica.." New York Daily News. September 8, 2021.

Mburur, Edward. "Email." Last modified October 2, 2022.

McFadden, Robert. "Suspect in Son of Sam Murders Arrested: Police Say .44 Caliber Weapon is Recovered." New York Times. Last modified August 11, 1977.

McGuire, Barry. "Eve of Destruction." BarryMcGuire.com. n.d.

Melissa, N., A. Rahmawati, M. A. Arfianto, E. W. Mashfufa, A. D. Kurnia, and N. L. Masruroh. "The Relationship between Body Shaming and Self-esteem in Students." *KnE Medicine* 3, no. 2 (2023), 488–499.

Merriam-Webster Online Dictionary. "Sadism Definition." Merriam-Webster.com. n.d.

Meslin, Richard. "Berkowitz says that he Faked Tales of Demons." New York Times. Last modified 1979.

Michaud, Stephen. "Ted Bundy: Conversations with a Killer." Author Link. Last modified April 2020.

Milgram, S. "Behavioral Study of Obedience." *The Journal of Abnormal and Social Psychology* 67, no. 4 (1963), 371–378.

"Mirror Neurons: How we Reflect Behavior." Association for Psychological Science. Last modified May 1, 2007.

Monica Lewinsky. "Ted talk. The Price of Shame." n.d.
https://youtu.be/H_8y0WLm78U.

Nemy, Enid. "Adopted Children Who Wonder, 'What was my
Mother Like?'." New York Times. Last modified July 25, 1972.

New York State Board of Parole. "The Parole report of David
Berkowitz." Last modified May 19, 2022.

Ouchi, H., K. Ono, Y. Murakami, and K. Matsumoto. "Social
Isolation Induces Deficit of Latent Learning Performance in Mice: A
Putative Animal Model of Attention Deficit/Hyperactivity
Disorder." *Behavioral Brain Research* 238 (February 2013), 146-53.

Parlamis, J. D. "Venting as emotion regulation. International Journal
of Conflict Management." 23, no. 1 (2012), 77–96.

Patchett, Ann. *State of Wonder*. New York: Harper 2011.

Paul, Annie M. "What we learn before we're born?" Last modified
November 29, 2011.
https://www.youtube.com/watch?v=stngBN4hpl4&t=864s.

Paul, V. *Rite of exorcism*. Roman Catholic Church, 1614.

The People vs. David Berkowitz. "The People vs. David Berkowitz."
n.d. https://thepeoplevsdavidberkowitz.com.

Perry, Todd. "Millennials and Boomers May Freak out over Social
Distancing but Its Gen X's Time to Shine." *Pop Culture*, March 2020.

Pert, Candace B. *Molecules of Emotion: Why You Feel the Way You Feel*.
New York, Touchstone1999.

Peyser, Andrea A. "A Mom Dies – Forgiving the Son of Sam." New
York Times. Last modified September 28, 2006.

Piaget, Jean. *The Psychology of Intelligence. Totowa, NJ: Littlefield*. 1972.

Plaut, W. G. *The Torah: A Modern Commentary.* Union for Reform Judaism, 2005.
p. 1403

Porrino, LInda J., and David Lyons. "Orbital and Medial Prefrontal Cortex and Psychostimulant Abuse." *Cerebral Cortex* 10, no. 3 (March 2000).

Pulaski, Mary. *Understanding Piaget: An Intro to Children's Cognitive Development.* Harper and Row, 1971.

Richardson, James. *Regulating Religion: Case Studies from Around the Globe.* New York City: Springer 2004.

Rider, A. O. "Fire-starter: A Psychological Profile. FBI Law Enforcement Bulletin." 49, no. 6 (June 1980), 6-13.

Roberts, Megan. "Satanic Panic in America's Greatest Forgotten Garden." Atlas Obscura. Last modified October 29, 2013.

Roeckelein, Jon. *Deindividuation Theory.* Amsterdam: Elsevier B.V.: Elsevier's Dictionary of Psychological Theories, 2006.

Rosewood, Jack. *Jeffrey Dahmer: A Terrifying True Story of Rape, Murder, & Cannibalism.* LAK Publishing, 2017.

Rousseau, Jean-Jacques. *Emile, on Education.* New York: Basic books, 1979.

Rudd, Ayden. "When did the Term Latchkey Kid Start?" June 2020.

Saldanha, D., N. Kumar, V. Ryali, K. Srivastava, and A. A. Pawar. "Serum Serotonin Abnormality in Depression." *Med J Armed Forces India* 65, no. 2 (2009).

Salvatore, Steve. "Columbine Shooter was Prescribed Anti-Depressant." CNN.com. Last modified April 29, 1999.

Saxon, Wolfgang. "Woman Dies in Mysterious Shooting." New York Times. Last modified January 31, 1977.

Scatliffe, Naomi, Sharon Casavant, Dorothy Vittner, and Xiaomei Cong. "Oxytocin and Early Parent-Infant Interactions: A systematic review." *International Journal of Nursing Science* 6, no. 4 (October 2019).

Schröder, A., G. V. Wingen, Nadine Eijsker, Renée S. Giorgi, Nienke C. Vulink, Collin Turbyne, and Damiaan Denys. "Misophonia is Associated with Altered Brain Activity in the Auditory Cortex and Salience Network." *Scientific Reports* 7542 (2019).

Scorsese, Martin. *Taxi Driver.* United States: Columbia Pictures, 1976.

Seltzer, Leon. "What Your Anger May Be Hiding?" Psychology Today. Last modified July 11, 2008.

Slepian, Michael. "The Benefits and Burdens of Keeping Others' Secrets." *Journal of Experimental Social Psychology* 78 (September 2018).

Smothers, Ronald. "Neighbor Who Got Threat Letters Was at Arrest Site." New York Times. Last modified August 12, 1977.

Solomon, Andrew. "The Reckoning." The New Yorker. Last modified March 10, 2013.

Spitz, R. A. *No and Yes: On the Genesis of Human Communication.* New York: International Universities Press, 1957.

Stoddard, Ed. "Violent Scripture May Increase Aggression – Study." Reuters. Last modified March 6, 2011.

Sullivan, Kelly. *Murder at Rocky Point Park.* Arcadia Publishing, 2014.

Sundar, Aparna, Frank Kardes, and Theodore Noseworthy. "Inferences on Negative Labels and the Horns Effect." *in NA - Advances in Consumer Research Volume 42, eds. June Cotte, Stacy Wood, and Duluth, MN: Association for Consumer Research* 42 (June 2014), 377-380.

Tashjian, SM, V. Fedrigo, T. Molapour, D. Mobbs, and CF Camerer. "Physiological Responses to a Haunted-House Threat Experience: Distinct Tonic and Phasic Effects." Psychological Science. Last modified February 13, 2022.

Taysom, Joe. "The Song That Split Up the Beatles." Far Out. Last modified April 23, 2023.

Terry, Maury. *The Ultimate Evil.* New York: Bantam publishing, 1989.

Turner, C. W., and D. Goldsmith. "Effects of Toy Guns and Airplanes on Children's Antisocial Free Play Behavior." *Journal of Experimental Child Psychology* 21, no. 2 (1976), 303-315.

Van den Dries, L., F. Juffer, M. H. Van IJzendoorn, and M. J. Bakermans-Kranenburg. "Fostering Security? A Meta-Analysis of Attachment in Adopted Children." *Children and Youth Services Review* 31, no. 3 (2009), 410–421.

Verplanken, Bas. "Habit and Identity: Behavioral, Cognitive and Affective and Motivational Factors of an Integrated Self." *Frontiers Psychology*, July 2019.

Verrier, Nancy N. *The Primal Wound.* Gateway Press, 1993.

Villanueva, Kristin. "Reduce Bullying by Cultivating Growth Mindsets." Mindset Works. Last modified November 21, 2017.

Vogels, Emily A. "Americans and 'Cancel Culture'." Pew Research Center. Last modified May 19, 2021.

Wang, Fushun, Jiongjiong Yang, Fang Pan, Roger C. Ho, and Jason H. Huang. "Editorial: Neurotransmitters and Emotions." *Frontiers in Psychology*, January 2020.

Watrick, Nancy. "Hardwired for Prejudice." New York Times. Last modified April 20, 2004.

Weiss, Robert. "The Reasons Someone Looks at Porn Matters." Psychology Today. Last modified July 18, 2016.

Weller, Chris. "The Texas Church Shooter Was 26 — And It Shows A Disturbing Trend About Millennial Men And Mass Murder." Insider. Last modified November 6, 2017.

Whalen, Andrew. "Mindhunter True Story." Newsweek. Last modified May 29, 2019.

Whitehead, Nadia. "People Would Rather Be Electrically Shocked Than Left Alone With Thoughts." Science. Last modified July 3, 2014.

Wiles, Jeremy. *Sing A Little Louder - Short Film.* 2015.

Winfrey, Carey. "Son of Sam." New York Times. Last modified August 22, 1977.

Wisengrad, Susan. "First Time Ever - The Startling Story of Son of Sam's Real Mother." *Good Housekeeping,* November 1978.

Zemeckis, Robert, Alan Silvestri, and William Ross. *Forest Gump.* USA1994.

Zilboorg, Gregory. "Loneliness." The Atlantic. Last modified January 1938.

Zimbardo, Philip G. *The Human Choice: Individuation, Reason, and Order versus Deindividuation, Impulse, and Chaos.* Edited by W. D. Arnold and D. Levine. Lincoln: University of Nebraska, 1969. pp. 237–307

.

Made in the USA
Middletown, DE
09 October 2023